A Passion For Piers

A PASSION FOR PIERS

Life and Community on a Small Island

Written and Compiled by

Patti Locke-Lewkowich

ISBN: 978-1-7782464-0-1

Blue Moon Publishing

Edited by Nancy Pearson

Cover design by Barry Tate

National Library of Canada Cataloguing in Publication Data

A Passion For Piers: Life and Community on a Small Island

Locke-Lewkowich, Patti – Author

I dedicate this book to past, present and future generations of Piers Islanders. And to the amazing community spirit that has made the island the incredible place it is today. I believe the following poem is the perfect message to honour the spirit of all islanders. Thanks to **J. Henley Earnhart**, San Juan Islands, for permission to re-print her wonderful poem.

If Ever You've Lived On An Island

If ever you've lived on an island
If ever you've lived by the sea.
You'll never return to the mainland
Once your spirit has been set free.

If ever you've smelled the ocean
Or tasted the salt in the air;
You'll know you've discovered a haven
That is uncommon, and precious and rare.

If ever you've watched the whales play
Or watched the eagles in flight;
You'll remember, again, why you live here
And why it feels so right

If ever you've seen the sunset
As the ferry passed the shore
You've seen the beauty of the island
That will be with you forever more.

If ever you've heard the seagulls
The waves, a foghorn, the winds;
Then you've heard the song of the island
And the peaceful message it sends

Indeed, if you live on an island
If you're lucky to live by the sea;
You'll never return to the mainland
As your spirit has been set free

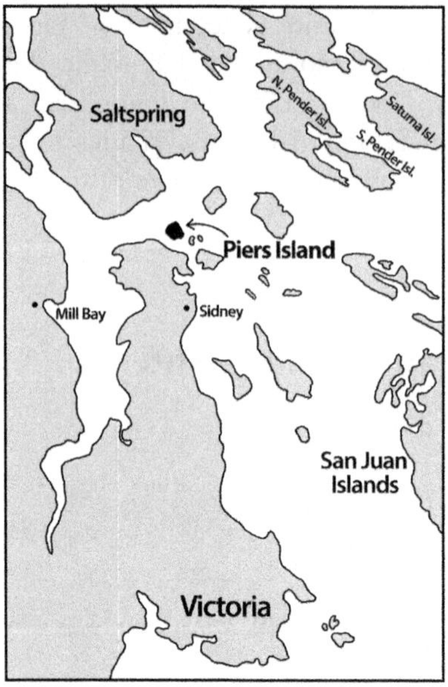
Saltspring
N. Pender Isl.
S. Pender Isl.
Saturna Isl.
Piers Island
Mill Bay
Sidney
San Juan
Islands
Victoria

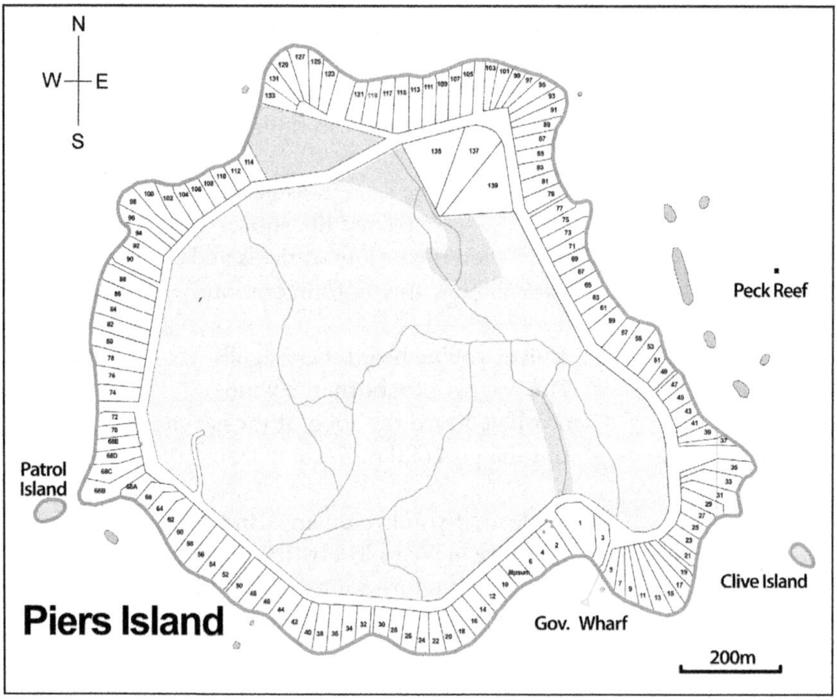
N
W
E
S
Peck Reef
Patrol
Island
Clive Island
Gov. Wharf
Piers Island
200m

CONTENTS

ACKNOWLEDGMENTS

A Passion For Piers is an islanders' book. It was written by over 100 Piers islanders and their family or close friends. I thank all those who provided their family's stories and dug deep into their treasure chests for photos and memories of the island.

The book is dedicated to all those who have lived on the island over the years, including the original Indigenous peoples, the Doukhobors imprisoned on Piers in a Federal prison 1932-1935, the families and owners from the late 1800s onward, and the people who have lived on the land since it was subdivided in the late 1950s. Piers has become the wonderful community it is today because of all of you.

I want to acknowledge the excellent book written by Piers islander, Harold Skolrood, in 1995 called *Piers Island: a brief history of the island and its people, 1886-1993.* Harold tirelessly wrote this book an amazing history of Piers Island. I encourage all readers to source out Harold Skolrood's excellent book for a thorough history of Piers. *A Passion For Piers* focuses on stories of Piers islanders rather than the history of the island.

I thank Vera Maloff for her excellent story of the Doukhobors on Piers, told through the eyes of her mother Elizabeth Maloff (now age 102). Elizabeth was only 11 years old when she was sent to a girl's Industrial school while her mother and grandparents were imprisoned on Piers. Please refer to the prologue of this book for Vera's Doukhobor story.

I am especially indebted to Nancy Pearson, for her tireless skills and flexible editing of over 100 different authors' stories. That was an amazing feat Nancy! I also owe my husband, Barry Tate, so much for his patience and understanding and his talented assistance with photos and layout, over the past two years. It has been my honour to be part of this project.

INTRODUCTION

"What is that island with all the docks around it? I wonder what kind of people live there?" Those were the questions I asked myself when I first spotted Piers Island. It was the early 1990s, and I had recently moved from Winnipeg, and was working as a counsellor on the southern Gulf Islands, based on Salt Spring Island. Five days a week, I returned home to Victoria, and passed that smaller 300-acre island by ferry. Some days I spotted people beachcombing on its shores and others enjoying the last rays of the day's sunlight from deck chairs. Brightly coloured kayaks and other small boats were tied up in front of small cottages or larger oceanfront homes.

The island looked like a paradise, tucked away between the metropolises of Vancouver and Victoria. Piers is a three-minute boat ride and then only five minutes by car to get to the small community of Sidney on Vancouver Island and 40 kilometers south to reach Victoria, the capital city of British Columbia. The larger ferries from Swartz Bay to Tsawwassen, Vancouver travel by the south and west sides of Piers, and the smaller ferries connecting the Gulf Islands like Salt Spring, Pender, and Mayne islands pass by the east side. Piers is a quiet place and has no commercial planes flying overhead, except for the occasional private float plane or helicopter.

The first time I stepped foot on Piers, it felt like 'home,' so serene and so peaceful. The tiny island, with its gorgeous white shell beaches, was peppered with beautiful Arbutus and Dogwood trees. I could see the sea everywhere around me, with the incredible array of Canadian Gulf Islands and American San Juan Islands with mountains in the distance. On that clear day, the majestic snow-capped Mount Baker was visible. The air was fresh and the place so quiet I could hear crickets. I felt like I was in another world when I tread softly in the peacefulness of the lush old forest in the centre of the island.

My husband Barry and I have now been full-time residents on Piers Island for over 25 years, and we both believe we found Utopia. It is a wonderful community of 135 properties, and there has never been cars (outside of a few work vehicles) or stores. The full-time population is approximately 125 which doubles (or more) during the summer with the return of seasonal owners and summer guests.

On the island there is a 'new' firehall, that also serves as a fire department training centre and a community hall. The only other non-residential building is the old firehall which is mostly used for storage. All the homes are located on McKenzie Crescent, a ring road around the island. It connects all the properties and the public beach area and takes about 30 minutes to walk around, but often more than two hours if you stop to talk to neighbours. Except for three non-waterfront lots, the interior of Piers is an undeveloped 150 acres of wooded paradise and walking trails, which is almost the size of Disneyland.

The 45 docks are private or shared, and there is a public dock for those islanders who don't have their own dock. The only way of reaching Piers is by boat. A private shuttle takes islanders on and off the island three days a week and it can be hired for private trips. B.C. Ferries does not serve Piers.

A Passion For Piers focuses on the stories from when the island was subdivided in 1959, when the larger community of Piers was born. Over the past few years, we have lost many long-timers' stories, either through death or through loss of memory. I felt it was important to preserve those memoirs and I wanted to hear the stories directly from the islanders themselves or their families (or neighbours, in some circumstances, where there were no families left). Some people say that Piers hasn't changed that much, but many say it has changed a lot.

Piers islanders (past and present) were invited to write their families' recollections in their own words. The only parameter was that they have been islanders for at least five years. I tried my best to contact former islanders, and I apologize to those I missed.

Some islanders responded with, "But I'm not a writer," and ended up submitting a wonderful contribution. Most wrote their own memoirs, while others asked me to interview them. Some families decided to remain private about their history and not submit a story. Some islanders wrote in prose, while others contributed poems. Stories were written from the eyes of a five year old to a 95 year old. This added to the variety and authenticity of everyone's experiences of the island. Each one of the writers spoke about their love for our community and their own 'Passion for Piers.'

Early Peoples on Piers

The island was originally inhabited by seasonal fishing settlements of indigenous families, primarily around various bay areas of Piers and surrounding islands. To this author's knowledge, their stories were 'word of mouth' rather than written. Unfortunately, no written stories and no living relations were located for this book.

Piers Island's early ownership history started in 1885 with Wilhelm Schmidt as the first documented private owner. This was followed by Sir Clive Phillips-Wooley 1901-1909 and the Harvey Family 1909-1959. There were two interludes in the Harvey family ownership. First, 1911-1918, Piers Island was acquired by Piers Island Syndicate Ltd. to develop the island with a hotel and resort, but a major fire (of a hotel being built at lot 113) in 1913, led to their returning the island back to the Harvey family in 1918.

In 1932-1935, the federal government expropriated the island from its owners (the Harvey family) for a Doukhobor prison. The government built two penetiniaries (one for males, one for females) to incarcerate persons of Doukhobor descent, who were arrested mostly for their actions of protesting in the form of nudity. This is a sad part of the island's history, which islanders acknowledge, but do not talk much about. In researching this project, I have had the pleasure to come to know Vera Maloff, who in 2021 wrote Our Backs Warmed By The Sun: Memories of a Doukhobor Life, her family's stories about being Doukhobors. These stories also include personal experiences of her grandmother and her great-grandparents who were all incarcerated on Piers. Vera has graciously written a special segment in the prologue of this book about her family's experience during their incarceration, as told through the eyes of Vera's mother, now age 102.

Piers was returned to the Harvey family in 1937. All of this earlier history is well recorded in the excellent research of islander Harold Skolrood (Lot 92) in his book *Piers Island: a brief history of the island and its people, 1885-1993*. This book is currently out of print, but copies may be found in various bookstores or online.

1960s THE BEGINNING YEARS

In 1959, the entire island was sold by the Harvey family to developer, John MacKenzie, for $50,000. He began to divide the island into more than 120 recreational lots. Mr. MacKenzie wanted Piers to be a special community and was adamant that the 150-plus acres in the centre of the island would remain an 'unattended forest' for the enjoyment of all owners. Although this concept was shunned by fellow developers (who thought he should develop the entire island), he gained a lot of respect from Piers property owners. In fact, a lot of the original owners bought on the island because of those acres of natural forest. The circle road connecting residences around Piers was named McKenzie Crescent as a tribute to him. At some time, a spelling error was made in the name ('McKenzie' instead of 'MacKenzie') that was never corrected.

In the beginning years, McKenzie Crescent was only a narrow path surrounded by trees and there was a bigger informal trail along the seashore that islanders used more often to visit each other. There have rarely been cars on Piers as they have to be licensed for the five-minute drive around, although there are a few work and fire vehicles on the island. There has never been any commercial development (no stores) due to restrictions in the bylaws. Piers remains a peaceful haven from the busy world so close-by.

In the 1960s, most of the owners on the island were only seasonal, camping in tents during the summer vacations and/or building small rustic shacks. Three or four families braved full-time living on the island and built modest cottages. These families included Peggy and John Mika (Lot 9) who were the first year-round Piers islanders, the Hams (Lot 23), Wally Bain (Lot 10), and Charlie and Paula Kent (Lot 32). Sheep roamed the island, along with a couple of horses belonging to the Mika and MacKenzie families.

The first lots on Piers were divided starting with Lot 1 (between the public dock and the public access road for loading barges on and off the island) and going west from there. A quirky part of the island's development is how the lots are numbered. When you enter the island at the government dock, which was added on the south side in 1962, all properties going south and west from the dock are even numbers, and properties going east and north are odd numbers. The map at the front of this book, illustrates this configuration. Visitors can initially be confused with this intriguing numbering system, but it works.

Those who bought in 1959 and the 1960s were eager owners, excited about their purchases. They often had to enter the properties from the water because their lots were so heavily treed. For some, it was years before they cleared their land enough to actually see the entire property they had purchased. Initial sales of vacant lots on Piers started at the hefty price of $2,000 to $3,000 and soared to $6,000 per lot by the end of the 1960s.

The houses built during those early years were often 'do-it-yourself' tasks or community projects where a few families would get together. Some cottages were basically constructed on one weekend with six to eight people working together, celebrating with a huge meal and lots of beer at the end of each day. The interior would then take months (or years) for the owners to complete. Lots of cottages in the early years were built with that community effort, although some people did use commercial builders.

The initial owners on Piers had few amenities. The water source in the early years was from shallow wells, or islanders brought water from their homes or various outlets on Vancouver Island. With the building of the BC Ferries terminal in 1959 at Swartz Bay, the developer John MacKenzie negotiated with BC Ferries for a water system with an accompanying telephone line to run under the sea between Vancouver Island and Piers. This project, providing both telephone and water service, was completed in April 1961. It would be another five years before power was connected in 1966.

There were various attempts to provide fire fighting on Piers and, in 1969 the Piers Island Volunteer Fire Department (PIVFD) was formed. Those first dedicated firefighters included Bob Clarke (Lot 55) as the first official Fire Chief, Peter Foulkes, Lionel Green, Rob Jarrott, Dave MacDonald, Dave Rees and Howie Sneade. A bench honouring those firefighters is located in front of the old firehall on Piers. The first Piers Island Association (PIA) meeting was held in 1959 with John McKenzie as President. The Piers Island Improvement District (PIID) was formed in 1965, with Reg Biscoe (Lot 2) as the Chair for the first three years.

Owners wanted to be kept informed about happenings on the island. Various island newsletters, welcoming new islanders and keeping all informed of building projects, were mailed out to many parts of the world where part-time Piers islanders lived. These 1960s informative newsletters were 'The Bulletin', Eleanor Destrube's 'Piers Island Gazette' and Peggy Mica's 'The Flotsam and Jetsam'. At the end of the decade, newsletters were replaced by PIA and PIID mailed correspondence that was informative, but certainly not as social.

The first Piers Island picnic was held in the early 1960s, pulled together with many volunteers, and the event remains a summer highlight. Islanders were dedicated volunteers in the beginning years and this community spirit and volunteerism continues to be an important part of Piers today.

Piers Island Princess: One of the early transport boats on Piers

Lot 2 - Reg and Alice Biscoe

Piers Island Memories 1959-1987

So many childhood memories stand out for us from our time on Piers Island: the friendliness of people walking along the road who were always smiling and saying hello; the community spirit and hard work at work bees for the volunteer fire department, the improvement district, and the firehall; the wonderful Piers Island picnics, and other community events; and the kindness extended in emergencies, such as transporting our dad to hospital when he had a medical emergency. Travelling back and forth to the island was always an adventure. We were taught to make a beeline when in the ferry's path - always respect the ferry! Our dog would travel in the back of the boat, while the cat had its own shelf in the cabin.

We made the journey in various small and larger craft from dinghies to our boat, *Jigger* (which Dad's brother Hugh has maintained and still uses). On occasion, we rode on the *Piers Island Princess*, a DUKW amphibious vehicle that miraculously made the trip across the water and was (for us children) an entertaining ride around the road on the island. Groceries, hay and other food for the horses, and in those days also propane tanks, had to be hauled across.

Raft building was a favourite pursuit of the children. Large logs washed in with flattened trunks, scrap wood was nailed on top, and the kids poled and paddled around the bay. One day, our father, dressed in suit and tie, had to go to Victoria for an important real estate business appointment. *Jigger,* was tied up to its buoy but the dinghy was nowhere to be seen. Our father negotiated passage on the raft with our brother Michael, who then poled the raft out to the boat, with Dad precariously balancing and gripping his briefcase, and mostly staying dry as he climbed aboard the boat.

We often had unexpected guests drop in for dinner. One time, our mother was cooking steaks on the hibachi, when the family dog seized the moment and two of the steaks and disappeared in an instant while her back was turned. The servings were a little small for humans that night, but the dog seemed quite satisfied. One evening, our brother Ian and his friend were at the southwest point for a fried chicken picnic dinner, which they left on the point while they went for a swim. Returning to shore for dinner, they found a vegetarian meal. Apparently, the seagulls were most delighted with their "chicken on the wing."

Reg Biscoe (in business attire) with family

Clam digging and oyster gathering were enthusiastically pursued. Once gathered, we put them in a bucket with seawater and our mother added oatmeal to the water so the shells would open, expelling any grit. It was always tempting to stick your fingers in the open shells and pull them back quickly before the shell closed again.

Our brother Ian once pulled up a large rock crab, which grabbed his finger, and then the dancing and yelling began. The crab was quickly smashed into crab "bisque," but the claw was still attached to his finger, and the yelling and dancing continued until the claw was eventually pried open and the inflamed finger tended to by our mother. She was fortunately trained as a pediatric nurse.

Horses Cheyenne and Silver roamed freely on the island and possessed a remarkable sense of humour towards riders, including our sister Anne. Silver, in particular, and Cheyenne on occasion would enjoy heading towards low hanging branches in the orchard, where the unwary rider could end up in a tree. Cheyenne liked to go for a satisfying mud bath shortly after being washed and groomed. When John and Peggy Mika brought their horse, Princess, to the island, she quickly joined forces to become a third conspirator.

One day, Anne and her friend, Kerry Lees, (niece of Bill and Belle Ham Lot 23, and cousin to Barbara Eckman, Lots 33 and 35), had tracked the three horses across the island, carrying bridles for Cheyenne and Silver. Horses bridled, they mounted and set off on their ride. Princess was in the lead, heading down the road, when she suddenly kicked back at Cheyenne. Anne, thinking he was injured, jumped down to assess his injuries and Kerry did the same. While they were assessing Cheyenne, the three horses took off whinnying with apparent humour, leaving Anne and Kerry in their dust. It was a long and dry trek to find them again on the other side of the island.

Young Biscoe Boys: Hugh (bow), Ian, and Michael (stern)

Early experiences on Piers Island gave us a formative upbringing and a unique sense of community participation, resourcefulness, and generosity. We will always be grateful for our time on Piers and are happy to hear that the community continues to be vibrant and evolving.

** *Author's Note:* Reg Biscoe, of R. Fraser Biscoe Realty, was Piers' first real estate agent from 1959, acting for Gulf Resorts Ltd., owned by developer John McKenzie. In 1965 Reg and Alice Biscoe took over sole proprietorship of Piers under the name Island Seafront Properties. Islanders still talk about how Reg spent a lot of time with interested buyers to make sure they would be suitable 'Piers islanders.' The public beach area on the island was known for years as Association Beach. The name was fondly changed to Biscoe Beach with the death of Reg Biscoe in 1988.

Lot 4 - Ken and Irene Gibbard

A Good 60 Years

As a young man some of my ambitions were to find a lovely girl and marry her, have a family, get or build a house, get a sizeable sailboat, and a waterfront cabin in the Gulf Islands. In 1956, I did meet a young girl, Irene, and we were married for 60 years. We had three great girls. In 1959, we bought a large sea view lot in Gordon Head for $2,000. I was only taking home $500 a month (for 10 months) as a young teacher but back then the lot only cost me four pay cheques. I really feel sorry for today's young people as the same lot would now cost a young teacher 10-12 YEARS of salary. In 1960, we moved into our new house, just a shell, and I finished it over the next few years.

About that time, I realized that we should get the Gulf Island property before a sailboat, for even then vacant waterfront property was a rare find. I figured that waterfront prices would escalate relatively rapidly. Boats, however, have a very high component of their cost in the wages of the boat-builders. I figured that my salary would basically match increases in general labour costs. Therefore, the cabin should come first, the boat later. We looked at several very steep lots on Willis Point Road and at some Salt Spring Island properties. I had camped on Piers while cruising in small sailboats as a teenager. I heard that Reginald Biscoe was selling Piers Island property, so arranged to go out with him and my father. We went out in a small boat rented from Randall's Marina, where the Royal Victoria Yacht Club out station is now. When Reg first began selling Piers Island property he had an old army duck - a small tank like amphibious vehicle, which he kept on the Dolphin Road lot. It was very convenient to drive out from town with clients, climb up onto the duck, drive down the ramp and motor across. On Piers he could drive up the ramp and take clients around the ring road. This ended before long as the system froze up because he did not properly maintain the lubrication and salt water got in.

At that time, spring of 1962, all of the south side and the southern part of the east side of Piers were sold. Reg had the next subdivision north up the east side surveyed but did not have the Ministry of Highways' permission to sell but said that he could take reservations when approval came through. It was a cool day when we visited and there was a northeast wind. The east side was unattractive. Reg showed us several lots on the south side up for resale and after another trip with my wife, we chose our present property, Lot 4. The cost, wow $3,000! A few years later Reg offered us one of the lots near 68D. The price $4,000. We were not prepared to pay that much for a speculation lot - if only!

There used to be a very old log cabin where the shelter at the head of the wharf is now. In the summer we camped on an old logging roadway which crossed our lot. One day when we were camping it began to rain. John McKenzie, who with a partner had bought Piers Island from the Harvey family, lived in the house on Lot 2 next door to us. He offered us the key to the log cabin to get out of the rain. We used it some that summer and fall.

In June 1963, I bought a truckload of 2 x 6 (full inch) by 18-foot floor planks from the O'Neil Glass building (about 1870) where the Yates Street parkade is now. I had these dumped at the Dolphin Road lot. A friend and I stacked most of them in one big bundle at low tide and at a higher tide towed the bundle across with a 5 HP outboard on a small wooden boat.

At the beginning of August 1963, I began the construction of the A-frame cabin. I chose an A-frame as the most efficient way to use the 18-foot planks. Each dimension of the A- frame is just a little less than 18 feet! One day of that early construction really stands out. I had the floor on and had made up the ten-A frames on the floor and then pulled them back behind the floor and stacked them. My wife came out with the two kids (Sandra was two years, Norma just over two months) and camped with me. The next morning we began setting up and bracing the frames. By lunchtime we had gone from a flat floor to a house. Well, not quite, but the shape was there. We actually had our first family weekend in the new cabin the following Easter.

There were at least six of us that often met that winter at Dolphin Road on Saturday mornings. We were all building cabins on Piers and hauling building materials across in small boats. I remember especially the Clarkes who took sand and gravel across in five-gallon buckets for their entire concrete foundation walls.

At that time there was no electricity on Piers. Water came from Swartz Bay by an aluminum pipeline. There were problems of incomplete mixing of the aluminum alloy causing pitting near the joints of the pipe sections. The line was completely trashed later when a BC Ferries vessel was testing an anchor winch. It failed and the boat steamed back to the Swartz Bay terminal towing the anchor, and our pipe! On Piers a plastic pipeline ran west and east of the ramp generally on old logging roads about 50 feet in from the shore. I lifted the line up over a log round on our lot and installed a tap.

Irene and Ken Gibbard

No one lived on Piers full time then. I can remember walking around the island on a Saturday night in the winter after dark and feeling fairly sure that I was the only person on the island.

After a few years the A-frame became too small for our family of five so I built a bed shed, as we called it, farther back on the lot. Some years after that, when we were still planning a full sized retirement house right at the waterfront, I built a 16 x 24 foot concrete floored workshop beside the A-frame. The full-sized house was never built as we both felt that we did not want to leave connections in Victoria. During the 1970's, I got a great deal of satisfaction from building my 130-foot jetty, ramp and float all with my own hands. The 1980 float finally broke up in a storm in December 2016.

The larger sailboat never came either as I found that the house and large garden in Victoria combined with Piers took all of my free time. I did build several small sailboats and in 1997 bought *Duchess*, my 22-foot black hulled, red-sailed boat, which is still around on the island.

I still come and go to Piers by canoe. For years we had a 14-foot aluminum boat with a 9.9 HP motor. As I got older the boat got heavier, so I downsized to a 12-foot boat. The motor got heavier, too, so I went to a 6

HP outboard. These got heavier, too, so now unless I come with others, I find canoeing both easier and more enjoyable.

When I was approaching retirement at age 58, it was generally considered that by age 80 one was old and I thought that I would be selling Piers about then. When I was 80 I was re-shaking the workshop roof by myself. Now 90 is here and I think that it is about time that I retired, from Piers. It will have been a good 60 years.

The Big Rock Story:

Piers Island was originally all forested. Imagine the first settler arriving with a few hand tools and, if he was relatively well off, a horse or two. What a job to clear land enough for a small vegetable garden, but he didn't stop there. Most of the present north and south meadows were cleared before 1900 in much the same way. Cutting down the big trees by hand and burning the stumps was not enough. There were many glacier-deposited rocks scattered across his land. If he had a horse, he would have made a stoneboat, a wooden sled. Probably before and many times after ploughing he would walk alongside the stoneboat throwing and lifting rocks onto the sled. He would have stopped the horse sometimes to roll larger rocks up a plank ramp onto the sled. When loaded he would have taken the sled to the edge of the forest and dumped the contents there where the rocks did not matter. In the middle of his north meadow was a large erratic boulder. It was about eight by 10 feet on the ground and eight-feet high. He could not move it so he used the area around it as a dumping place for some of his stoneboat loads.

This ice age glacial erratic is what my family called 'The Big Rock'. When the kids were small we would go over to The Big Rock after supper a few times a summer. At first we had to help the kids climb up the larger rocks left by the farmer, then up the steep slope of the Rock to the top. There we would all sit in a row as sunset approached and watch the deer come out of the forest onto the meadow to feed. At this time, the Rock stood high up in the meadow grass and we could see all around. Finally, we would slide down the Rock and head home. It would be quite dark in the forest between the north and south meadows. Then we had twilight in the south meadow. The kids were quite ready for bed after these evening outings.

Where is The Big Rock today? One of my daughters recently started going to Piers again. She walked through the north meadow, but didn't see it and asked me where it was. I hadn't seen it for years but soon found it. It was completely hidden by very tall roses, wild crabapple, and hawthorn trees and other growth that had grown up in the 45 to 50 years since we went with the kids. If you walk up through the orchard about 50 meters past the last fruit tree, you will see on the left the beginning of clearing the growth to reveal The Big Rock. In August of 2021, the Piers Island Association gave approval for clearing the invasive growth to at least allow sight of the rock and access to climb it. Hopefully new generations of families will enjoy the Rock as we did.

Ken on the Duchess

Lot 9 - John and Peggy Mika

Saving The US Navy!

In 1965, we saw an ad in the *Victoria Times* newspaper where John worked, advertising an open house on Piers Island. Reg Biscoe took us across to Piers with John's mom and we bought two lots that same day. We camped on the lots at first and then the house at Lot 9 came up for sale and we bought it. The house was originally owned by Clive Wooley and family. We added onto the house over the years. We had a horse and two goats that roamed freely on Piers with Reg Biscoe's daughter's horse.

We were the first full-timers (throughout a full year) on Piers from the time when it was subdivided. John worked at the *Victoria Times* newspaper Monday to Friday, and he stayed in the city with friends while I stayed totally alone on Piers, with no other islanders around. John joined me on weekends. I was the one who drove the boat and I would drive John to and from Piers. I became the 'water taxi service' for anyone who called on me. It was okay at first when there were just a few people, but then all the part-timers started calling for rides, too. It got too much, and it was a free service, too. I didn't take any money. I guess that was kind of stupid.

I remember an amazing story in October 1967. It was a weekday and I knew that I was the only person on the island. It was very foggy. I heard a noise that sounded like a diesel horn, and then I heard a voice but couldn't see a thing because of the fog. I went outside and heard someone saying, "Pardon me, Ma'am, but where are we?" It turned out there were three men walking the shore who were members of the US Navy, stationed in Washington. They had been doing some training in Nanaimo. On their return, they got lost in the fog and their 70-foot ship got grounded on Piers after coming within inches of hitting the Salt Spring Queen ferry. They had no radar and tried to find their way by compass only, which they found out was not functioning, leaving them stranded. The only map they had was a large one covering the whole area, that showed Piers Island as a small dot.

I invited the men to our house for tea. When I realized that they had been lost for hours, and hadn't eaten much, I fed them sandwiches. They were so thankful. Their captain was very embarrassed they had gotten lost. I had a rough map of the area under a glass on the coffee table in the living room. They used that as their guide and left hoping that they had gotten the directions right to reach Friday Harbour, Orcas Island, Washington, where they were planning to spend the night. I hoped they made it too!

We loved throwing amazing New Year's Eve parties. It was always a potluck and all the full-timers came. At the beginning, it was only us, the Hams (Lot 23), the Eckmans (Lot 33) and the Ferries (Lot 117). In later years, other full-timers and part-timers started attending. Everyone dressed up in tuxedos and long gowns and had a good time. Sometimes people had a bit too much to drink and got lost. One year, the revellers searched all over Piers for one person and found them curled up in a closet fast asleep.

I also had a full-time bakery on Piers. After four years, I was weekly baking 50 loaves of bread, more than 20 pies, lots of cakes and dozens of cookies for the kids who had saved up their allowances all week. Over the years Piers full and part-timers ordered all their weekly bakery needs from me and, even when I raised my prices, they still ordered. Finally I was totally exhausted and put a sign up saying 'Closed due to too much success!' Thirty years later, I was approached in James Bay, Victoria, by a former Piers kid, who recognized me as the 'Cookie Lady' from Piers.'

We moved to Victoria in 1969 when my dad died and we needed to help my mom. We sold Our Piers home in 1972. Piers still holds many special memories for the two of us. We recently moved to a senior's home in Sidney. We hope we can see Piers between the trees when the leaves fall.

Peggy and John Mika, 60th anniversary 2015

Lot 15 - Lionel and Deanna Green

40 Years Of Adventures On Piers

(written by Deanna Green)

In 1968, we found Piers when we visited the Gait family (Lot 87). I walked around the island and found some empty lots for sale and then we contacted the owners to see if they wanted to sell. We started negotiating with the original owner of Lot 15, Mr. Keay in the fall of 1968. However he couldn't make a decision until he spoke with his son. Maybe the son wanted to buy the property? Mr. Keay's son worked in a remote part of northern Canada and there were no cellphones or emails in those days or any way of reaching him. Negotiations weren't finalized until Spring 1969 - over six months of negotiating the sale from start to finish!

We built our summer home on Piers and enjoyed 40 years involved with the island and its development. A number of special 'boat' memories stand out for us. Over the years, Lionel worked on and built many boats from a little *Squirt* speedboat to a 38-foot sailboat. Lionel was a gifted craftsman who has left a tiny piece of himself with many people. He was never without a project and was fondly referred to as the 'Inspector' or 'Mr. Fix-it'.

Lionel built a greenhouse at his home in Victoria for one of the islanders, Mrs. Ham (Lot 23). He brought the greenhouse across in a small boat at dusk one summer and presented it to a very surprised Mrs. Ham the next morning. She loved that greenhouse for years. We remember another neighbour, Bill Scoones (Lot 29) who was transporting a cement mixer to Piers with an eight-foot dinghy. He was going so slowly that the BC Ferries vessel actually had to stop and go around him. Another islander family, the Ferries (Lot 117), were bringing across a huge load of plywood in a small boat to Piers. They underestimated the ferry wake and the wood fell overboard as they watched it all float away.

We enjoyed our summers and weekends on Piers Island with our children for many years until we left the island in the early 2000s. Our son Lenny Green and his partner Deneen Cunningham bought the property and enjoy it very much.

Lionel and Deanna

Lenny and Deneen

Lots 31, 33 - Barbara and Howie Eckman

Four Generations And Over 55 Years Enjoying Piers

My Mother and Dad (Bill and Belle Ham, Lot 23) moved to Piers Island before us, in the early1960s. Dad knew the Biscoe family and Reg showed them some places on the Saanich Peninsula, but they couldn't afford anything there. Then Reg said he could show them Piers Island and they bought soon after that. We visited my parents and fell in love with Piers too. We bought our property around 1963 and we stayed at Mother and Dad's cottage while our place was being built.

Mother and Dad were the second full-timers on Piers. Dad was the first unofficial Fire Chief on the island. They gave him a hat and he was be responsible for watching for fires. He did put out a couple of fires on Sunday evenings after part-time people had left to go back home. Dad took his 'unofficial' job very seriously. He also read all the meters around the island. Our friends Michael and Suzanne Ferry came over to visit us on a beautiful sunny autumn day and got excited about Piers, too, and bought Lot 117. They said, "If it's good enough for you, it's good enough for us."

The power just came in on Piers the year Mum and Dad moved into their home full-time in 1966. Dad had a little aluminum boat that he used to go fishing at Cowichan Bay. He had retired from the bank in Vancouver. Before they would come over to Piers, they would always telephone Dave at Queens Payless (in Sidney) and every week Dave would go and deliver groceries to the end of Barnacle Road wharf. That's how we got our groceries. After awhile Mum wasn't that well, so friends lent them an apartment in Victoria and they moved off the island in the late 1970s.

We came over one New Year's Eve, and there was no power. We came over with the Ferries and we were all staying at our house. There were lots of children, and the men were trying to thaw the water line, because in those days the water line was not buried, but was above ground. They got it thawed out right at 12 midnight, so we sang 'Happy New Year' and then we all went to bed. John and Peggy Mika (Lot 9), The Kents (Lot 32), Mother and Dad (Lot 23) and us were the only ones on Piers that New Year's Eve. We had a 'New Year's Black Tie' dinner party at the Micas! For a number of years in the 1960's, Mother and Dad used to have a New Year's Day party and invite whoever was on the island. It was a great community then. In the early 1970's, our daughter Deborah had her eighth birthday and we invited eight little girls (mostly part-timers). There weren't that many boys for our son David and there were few permanent residents. Peggy Mica made and sold bread. She had a huge oven for that and lots of people loved her baking.

There was the time when Margo Morrison (Lot 35) nearly gassed herself with a gas heater. Most everyone called her Mrs. Morrison. She was so independent she ran her own boat and swam in the sea nearly every day she was on Piers. Our dog Megan, a golden retriever, started barking and barking one morning. Howie went over to find Mrs. Morrison lying on the kitchen floor. Howie and another neighbour got her in their small boat; she was very heavy because she was unconscious. They took her to the Saanich Peninsula Hospital on Vancouver Island where they saved her life.

We bought Lot 33 first when we came to see Piers Island in 1963. Then Lot 31 next door came for sale awhile later. There was a man who owned this lot and he had a small shed on the property with some tools. He actually wanted more money for the place because there were tools on the property, but they really weren't worth anything. We had one week to buy the lot next door because the man needed the money right then. We purchased it to share with Bill and Barbara Scoones (Lot 29). When Bill and Barbara left, we had to buy out their share of Lot 31.

My husband, Howie, was a stock broker and worked for the same company (Scotia Bank) for 50 years. I never worked outside the home. After high school, I went travelling with a girlfriend from England who had inherited some money. We hitchhiked all over Europe. I had learned to sail at Maple Bay. I met Howie at a fancy dance party and the rest is history.

Some of my favorite memories of Piers are just 'silly little things'. I was volunteering for the picnic, and we asked people to bring onions, and to rinse them so they would be easier to fry. There we were trying to fry up these soggy onions; that was a mistake. Another time, I remember a party and being in a boat. We had to dress up like Piers Island, so we were dressed up with branches coming out of our head. We were supposed to dress up with natural things from Piers. The parties were always great on the island, especially at the start of the Fire Department. The Sneade's son (Lot 41) built our guest house and the drawers were beautifully done because he was a cabinet maker. The Piers picnics were so much fun with all the kids. My grandkids are now 12, 14 and 26 years old, and they have been visiting Piers for years.

I had a detached retina that was mis-diagnosed, so I can't drive now. I just put on my backpack and take the bus from Vancouver (and sometimes a taxi) and ferry to get to Piers, but it is worth it to be here. Luckily, I can still walk well and I even take my cat Whiskey with me, but I found out that cats aren't allowed on ferries. It is now difficult for me to get over the ferry ramp.

For the longest time on Piers, we didn't have any phones in the houses. We just had one phone at the government wharf. The teenagers would be lined up to make calls, and adults hardly ever could use that phone.

Linda Clarke (Lot 55) nearly always won the ladies' nail-driving contest, but in 1982, she missed the picnic, and that was the only reason I won that year. That was a highlight for me.

We will all keep enjoying Piers as long as we can.

Howie and Barb Eckman

Lot 32 - Charlie and Paula Kent

(from an article written upon Charlie's death January 1998 by John Mika, former Piers Islander Lot 9) * with Permission of Times Colonist.

'Charles and Paula Kent became early permanent residents retiring to the island as their only home in autumn of 1965. Charlie, as everyone called him, had immigrated from England as a young man and became a versatile citizen - farmer, shipyard foreman in Victoria, salesman, barge builder in the Arctic, apartment owner, fisherman and businessman were just some of the roles of his successful life.

He was an easy-going master craftsman with a genuine interest in all people. He met and married a passionate idealist who gave more than she received. So, naturally their kitchen became a centre of operations for newcomers - introducing them to island life, arranging water taxi service (free), helping plan erection of homes or docks and on and on. But they were concerned that all should absorb the island way of life to ensure its survival. Governance was key. Of course, they did their stints of service on the Piers Island Association and the Improvement District executive.

But even more important, they gently persuaded numerous others to take the time and make the effort to do likewise over the years. Ideas are never so powerful as when embodied in the lives of individuals who illuminate them. This co-operative sharing of leadership and service lead to astonishing improvement: a water line across the channel from the peninsula; a huge reservoir on the island; a newsletter; a federal dock; cross-channel telephone and hydro connections; annual children's picnics; a firehall and volunteer brigade (an oil delivery truck was converted into their first pumper); even a community centre.'

** *Author's Note:* Paula Kent was Piers Island's first Secretary-Treasurer. (1972-1979 and 1984-1986)

The lower reservoir was dedicated to Charlie Kent - 1976

Charlie and Paula Kent

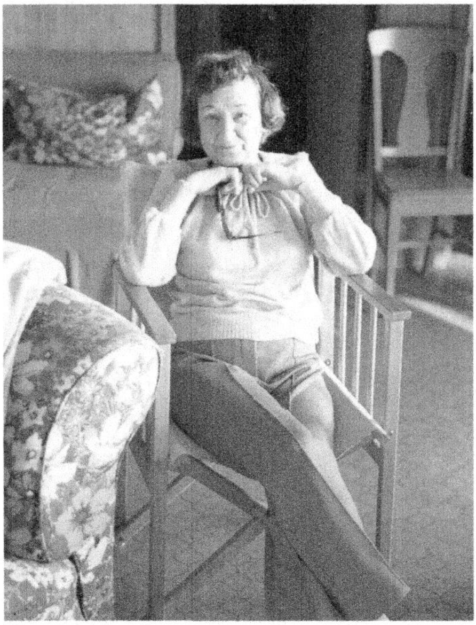

Paula Kent

Lot 35 - Mrs. Morrison

A Very Special Lady!

(written by previous neighbours Jim and Debra Hills)

Mrs. Morrison and her husband purchased their cottage as a kit, and set it up themselves on Lot 35 around 1963 to 1965. This was a primitive summer cabin with only an outhouse, no running water or power.

She told us she would swim from her little beach on lot 35 to Clive Island every day when she was younger. She said her greatest joy living on Piers was watching the ferries sail back and forth in front of her window at night through the gap between Clive and Knapp islands. The cottage would vibrate, since it was set on 8x8x16 concrete blocks. She often said, " The walls seemed so friendly." After we purchased her cottage around 2002, we felt the same way about the ferries because we could almost reach out and touch them.

She later got propane installed in the cottage for a gas stove and gas lights. On one occasion, after her husband had passed away, she was overcome with propane fumes and stumbled out onto the side porch, where she collapsed. Thankfully, the Eckmans (Lots 31 and 33) heard her moaning and called for help. She recovered in a Victoria hospital.

When we purchased Mrs. Morrison's cottage, she stipulated she would only sell it to us if all of the funds could be donated to a non-profit orphanage in Haiti. She got the BC Government to allow her to use all the funds from the sale to go towards that cause.

Mrs Morrison was a religious woman and Deb and I would visit her in her home in Victoria, often on Sunday afternoons, just down the street from Emily Carr's home. We'd listen to her stories about Piers and Victoria during the early years, munching on chocolate cookies and sipping tea. She was a very special lady.

Hal Weaver, Mrs. Morrison, Coco Eckman, and Mrs. Morrison's niece

Lot 37 - Burpee MacLennan

And The Old Firehall

(told by Bob Clarke – Piers' First Official Fire Chief)

In the mid-1960s, Burpee MacLennan and his wife purchased Lot 37. Burpee was a serious diabetic and could not attend various work parties and training for the Piers Volunteer Fire Department. (PVFD). Burpee willingly helped complete difficult jobs by himself in his own time. Firstly, he raised and set the firehall flagpole. He also rigged and raised an urgently required fire hose drying rack high in a fir tree. Burpee was a well-respected and valuable member of the PVFD. It was a sad time when he passed away.

The original firehall was built across the road from Burpee's lot. At the Annual Piers Island Association (PIA) meeting in 1968, desperate to finally succeed bringing good fire protection to Piers, the members willingly agreed to the conditions this new fire committee demanded - that they would have 'carte blanche' authority to build the fire department. The committee, working within the established $10.00 per owner yearly budget, would make all decisions without any interference. This was necessary since annual PIA meetings had shown how difficult it was to make even minor decisions.

The location of the firehall was chosen as a temporary site for a good reason. The fire engine was a converted 1953 GMC oil-delivery truck, which had an old 6-volt battery system. If accidently flooded when started, the battery did not provide much juice for extra attempts. The main firemen were aware of the problem and usually avoided the flooding problem. It was too easy for others who were not aware to fail. In this temporary location, if necessary, the fire truck could be hand pushed out of the hall and coasted down the hill to start. When the truck was in use as an oil truck, it was started in the morning and never turned off as it made its rounds. In our second year, a visitor to Piers who was a farmer from Alberta, told us how back home they overcame the starting problem with these trucks. He told us to go to a local battery shop and ask to have an 8-volt battery specifically built. We did and this, with the extra two volts, completely solved the issue.

The committee had also chosen a site for a permanent firehall to be built hopefully, in five years time. This site was in the triangle at McKenzie Crescent and Blackberry Lane. Interestingly, we had no opposition to the two firehall sites chosen. However, the permanent firehall was not to be realized until 24 years later. This time it was a hard time battle to decide on a second location. Serious opposition year after year delayed progress, a main point being that Piers did not also require the new hall to be a community centre. It was finally sold to the community as a firehall with a training room. The facilities have become a great community centre with a perfect location.

Bench in front of the old firehall

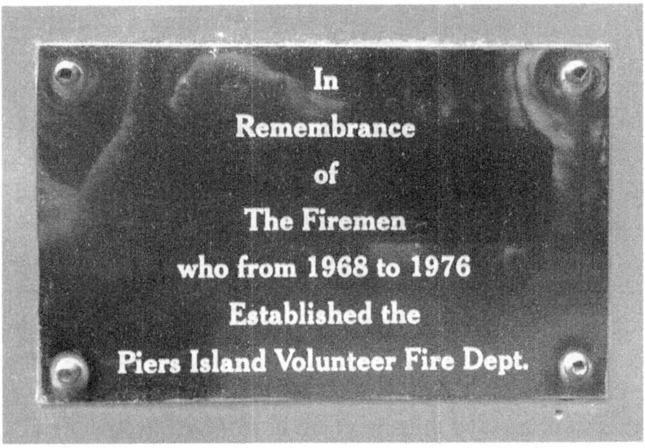

Lot 38 - Fran and Miles Primrose

Remember About Piers?

Yes I remember a lot.
Our parents, Miles and Fran Primrose, bought two acres in the middle of Piers Island in the 70's.
I was a very small little kid. A horse crazy girl.
I got that bug from my mom.
Before I owned a pony, I was a pony. I trotted and galloped.
Jumped and whinnied.
Cut out dozens of horses from magazines.
Northern Dancer, Secretariat, Bask and many coloured horses.
Piers had a lot of opportunity for getting a horse.

Tidbits of memories and stories.
One was my parents running along behind Charlie Kent with him yelling and hollering at them from behind the wheel of a tractor.
Telling them to get the next rolling pin from under the cabin around to the front. They were skidding it to the farm. The farm being one of the three pieces of private property in the middle of Piers.
Friday nights going across to government dock on Piers on Dad's boat, the Just Lovely.
We would walk up the dock and get the wheelbarrow. Load it with tools and food.
I remember the long walk to THE OTHER SIDE (the farm).
Remember I was little.

We slept on the floor of the cabin with the red lights flashing off of the top of Salt Spring.
We ate KING apples from trees that had survived Doukhobor days.
We were told a lady on another island used to watch through binoculars the men swimming around the edge of a fence to the ladies side of Piers Island.
What for?

A PASSION FOR PIERS

The pony came in a single wide horse trailer behind my dad's truck on a barge.
A free lease on an Arab/Welsh-cross called Frijole was mine!!!!
Mom made me wear a helmet. Wasn't wearin much more. Gumboots, oh yeah. I looked a poor sight. In my head I was on a big stallion running free.
Helmet got a big hole in it while on my head. I was going warp speed after snapping a twig off a tree for a crop. That pony found higher gears. We were off. Nearly took my head off on a low branch.
I rode all those trails and beaches. Never picked up poo or worried about leaving tracks.

I was terrified of snakes. Piers was loaded with them. Those ones the size of my skinny arm. The colour rhyme...taught me to be wary:
Black beside yellow could kill a fellow. Green beside red was a friend of Fred. Something like that. They were all dangerous. But up on that pony wearing the helmet and gumboots, I was safe.
So many memories.
Driving a flat deck/towtruck thing we named Big Red. I can't believe we could drive that. Even in the middle of the island.
Had lawn chairs on the back. You had to hang on and stop laughing. Too much fun.
Driving a standard yellow pickup my dad said I could. Driving a red cub Farmall tractor. Absolutely found freedom again on that.
Every time I found enough quarters I would ride my bike over to George's for honey bars. Sticky
hard little granola bars made with his honey.
Being super shy of the Lauener boy Michael. Shy but curious.
Picnics and Fishing derbies were huge events. Midnight madness dances at the old firehall later.
There were dirty nudy calendars in that firehall. We looked at them more than once.
Running back and forth to Sidney, Dolphin Road, Canoe Cove in Boston whaler.
Few times tied all our dinghies head to tail and towed them out to the strait. Sat out there and waited for ferry to go by so we could ride the rollers.
Rowing out to Arbutus island to walk around. It had arbutus trees on it
A lady across the way lent us her small boat for running back and forth.
Mom and I hit a deadhead one evening heading back to Piers. Mom yelled “Keep going!”
The next morning it was hanging by its ropes under water. Oh boy.

Painting clam shells with paint that dried too fast.
Sleeping outside under stars and the glow of ferries, with a few girls on the front lawn. The lawn that is no more.
Making peanut brittle in a cast iron frying pan. I always burnt it and always ate it.
Making little pens and corrals for imaginary horse.
Going to Sidney to buy school supplies. Worst feeling.

Family names of then:
Herbert, Kent, Ross, Tidman, Perry, Barber, Gate, Lauener, Scholefield, Forseth, Currie, Scoones, Popp, Green, Willmore, Brin, Omara
One day a lady took a picture of my pony and gave it to me. I think her name was O'Mara.
Party line was exciting. Mom made us swear never to listen to other conversations. Sometimes it was impossible not to.
Charlie Kent and his wife Paula were so good to us kids.
He was the mayor of Piers.
Part farmer, fisherman, builder, politician, leader, inventor.
His grandkids were Brenda, Brian and Ricky.
The man that owned the neighbour's place before Mr Brin saw me one day and offered me flippers and snorkel. I wasn't exactly thrilled. But when I look back it was so kind. If it had been an old lead rope or halter I would have been smitten.
I was so shy.

My parents Miles and Fran Primrose gave my sister Tia and me the best childhood growing up.
Everything was for us. Life is great and I am grateful.

Miles and Fran Primrose

Lot 39 - Dave and Sonia Rees

Many Fond Memories

(written by Sonia Rees)

We purchased lot 39 on Piers in 1965. We camped for awhile and then completed building our dream home. We moved to Piers Island as permanent residents in 1978. Our youngest son Paul developed a condition which required hospitalization off and on for three years, so we had to move back to Vancouver Island.

We were living in paradise on Piers until all activities of daily living became more complicated and a chore, so we had no choice but to move off the island. I still remember that last day with much sadness. Many fond memories still remain with me and always will. Piers is a great community.

My grown children wanted to tell their 'Piers story' in their own words:

Sonia and Dave

I remember my childhood on Piers

Vincent Rees (eldest son)

I remember the smell of the trees all around.
I remember the sound of the waves on the beach and peaceful afternoons watching the ferry go past and waving to the passengers. Sometimes they even waved back.
I remember the smell of the fireplace burning gently and keeping us toasty warm, along with the calming sound of the rain on the roof as I nodded off to sleep.
I remember the excitement as the salt water sprayed against the windows during a good winter storm.
I remember chasing frogs and watching slugs on the land and jellyfish and crabs on the beach.
I remember there was always a colourful cast of characters popping by.
I remember trying to get the bunny ears on the television to pick up Saturday morning cartoons and I remember wondering when the neighbours would get off the party line.
I remember the Terry Fox run and what a bonding experience it was for everyone on the island to rally together in support of a good cause.
I remember the work parties and the sound of chainsaws clearing trees and the laughter over cheap beers at the end of the day.
I remember the wheelbarrow. We sure put it to work, hauling goods and supplies back and forth from the government dock.
I remember climbing on the fire truck at the volunteer fire station and pretending it was some sort of spaceship cruiser taking me on some great adventure.
I remember digging for clams and eating them up with fresh butter on the deck with friends and family.
I remember the annual island picnic and the fishing derby. I have a confession to make I never did catch that fish myself and never should have won the fishing knife when I was six years old. Dad caught it.
I remember the tree fort we had with a pulley system we used for bringing snacks and other supplies.
But mostly I remember the laughter. Time stood still in those days and we had time to live in the moment and be free-spirited and just laugh… all day long!

A day in the life on Piers as a five year old

Paul Rees (younger son)

Piers Island: The excitement would grow in the early morning hours when my parents would be loading groceries, supplies, clothes, and toys into our maroon station wagon (Pontiac Parisienne) which visually resembled a hearse but was full of life. We would eventually all be loaded into our family car including our young black lab, who in those days would keep on jumping back and forth from the front bench seat into the back. I remember her whining as dogs do when excited as we neared Canoe Cove where our boat was docked. Like her, I could sense and knew where we were going and the traditions and rituals that would come next. They were always brisk mornings and our boat was located at the furthest possible point from the parking lot, which made the anticipation of the adventure we were about to embark on even more exciting and painful all at the same time. My father would make what seemed like 20 trips from the car to the boat. I would stay with my brother while my parents loaded and packed the boat, looking over the edge of the dock for any possible signs of sea life.

The Departure: Finally, we were all loaded into to our small boat wearing big smiles and life jackets (I hated to put one on). Dad would slowly pull the boat out and it was an amazing feeling to be so young, riding in a boat on top of the water - more importantly knowing what was about to happen next. We cleared the dock and set out on the open water for what was probably a 20-minute boat ride. Once we were clear of the nearby BC Ferries terminal, the adventure that is Piers Island took the next step. I sat in the back of the boat mildly getting sprayed from the water as our family boat cut through the waves. Then Dad would look over his shoulder and give me the nod and the smile. A rush of excitement would run through my body as I jumped and ran all the four steps to his 'captains chair.' For the next five minutes (which seemed like an eternity), I got to sit on his lap and captain the boat - navigate the waves, avoid the kelp and the driftwood, and on occasion heroically sail the ship over the ferry waves of a recently past vessel. Eventually I would help our family safely arrive at our dock.

The Journey: We never had our own dock in front of our house so we arrived at the community dock, even though there was always a dock in front of our house, or at least a half built one. There was a small shed at the top of the road where we kept the biggest wheelbarrow I had ever seen. I loved the shed/cabin. It was always locked and showed no signs of anyone having entered it in decades. With cracked windows and spider webs everywhere, it was so alluring and there were so many things to potentially explore and see. I could hardly wait. Everyone would help make the multiple trips from the boat to the shed to load up the wheelbarrow. How my dad was able to pick it up and walk with it was beyond me. The entire way to our house was UPHILL. I had to walk it along a gravely dirt windy road. The only downhill part was the path to our house. There was a 'fire station' by the entrance to our house that I had explored many times by myself and with my brother and was the marker that we were almost there.

The Arrival: I remember the excitement as we arrived at our oasis. Walking past the treehouse that our parents built, watching my dad navigate this tank-like wheelbarrow filled with what seemed like everything we owned down this bumpy, twisty-turny trail until we arrived at our home. The best part of the Piers Island adventure was about to happen for me - in my-five-year old mind. We had a huge, gorgeous deck that ran along the side of the house, yet there was four by four piece of wood (that had certainly seen better days) that served as a "ramp" from the yard to the deck, so the wheelbarrow could seamlessly pass. However, the tradition which never failed:

I would run with anticipation to lift up this piece of wood to see or find my magical friend . . . and it never once failed me. What you would find underneath this innocuous piece of wood was a magical kingdom that was home to the biggest frog you would ever see in your life. With no fear, I would pick him up triumphantly and show him gleefully to my Mother and in turn, he would pee all over my hand and arm.

The Adventure: From here the next few days would be a blur. I remember:

Waking up in the morning and going to the beach and exploring. Turning over rocks to see crabs and eels
Digging for clams
Catching snakes of all sizes (Mom wasn't a big fan of that)
Exploring the centre of the Island, following trails and on a good day finding deer roaming in a clearing
Watching from our massive living room pods of killer whales jumping in the ocean
Enjoying the ambiance of the last ferry's light sailing past our home

The sense of community, comradery and life like no other. When you were there - life, adventure, and family were all that mattered.

Piers! Thanks for the memories!

A life-changing time

Rob Rees (nephew)

How can I forget my memories of Piers Island? I am so fortunate to have two special people in my life who provided me with a wonderful and adventurous time as a young boy. These people are my Uncle Dave and Aunty Sonia. I so remember going over to my Aunt and Uncle's house early in the morning as we all packed our gear and headed to Piers Island. This was long before the house was built and we would all camp in our tents and watch all the excitement going by: the ferries, various boats and lots of wildlife.

I remember getting up at first light as a kid and getting in the rowboat and rowing about 300 feet off shore where there was a reef. I would jig a rock cod or sea bass and that would be the barbeque in the evening. I remember big cookie sheets with steaks marinating in wine too. After fishing and breakfast, I would often hike around the island and go through the old apple orchard in the middle of the island to see deer. Then I would visit people like the Hams, the Friedenthals and many more whose names I can't remember. There was always something to do. Those days being bored never crossed this boy's mind.

Many times Uncle Dave would take me salmon fishing and cod fishing. These memories I cherish and I can relive them at any moment. How could I have forgotten the Sneades? (Lot 41). They were amazing people; Howie was an incredible fishing lure maker. Howie's lures could outfish anything on the market. I remember we dug some clams and took them over to Joe Friedenthal's house (Lot 49) where he taught me how to steam clams with wine and herbs. They were delicious and I still cook them that way today. Joe's wife had a little dog she called 'Little Bit'.

I always remember the first Piers Island fishing derby. I caught a big dogfish, which was fun, but the winner had caught a 99 pound Skate. It was the first time I ever saw Skate prepared before. I will never forget going to Princess Margaret Island (now called Portland Island). The cod and green ling fishing there was something you can only dream about now. We used to bring back potato-sacks full of fish. We had so many good fish cookouts there! As a young boy I felt like Robinson Crusoe on that island. It was heaven to me. All those wonderful summer days filled with laughing and everyone enjoying themselves are some of my fondest memories of being young. I can't think of one single bad time there, so Heaven is the right description.

I remember when my Uncle Dave and my Dad went fishing one hot summer day. When my Dad got home he was walking very bowed-legged. I asked him what had happened. He said after a long day in the sun he lay down to sleep. The problem was he left the fly open on his shorts and I guess he was not wearing any underwear. He had sunburned a very sensitive spot on his body. Did we ever get a laugh out of that one.

The last memory I have of the Island was Uncle Dave inviting a bunch of my cousins and me, for a day and night on the island. We had a riot and a blast. I owe my Aunt and Uncle a great debt of gratitude for allowing me to share in this wonderful and life-shaping time.

Vincent and Paul Rees (sons)

Lot 41 - Howie and Helena Sneade

Treasured Memories Of Piers

(written by Ken Sneade)

In 1963, my Dad Howie built a 17-foot Brandlemire and that began our boating days around the Gulf Islands of B.C. Dad would pack up my brother Kerry and our two sisters, Debbie and Janet, along with my mom Helena. My Dad's first boat he owned was called *Burma* and he named a lot of his subsequent boats Burma after that.

This was our regular Friday night tradition. We would stop at Sidney and we all got Dairy Queen ice creams while Dad fuelled up the boat at All Bay Marina. All aboard, we headed out to discover Piers Island. Dad saw a For Sale sign on one of those summer nights. It was for a home listed by the realtor, Reg Biscoe, and the rest is history and the beginning of our life on Piers.

Dad and Mom bought Lot 41 on the east side of Piers and right away we started camping out and pioneering on the lot. We shuttled groceries and all our camping supplies and lots of other stuff in a wee dinghy. The first thing Dad did was to build a staircase from the ocean's edge up to the property, to provide us access. It was very wide, built with two logs that he winched up from the beach. In the late 1960s, Dad built a 600 sq. ft. cabin for his growing family and soon we had two more sisters, Charlotte and Stephanie.

Dad was a very social guy, inviting friends Dave and Sonia Rees and Dougald McDonald to Piers and meeting lots of other islanders: Peter and Grace Folkes, Bob and Linda Clarke, Joe and Flo Friedenthal, Bill Scoones, Lionel and Deanna Greene, Brian and Joanne Sibley, Rob and Edith Jarrett -- all of whom formed close friendships bonded through their mutual fondness of Piers Island.

It was great times every summer. I remember a close neighbour Burpee MacClennan (Lot 37) who became instrumental in building the first Piers Island Volunteer Fire Department structure with his cable riggings, and block and tackle approaches. Then my dad converted a 1953 Chevy five-ton oil tanker into the first Piers Island fire engine - a red fire truck!

All sorts of things were happening then. Cabins were being built, families were summering. The first boat for any child was as exciting as getting their first bicycle. Summer traditions were established, such as the annual Piers Island picnic in August, with endless corn on the cob, hot dogs and burgers. There was enough ice cream to feed the 100 or so people who had become the Piers Island community, both full-time and part-timers.

Howie Sneade

By 1990, our small cabin at Lot 41 had become a large three-bedroom home with Dad's signature skills throughout. The face of Piers Island had seen many changes, but the essence of the island had remained the same. My dad and his second wife Diane sold the Piers lot in 1998, but they remained in touch with lifelong friends our family had made on the island. I still boat over from Salt Spring Island when I can, to catch up with friends on Piers. The treasured memories I have of Piers Island will always be close to my heart.

Sneade family on the Burma

Lot 44 - Maurice Destrube and Eleanor Sandman

A Skilled Builder In The 1960s On Piers

(told by Rob Destrube, Maurice's nephew from Victoria, B.C.)

Uncle Maurice Destrube and Aunt Eleanor Sandman bought the property on Piers in 1959, and he built a log house on the property when he was well over 75 years old. I recall him falling off a ladder and, I believe, breaking a leg in the process. Maurice had built a number of log homes in Alberta over the years (one is a two-story log house that was moved to become the major part of the museum in St. Paul, Alberta). As a result, he was a skilled builder when he built his cottage on Piers.

I personally remember the long dirt road all around Piers at the time when I visited the island in the mid 1960s.

Maurice's brother (my dad) (Guy or George) and his wife also bought two properties on the east side of Piers in the 1970s (for $5,000 or $6,000), and offered it to my brother and me. We both declined due to the huge expense, and both lots were both sold a few years later. Destrube Place in Cordova Bay is named after Maurice Destrube.

According to *Pioneering in Alberta: Maurice Destrube's Story (1981)*, published by the Historial Society of Alberta, Maurice had written the following about the property on Piers:

"Sometimes it seemed a hard venture for a man of my age, but I enjoyed doing it in spite of the very hard work. When the cabin was completed we decided it deserved a name, so we called it 'Notre Folie.' The sign, carved into a cedar lot, hangs from a post by the road. To begin with we had no amenities. We carried our drinking water each time we went over there. Now it has become disgustingly civilized. We have plumbing, electric power and light, and soon we shall be looking further afield for piece and quiet. Later I added on a living room, kitchen, bedroom and a wee bathroom. So I am back to where I started. My first home in Canada was a one-room shack with a sod roof and mother earth for a floor. My present log home on the island is rather more sophisticated."

Maurice Destrube (photographed by nephew Rob Destrube)

Lot 50 - Mary Tucker and Enid Houghland

Mary Tucker has been described as, "Queen Mary", the "Matriarch of Piers" and many other endearing names. Mary was no wimp, having built her own home in the 1960s, drove her own boat (including a number of boat rescues) until age 89, and lived independently on Piers until after her 95th birthday celebration. She was tough, funny, cantankerous, opinionated, mischievous, thoughtful, generous, wise and dearly loved. She was the oldest and the longest full-time Piers resident (age 95) when she left the island in 2019, and proud of it. For years, Mary shared the home on Piers with friend, Enid Houghland, who left due to illness in the late 1990s.

Mary had lots of stories to tell but, of course, when I tried to interview her for this book, she kept changing the subject to other people's stories. Since she passed away in Sidney in 2020, there is no story directly from Mary. However numerous people wrote about this special island woman in their own *A Passion For Piers* stories. There are also a number of photos of Mary throughout this book, which show Mary's strong and diverse attachment to the community.

Mary loved Piers and she especially loved the nature – the environment and the animals on and around it. She was an ecologist before it was trendy to be one. According to Peter Arcese (Lot 80), who is a biologist with the Faculty of Forestry, University of British Columbia, Mary spoke to him on many occasions about the island's plant life. With Peter's permission, he has shared a letter that Mary wrote to him in July 2000 outlining the history of Piers' flora "before the coming of the sheep and us." I believe this letter is a wonderful tribute to Mary, and displays her passion and love of Piers.

July 13th/2000

Peter Arcese
80 McKenzie Crescent
Piers Island

Dear Peter
Trish Ross asked me to write and tell you how the island used to look before the coming of the sheep and us
I have listed the plants and animals that have either gone or become scarce.
Please remember this is only my opinion of how it used to be.

1. Meadows both north and south
bats, swallows, butterflies, rabbits, deer, a few skylarks the edges of the meadows had plenty of wild strawberries

2. Waters edge and cliffs
deer, mink, Kingfishers, otter, osprey, hawks, cormorants, hens & chickens lots of ladyslippers (especially Harry Point), humming birds, lilies and chocolate lilies, false boxwood.

3 Lower Reservoir Area
trilliums, wild bleedingheart, swallows, salamanders, butterflies

4. Upper Reservoir Area
was like a tropical jungle with many strange flowers and insects not found on the rest of the island – a delightful place to walk quietly through.

5 Centre of the island & roadside
Bats, Salamanders, snakes, owls, lilies and chocolate lilies, oregan grape, pigeons, hawks,

5. Centre of island and roadside (cont.)
coral root, rattlesnake plantain, spire orchid, wintergreen, false boxwood, candy stick, pine sap oregan grape, indian pipe, wild strawberries, daisies down centre of road.

6 Biscoe Beach
before draining had miners lettuce and was a fly-away area for many ducks

7 The water's edge & shoreline
oyster, clams, swans, of course many more ducks etc and Kelp beds.

Sincerely
Mary Tucker.

P.S Thank you for your report on the centre of the island. I think it has been long needed and was excellent.
MT

Mary Tucker

Enid Houghland

Lot 55 - Bob and Linda Clarke

Our 'Piers Island Highrise'

In October 1962, my brother Frank Clarke and his wife Judy, my girlfriend Linda (Slocomb) and I were taken on a tour of Piers Island by Reg Fraser-Biscoe, the real estate agent. We all fell in love with Lot 55 with its sandy beach. Reg arranged with the owner John McKenzie, easy terms for Frank and I to purchase the lot. Frank had just finished an apprenticeship in carpentry. We were then busy every weekend until the Spring of 1963, clearing the lot of many large fallen trees and overgrowth.

April 1963 saw the start of our 'dream cabin' in earnest. We devoted all week-ends and many week-day evenings after work in Victoria. All heavy Navvy Jack and building materials were carried over in a small 14-foot boat. The front of the cabin rose three stories and Reg, passing by with prospective customers, named it the 'Piers Island Highrise'.

Other islanders started asking for Frank's help in building their cottages. In 1964, Judy and Frank decided to move to Piers full-time with their baby son Frankie. Frank was kept very busy building on Piers and community volunteering with Judy. Soon along came their daughter Debbie. While they loved life on Piers, the income made was just not sufficient. They made the difficult decision to sell their share of Lot 55 to me in late 1966. Linda and I got married later that year. Our priority was to keep the Piers cottage as a vacation home. Fortunately, we were able to purchase a permanent home in Saanich. From babyhood our son Wayne and our daughter Wendy grew up spending every possible time on Piers Island.

In 1968, an accidental fire raged almost to the point of destroying our cabin. Neighbours rushed to help and saved the day. All of us were thoroughly upset that the Piers Island Association directors had failed promises to provide some fire protection. Our group decided to get some fire equipment for our own protection. The directors quickly arranged that we form a Piers Island fire department. Another offshoot of this endeavour has been our wives forming the 'Piers Island Progressive Dinner' — an event enjoyed for more than 50 years. (This is well-covered in Harold Skolrood's book, *Piers Island: A brief history of Piers Island, 1886-1993.*)

Linda's sister Jane and husband Les Grant and their family have enjoyed Piers with us for many years. Together with our Son Wayne, his wife Sylvia, their son Dayton, and daughter Jordyn, and with our daughter Wendy and her husband Rob, we all continue to love Piers Island.

Dorothy Hubin, Jane Grant, Les Grant

Sonia Rees, Jean Thompson, Linda Clarke

Fred Thompson, Harvey Hubin, Edith Jarrott

Lot 56 - Grace and Svend Mariager

A true Craftsman And Community Involvement

(told by granddaughter Dawn)

In the 1970s, Grace and Svend Mariager bought the pan-abode cottage on Piers at Lot 56. Shortly after they moved in permanently. In 1976 Grace's son Bruce got married and they went to the cottage for their honeymoon. The little boat that Grace and Svend said they could use had been stolen from the Piers lot on Dolphin Road, so they had to rent one to get to Piers. Bruce says it was a very basic cottage at the time they were on their honeymoon.

Grace and Svend lived in that very basic cabin for a few years, until Grace agitated for a new home and Svend said "Yes". BUT, first he had to build a large workshop to make some equipment. THEN, he built a major horizontal band saw on steel tracks to cut some lumber. THEN, he spent two or three years pulling logs, 'high floaters' up from the ocean, using a winch assembly he built. THEN, he spent another couple of years milling the logs into planks to build the house. THEN, he built the house. The project took awhile…

They belonged to the Lifeboat Society while living there, and were called out on numerous missions to help stranded boaters, at all hours of the day and night.

Svend used to get furious with the BC Ferries for going too fast through Satellite Channel and he would clock their speed and radio the Ferry to scold them. Svend and Grace were very community minded volunteers and involved in the Firehall and the water maintenance on the island.

Grace's love was her garden and she was proud of listing the produce she had grown, of the food on your dinner plate. Keeping the deer out was a big deal. Also, they enjoyed picking all the wild berries on the island, and relished all the seafood they caught. Piers Island was a very special part of their lives.

Sven and Grace Mariager

Lot 61 - Fred and Jean Thompson

Wonderful Island Living!

We bought our lot on Piers Island in July 1965. We had been visiting a friend in Victoria who had just come back from Piers Island and we asked, "Where's that?" Since we had been looking for a recreational property and loved boating, we thought about it and decided to visit the island. Because we had young children, Fred went to see Piers first with a friend of his and they hiked all around the island. Near the site of the government wharf, they met a guy and asked him if he knew who sold property on Piers. The man said, "Actually, I do." They were talking to the realtor Reg Biscoe (who lived at Lot 2).

Shortly afterwards, we came to Piers with our three children in tow (Bruce was a baby). Reg's wife, Alice, said that she would look after the kids, while Reg showed us houses. We were there three times, and then decided we wanted to make an offer on Lot 6l. We got it for $3,200. We were still living full-time in Victoria, but spent most weekends and vacations on the island. Fred found out that Charlie Kent, who he knew from the work in Victoria, lived full-time on Piers.

It was wonderful living on the island. We camped in the early years and built a cottage that we expanded over times. We moved to Piers full-time in 1991. At times, when our boat or motor wasn't working, all we had was a tiny eight-foot Sabot (a small sailing dinghy) to transport our three kids and us and all our supplies to and from Piers. So, we had to make many trips. We got swamped over by the ferry's waves more than once. We had to pack up from the beach and put all the wet stuff in the back of the station wagon (including wet sleeping bags and wet tent) for our trek home.

We really loved boating. Fred got involved with Sabot boats on Piers. He built a wooden one and then we bought two more plastic Sabots. At one point Fred took 10 sailboats in a line and towed them all the way from Dolphin Road (on Vancouver Island) to Piers. In the late 1960s to early 1970s, Fred was instrumental in arranging for someone to teach dozens of kids and adults how to sail those Sabots. Over the years we acquired a 14-foot open aluminum boat for most of our commuting to and from Piers. We also had a 16-foot Hobie Cat (a small sailing catamaran) with two pontoons together plus a trampoline on top. The whole family had a riot.

Our progressive dinners were so special. A number of Piers families got together and we all shared different courses going from one house to the other. We started at one house for drinks, then another for appies, then another for the main course, and ended with dessert. Especially memorable was when Rob and Edith Jarrott (Lot 80) arranged for a belly-dancer to come to the island for one of our dinners. The progressive dinner members were Howie and Diane Sneade (Lot 41), Joe and Flo Friedenthal (Lot 53), Bob and Linda Clarke and Jane and Les Grant (all from Lot 55), Dorothy and Harvey Hubin (Lot 58), Dave and Sonya Rees (Lot 39) and us. We dressed in a special theme each time. For one dinner, we dressed as pirates and had a cannon (at Lot 41) that shot toilet paper. Dave Rees hired a herring skiff and put the cannon on it and from the sea he shot toilet paper back to Piers. It was all such fun.

On our twentieth anniversary of the progressive dinner in 1988, we told people "Just bring your suitcases, and toothbrushes." No one knew where we were going. We rented a huge boat with a captain and booked rooms in a hotel in Cowichan Bay to celebrate. We also went on a real cruise together from Victoria down through the Panama Canal in 1993 to celebrate our twenty-fifth anniversary. The progressive dinners are still going on, but we get together now for dinners in our homes or at restaurants.

Now we are now living in a condo in Sidney and still looking out at the water. Our time on Piers was some of the best years of our lives for our whole family. We have so many memories we will never forget.

Pancake Breakfast Crew (left to right)
Al Morrison, Pauline Poulsom, Pat Phillips, Jean Thompson, Bob Clarke, Dave Poulsom, John Currie

Fred and Jean Thompson

Lot 69 - John and Ann Herbert

How We Found Piers Island

In the early 1960s, my brother Fred and I were searching for a summer cottage property. We saw an ad by Fraser Biscoe in the Vancouver Sun newspaper describing property on Piers Island. Fraser agreed to pick me up at the old government wharf, which was located where the B.C. Ferries vessels now dock.

He explained to me that he was only selling lots in blocks of five and he took me to the lots that were still for sale. We chose the property at Lot 69 and agreed to buy it. He wanted a deposit and we agreed on $300; however, the only problem was that I had to borrow $100 back because I did not have the price of the ferry ride home.

Thanksgiving dinner on Piers has always been a special time for our family. For many years we would gather the family together for a traditional Thanksgiving dinner at the cottage. There often were around 20 hungry mouths with extras being various girlfriends or boyfriends and often some of the Skolrood (Lot 92) clan, since Ann and Isabelle Skolrood were sisters.

We would move the picnic table inside from the porch and move a chesterfield and chairs up to the fireplace for maximum room. We were now set for the banquet. One particular Thanksgiving was especially memorable. Just when dinner was ready to be served and everyone was seated, the power went out. Luckily Ann and I had saved coal oil lamps from each of our cottages. These were placed throughout the cottage to give a lovely glow. At that point our little granddaughter piped up, "Grandpa, can we do it this way every year"?

John and Anne Herbert

Lot 80 - Edith and Rob Jarrott

Fishing Derbies And Slugfests

(told by son, Michael)

My parents, Edith and Rob Jarrott moved to Piers in late 1969. I was born in 1972, and as a kid, I loved Piers. I was always a real 'water baby'. We put up the second dock on the west side of Piers. The process involved pouring concrete trusses from a helicopter. Howie Sneade (Lot 41) hand scuptured trusses with a 6" grinder; Dad and Howie were good friends. Unfortunately, we sold Piers after dad passed away summer 1997.

My favourite memories of Piers were the picnics and fishing derbies. Howie Sneade would show up in his swimming shorts and fur coat (mostly for the fishing derby). We would have a big party on the beach after the fishing. I remember Reg Biscoe camping on the bay at Patrol Point, on the white sand beach. He often camped in his boat. The fishing derby was a childhood 'right of passage' each year, and we would fish and fish and fish. There was a rule of the derby that you had to be in sight of Piers Island for the fishing. In the late 1980s, we fished James Island (around Powder Wharf where explosives were shipped to Victoria and Sidney) and Coal Island, where we could still see Piers. Howie made the Swartz Bay ferry fishing area popular for mackeral years ago. We all liked 'the wall' of Pender Island. Near Fulford on Salt Spring Island, we caught a lot of cod.

The parties on Piers were always great. My parents were part of the 'Progressive Dinner.' All the 'progressive people' were the most memorable people on Piers. We had the Turkish dinner at our place. I sat behind Joe Friendenthal (Lot 55). He was smoking two cigarettes at once watching the dancer. We used to play poker at the Sibleys (Lot 27) and they had great New Year's Eve parties. They had a little rec room, which looked like an English pub. I served adult drinks from behind the bar when I was still a kid. The Sibleys moved off Piers via helicopter and the pilot then brought trusses over for the Yearwood's house (Lot 84) on the west side, instead of going up the steep hill. John and Diane Currie (Lot 86) brought house lumber in by helicopter too.

Sven Marianger (Lot 56) was a real craftsman. He was a Swedish machinist and in the early 1980s he made a three-wheeler power wheelbarrow - Gerry Kristianson still has one. My dad hired him to do drain rocks and he used his three-wheel barrow. He had his own sawmill and had quite a shop. He was very handy. Grace Mariager and my granny were in girl scouts together.

The early 1980s were crazy years for slugs. As a group, we declared a Slugfest. We decided we would walk around the island with a stick and a piece of tin, and would stab all the slugs we could find. Mary Tucker (Lot 50) was the most ruthless. One year the bullfrogs were so big (six inches) that they would take us out on our bikes.

After we moved away, I've been back to the island a couple of times. Mr. Peaker (Lot 5) recognized me right away and picked us up in his golf cart and gave us a tour around Piers. Mr. Peaker used to always be the MC for the Piers picnic in the 1970s and 1980s. I visited the Hubins (Lot 58), the bench at the old firehall, and of course, Biscoe Beach. I recognized Mary Tucker right away with her hands behind her back and her head down, chuckling away. My grandmother and Mary Tucker went to school together, so they had known each other for a long time. My mom's Dad and Mary taught in Trail, B.C. together years ago, and then they taught together in Victoria. Mary Tucker was one of the originals.

Mike Smart (Lot 6) helped build a pirate ship for one progressive dinner. One fishing derby or picnic Mike was water skiing and broke his Achilles heal. I loved waterskiing with my Lifetimer boat. Howie Sneade fired off a canon on us at the water one time. It was all a lot of fun.

Living on the west side of Piers, I remember wonderful sunsets. I now live in Point Grey, Vancouver, just up from the yacht club. My wife's family has a place on Bowen Island, and we face the same direction as we did on Piers. So, I still have the cottage experience. However, I still have a tear in my eye when I go by Piers on the ferry. I kept my dad's bike from Piers Island. Dad used to carry my sister and me around the island in the basket of the bike. So many memories…

I do have a confession to make after 40 years. I cheated during the Terry Fox run one year on Piers. I was only 10 years old and I still feel badly. My mom Edith added one more thing she remembers about Piers. I won a prize in the Piers Fishing Derby. It was a cigarette lighter and I was only five years old!

Jarrott family

Lot 87 - Pat and Doug Gait

Fifth Generation On Piers

We were coming back from Vancouver on the ferry, and saw a sign on Clive Island, that said "Property for Sale on Piers Island." Doug's mother Margaret, Doug and I (Pat) bought Lot 87 in March 1965. The first thing Doug built was an outhouse, since we needed it with five children, aged two to ten years old.

We tented the first summer and got rained on a lot. The next spring Doug built a four bedroom cabin with no power. He felled trees with help from the Denalics, for the stringers that are still under the cabin. Later he built a one bedroom cabin, with a workshop in the basement. Doug thought it would keep the kids out of the fridge. It didn't work.

In the summer, Doug commuted to work Monday to Friday, and after supper it was 'water-ski time.' The children learned to swim, fish, ski, dive and sail. We all have enjoyed the fishing derbys, picnics, the walkabout and Moonlight Madness dances. We had many birthdays and anniversaries on Piers. Our granddaughter Erin married Zach on Piers. We have many good friends: the Dwyers, Changs, Joneses, Neidigs, Thompsons, Formans, Duffies, Morrisons, Bert Johnston, the Watsons and many others who we met on Piers over the years.

We are now on our FIFTH Generation on Piers!

Pat and Doug Gait

The Gait Family

Lot 88 - Mike and Heather Siska

(Heather 'in spirit')
Reflections On Piers Island

Our love of the Gulf Islands started with my late wife Heather's high school summer camp experience on Gambier Island. In our quest to find a place with similar enchanting geography, we had met Reg Biscoe who introduced us to his Piers Island development and his vision for the island. Reg always tried to foster ownership by a diverse group of people who could see and understand his vision. The final plan developed was restricted to waterfront properties only and three properties developed inside of McKenzie Crescent. The decision to develop the interior lands as a shared natural forested area for the residents was an important factor in our decision to purchase our property on Piers. We became hooked on the potential and the lifestyle that the island offered. After reviewing several properties we purchased Lot 88 in 1967, which was the beginning of our summer life and experiences on Piers Island.

We purchased our property on the island before we purchased our residence in Victoria. Now with two properties we had no money to build, so we camped for a number of years on the site of our cottage. When you're young, tenting has its joy and if set up reasonably well for the summer - a good tent, lawn chairs, barbecue, kerosene lantern, a safe water supply at the road, and a good outhouse - it can be marvellous. What more does a new summer resident want or need?

Reg Biscoe was eager to hand over the administration of the island to the Piers Island Improvement District [PIID]. It was an honour to serve as a trustee with Fred Thompson (Lot 61), William McNutt, Paul Dwyer (93) and Gord Jones in the years 1968 to 1970. The community required a good water system and the Trustees at that time were challenged to complete a permanent and safe distribution system with standpipes for a measure of fire protection, a wood stave reservoir for storage and access for operation and maintenance. Developing any project on Piers is not an easy endeavour and often fraught with controversy, but in the end islanders always find a path forward for the benefit of everyone. There are many challenges in self-governing but through the democratic process unique to the island, it is a rewarding way to give back to the community. I would encourage all islanders to be involved in the island's governance.

Our plan was to 'stick build' our cottage using salvaged material where possible. During the 1970s, many redevelopments replaced the older turn of the century houses in Victoria and we were able to salvage flooring material, leaded and stained glass windows, doors, asphalt roofing ($5 for our first roof!) as well as native stone from our property and our neighbours, and a few timbers, which were plentiful on site. With a growing family and always limited by money, we were able to complete the cottage over many years through perseverance and love of our dream. The architectural features of our cottage were designed around summer living and outdoor life on the deck of our west-facing property. Both our sons and a few other extended family members, contributed to building our cottage, making it a truly family affair. Our former neighbour Bob Jarrod (Lot 80) completed the electrical and occasionally a few helpful hands were lent by others on Piers, including Harold Skolrood (Lot 92), John Currie (Lot 86) and Jorge Boehm (Lot 82).

Boating to and from Piers is part of the allure. Both our sons enjoyed boating and the marine environment around the island and also nearby to Patrol Island, Arbutus Island, and Salt Spring Island. I would be remiss if I didn't mention the early years of good fishing with many enjoyable hours trolling and jigging in the nearby waters.

The centre of the island is unique to the development and has played an important part in our island experience. The trail system has played a fun part for all of us, especially our sons and grandson. Hiking and mountain biking the trails have been a highlight of family activities. Spotting a deer trail directly opposite our property, I cleared off the dead branches and small dead falls to interconnect the west side to the summit - a unique feature on the island. The Piers Island Association (PIA) has nicely improved this trail to become a part of the interconnecting trail system. The centre of the island is unique to Piers and offers nature's beauty to all of us. Preservation of the island's natural ecological system is now being addressed and will be a gift to all of us to enjoy in the future. Some specific trees, including rare Garry Oak and Arbutus and others, are being challenged to survive as the second growth coniferous trees become dominant.

Pioneer Sir Clive Phillips-Wolley (on Piers 1901-1909) established an extensive orchard on Piers and a significant number of trees survive. It was a joy to spearhead and be a part in managing and expanding the orchard. With an irrigation system installed by the PIA, the future operation of the orchard can be maintained with relative ease. Thanks to Sandy Brunham (Lot 64) for continuing this legacy.

Beachcombing is a favourite pastime for our family, may it be shells, sea glass, the island's sedimentary geology or the long ago sea life trapped within the layers. We've always enjoyed bird and whale watching, and discovering the diverse flora and fauna of the island during the many walks and explorations. Heather loved photography and Piers was her oasis for many spectacular sunset scenes. Being on the west side means savouring the late afternoon, and bathing in the intense afternoon sun amplified over the reflecting water. The seasonal traverse of sunset timelines highlighted by the southern shoulder of Salt Spring Island was a reminder of the seasons coming and going.

Heather loved the solitude of Piers in the fall and winter. She spent many times writing, enveloped in the natural environment offered by Piers. It is easy to understand why the Gulf Islands, including Piers, attract many writers, artists and sculptors.

Piers Island was and is our getaway from the hustle and bustle of Victoria. Island living requires resiliency and a passion for the quiet way of life on a small island. Those who discover its secrets find it a paradise away from the adjacent urban world, yet still close enough to civilization to not feel isolated.

The significance of Piers to our family is spiritually enhanced as Heather and her parents rest at sea in the waters near Shute Reef. It's a reminder that we are here to enjoy the beauty of the place but only passing through in our journey on this precious earth of ours.

As I start to approach my middle 80s, it's time to assess the future. Piers requires a level of fitness and agility but knowing when to move on is always a personal choice. Our youngest son Jonathan and partner Melissa love the island and intend on continuing our family's cottage life on Piers. While it is too early to tell, perhaps in the future our grandson Brandon too will also fall in love with the island.

Warm regards to all islanders past and present - sunshine passes, shadows fall, and loved memories outlast all.

Heather and Mike Siska

Brandon, Jon, Melissa

Lot 89 - Laird and Gillian Jones

Endless Good Times

Laird bought Lot 89 on Piers Island in 1964. My brother, Chris Scott, and his friend, John Stenstrom (Lot 99), co-owned a new business called *Fleet Boats*, a water taxi-mail delivery service based in Van Isle Marina in Sidney. One of the fleet boats, *Sayonara*, was a 22-foot mahogany runabout with a 300 hp engine. In the 1960s, they travelled regularly to the Southern Gulf Islands to deliver passengers, supplies, and the mail.

On one memorable day, Laird, an employee of *Fleet Boats*, took realtor Fraser (Reg) Biscoe to Piers. Laird was given a tour of the island and subsequently bought Lot 89. We built a small cabin with the intent to build closer to the front of the property, but that has not materialized….yet.

Laird and I spent many summers at Piers with our children, Mike and Megan, with only basic amenities. The updated outdoor shower still exists today with a fantastic ocean view. Our days at Piers were filled with recreational activities, including boating, water-skiing, knee-boarding, tubing, fishing, shrimping, exploring the beaches, daytrips to Sidney Spit, ice-cream cones at Nan Patterson's store in Fulford Harbour, the Hoyte's honey bars, axe-throwing, walking on stilts, coffee and happy hour with the neighbours, and many more memorable times with friends and family.

Sadly, Laird passed away in 1998. Since then, we haven't been to Piers as much as we used to. Mike, his wife Susan, and their kids Connor and Amara love spending time on Piers in the summer. I have been so fortunate to enjoy the companionship of Scott Denoon (Lot 131). He is affectionately known to Connor and Amara as "Grampa". Megan and her husband Ian, and their special grand-dog Gaia, come from Calgary whenever possible.

Piers is a wonderful community to be part of. Endless good times with family and friends at Piers have been unforgettable! We are looking forward to creating many more memories.

Lot 92 - Harold and Isabelle Skolrood

Valhalla: Just about the best place on earth

(written by Doug Skolrood)

It's not difficult to picture what Piers looked and felt like when we (children Sharon, Ron, Sheila and Doug) were young, after our mother and father built their simple cottage on the west side of the island. Very little has changed in the years since 1967. It still feels a bit isolated - an almost framed view of Salt Spring and Satellite Channel - with the forest behind you. All surrounded by spruce, cedar, lazy-looking arbutus and ferns straining to reclaim the small area cut back for the cottage.

Like almost every other resident, our parents' first exposure to Piers came as guests of established islanders: in this case, our mom's sister Ann and her husband John Herbert (Lot 69). Having enjoyed childhood summers at their own family cottage in Tsawwassen, the sisters already knew the joys of a hideaway by the sea. Having grown up on the windswept Saskatchewan prairie, the charms of the Gulf Islands must have seemed like a beautiful and lush revelation to our dad. They quickly chose to build their own place nestled in a small cove on the less-populated west shore of the island.

For years, our family boat at Piers was the *Goose Feathers*, an open 16-footer that ferried groceries, laundry and guests to Piers. It was the only small boat around with its name proudly emblazoned on the bow. It was ungainly, unwieldy, weighed down by multiple coats of fiberglass - and a well-loved part of life at the cottage.

Younger brother Doug remembers being out alone one day in *Goose Feathers*. In those days, ferries heading into Swartz Bay created huge, 'roller' waves which slowly washed away the banks of the island. More crucially, they were an absolute thrill to jump over in a boat. Changing course to intercept the ferry, he remembers zipping along beside the great white hull searching for rollers - and instead finding a storm of churning, swirling foam and steep waves kicked up by the propellers. Immediately, boat and boy went airborne, with boat gaining marginally less altitude than boy. He came down in a heap by the bow, soaking wet, bloodied and with a literally flooded motor. Upon bailing for half an hour and restarting the motor, he returned home to tell his mom he'd "lost his grip getting out of the boat," which was technically the truth.

Younger sister Sheila recalls Piers feeling like "a real-life version of the 1970s television series Fantasy Island," where almost-weekly episodes inevitably began with dad travelling across to Dolphin Road to bring back a boat full of guests. As 'da boat' arrived back at Piers, the newly arrived friends and family were unloaded onto the beach carrying their luggage, sleeping bags, swimsuits and great expectations. Luckily, Piers would never disappoint.

All our visitors stayed in true luxury - shoehorned into the tiny two-bunk guest room. They'd then fill their days building log rafts, racing through the centre of the island, having water fights on giant inner tubes with homemade wooden paddles, then collapsing on the beach at sunset with lemonade and hot dogs around a fire. At the end of their stay, our happy guests were loaded back onto the boat, returned to their car, and we'd head to Sidney to restock, do laundry and await the next arrivals. "Smiles, everyone... smiles!"

Older brother Ron remembers a slightly different aspect of being invited out to Piers. Like every other cottage, Lot 92 was a constant work in progress. What many people would call guests, dad sometimes considered labourers.

While visiting kids may have spent their days swimming and exploring, adult guests frequently found themselves painting, hauling materials up from the beach, helping to dig trenches - or worse, a pit for the septic tank - and generally pitching in to maintain and improve the cottage. While in law school, Ron proved he was his father's son by inviting a crew of friends out to Piers with the promise of sunshine and beer - and also put them to work cutting firewood all weekend. Later on, another friend visiting from England was brought out to experience Gulf Island hospitality, which included a harrowing trip in *Goose Feathers* balancing a new wood stove and, of course, hauling it up from the beach to the cottage along with their luggage. Every guest leaves their mark, and takes a little bit of Piers charm home with them.

Originally paying homage to his Norwegian heritage, our father named the cottage *Valhalla,* the heavenly Viking hall, a just reward for a life well-lived.

While many things have changed and the sturdy little *Goose Feathers* is gone, *Valhalla* has for the most part remained unchanged since the early days; every member of the family seems content to have the cottage remain as they remember it. Discussions come up, with the more progressive and ambitious proposing upgrades and the more sentimental and stubborn countering with a literal and figurative fresh coat of paint.

Nobody has the heart to make wholesale changes, instead happily returning to enjoy the cottage as it's always been. It's our family's favourite retreat, and still a source of great memories as three generations regularly gather for special holidays and weekends.

Our father would be happy to see that his children and now his grandchildren, still see what he and our mom originally did - a quiet little corner of heaven, and just about the best place on earth.

Skolrood family

Lot 93 - Paul and Helen Dwyer

The Pride Of Building A Cottage

(written by Paul)

In the early 1960s we visited friends Peggy and John Mica (Lot 9) on Piers. Helen had worked with Peggy at the former St. Joseph's hospital in Victoria. We were introduced to Piers Island realtor Reg Biscoe, and shortly afterwards bought Lot 93.

Although I had never used a chain saw before, I cleared the lot so that we could build our cottage in 1965. Reg Biscoe had a small barge that Piers Islanders could use to move things back and forth, and for several Saturday nights on that first summer, I borrowed that barge and moved logs from our lot to Barnacle Road. Because I felt safer hauling the barge with my small 14-foot boat when the ferries were not running, I would use the barge from midnight till 3 AM! We bucked up that wood for firewood for years to use at our Victoria home, and still have a bit of that wood left.

I built the Piers cottage myself, and I take pride in that. I am also proud that I only slipped off the roof once. We hired a lot of professional experts on the cottage for the electrical services and other amenities, but a lot of it we did ourselves.

I remember when our son Michael was young (age eight or nine) and a friend of his would come over every weekend to Piers. The two boys would roam around exploring 'every nook and cranny' on the island. Michael and his wife Anne now own the cottage on Piers.

start of cabin 1965

Paul, Tia, Helen and Liam Dwyer

Lot 96 - Ted and Theresa Stevenson

Piers Memories

(written by son Kelly Stevenson)

The Stevenson family was introduced to Piers Island by the Tredger family (Lot 107) in 1967. Fraser (Reg) Biscoe (Lot 2), the island realtor, took us around to view properties in his boat *Jigger*. He would drop anchor and row us ashore because this was easier than crawling through the bush from the roadside. I only remember there being the government wharf and Charlie Kent's (Lot 32) wharf at the time. The west side of the island was the last section to be opened up to property sales and was the only quarter section that did not have electricity. We purchased Lot 96 that week and the fun began!

We built the cottage the next summer and there were no other houses on our corner of the island. Many properties had tiny summer shacks or tent platforms with outhouses for the summertime owner's use. There were only three full-time residents back then, Charlie and Paula Kent (Lot 32), Wally Bain (Lot 10), and Hams (Lot 23). Every time we arrived at Piers, we would visit all three families and their doors were always open with no such thing as a short visit.

The road was more like a cart path with grass growing down the middle, often winding through a tunnel of overhanging branches. I remember lots of toads hopping along the road and the croaking chorus at sunset from every direction.

There were two horses that roamed loose around the orchard that we would entice with apples over to the big 'orchard rock' from which we would hop on for a gentle bareback ride to the beach.

My fondest memories of 'the way we were' was that there was a foot path that went all around the island in the front of the properties. Everyone would greet each other and catch up with the local chatter. It was a marvelous way to see the whole island and appreciate the tremendous views from all sides. It was also the way we kept an eye on each other's properties.

There were often 'progressive work parties' where a group would go from property to property and do odd jobs together, which often included meals and beverages. Work parties went into the late hours and often continued the next day. Many great accomplishments were appreciated by all.

Long before golf carts, we got around by small boats which we would beach or a number of minibikes appeared on the island to be used by the children by day and the parents by night.

Once on Piers, the only communication with the outside world was a pre-arranged telephone call at the government wharf payphone.

As children, we would often camp out at the beach or in the centre of the island, with or without tents. Forts were everywhere and hide-and-seek would last for hours. Our days were spent waterskiing and fishing with unforgettable success.

** *Author's Note:* Kelly says his mother Theresa was the lead in designing and establishing the Stevenson home on Piers. Both the Stevenson and Tredger families still own properties on Piers.

Ted Stevenson and Mary Tucker

Brenda Allen and Kelly Stevenson

Lot 112 - David and Pauline Poulsom

Pioneers in a New Land

(written by Paula Davis and Craig Poulsom)

The Poulsom family - David and Pauline, Paula (11), Dave (eight), Craig (four) - landed on Piers Island July 1966 at Lot 112. Our story covers the first 10 years, before our current cottage was built in 1976. For us, it was to be the start of a lifelong relationship with Piers. We felt like pioneers in a new land. Being seasoned campers already, we saw this as a new adventure.

We have many fond memories of early years on Piers. As it turned out, we had lots to keep us busy:

- Playing on the Association Beach (now Biscoe Beach). Beachcombing, finding baby crabs and bullheads in the tidal pools, digging for clams that you could eat.
- Exploring the woods at the Doukhobor camp, the old water tower, and the orchard.
- Swimming with our homemade wooden paddleboards, and Sabot sailing lessons.
- Great walks with Mom to Harry Point. There were only two cabins there at the time, and spring and summer flowers grew in abundance.
- Picnic excursions with the Forseths to Sidney Spit for crabbing and playing in the soft sand and quick trips to Russell Island for a few oysters.

From our place it was a 'short' excursion through the meadow and the woods just to make a call from the old payphone at the main wharf and to check for mail. We were always excited to see if we had letters from friends.

There were two main structures that Dad had to build right away to make our life on Piers somewhat comfortable. The first amenity was a plywood tent floor; the second was a makeshift camp/kitchen shelter fashioned out of a few small trees and a plastic tarp. We had a stone hearth fire pit for heat, a Coleman stove for cooking and a Coleman lantern for light, since there was no electricity yet.

Within a year or two, Dad built a second tent floor for the kids (it was very exciting to have our own space), as well as a proper kitchen shelter that we nicknamed the Birdhouse (it still stands today as our woodworking shop). Mom created many, many meals using the old cast iron coal/wood stove that Dad brought over from Vancouver Island. Pizzas, blackberry pies, and clam chowder made with beach clams, were just some of the delicious dishes Mom managed to create.

We always loved watching the clams in the cleaning bucket. We let them sit for a day in seawater and added oatmeal to help the process. What a funny thing to remember.

The Birdhouse was a gathering place for dinners with our neighbours and card games when it rained. How did we fit 12 people in that small space?

Another 'luxury' that we enjoyed was our outdoor shower shack. What a treat it was to get a few minutes of hot water from the black garden hose coiled up on the ground. Solar heating in the 1960s!

The smells of the beach and the forest, musty canvas tents, wood smoke, and oddly, white naphtha gas, and chain saw oil, all evoke vivid memories of those times.

For years it seemed we had that little slice of Piers to ourselves and the Forseths, being book-ended by the two Docs (Stevenson and Scholefield). Although we were only a short distance away from civilization in nearby Sidney (trips to the Sidney Bakery for a Charlotte Russe, Tanners for some comic books, and Harvey's for fishing tackle), Piers provided a tangible retreat, away from cars, concrete and the masses.

As we all know, time marches on and we see changes to the places that are part of our lives. Some are small, some big, but the things most important to us have not changed. The eternal beauty of the ocean, the chatter of the birds during the day, the silence of the forest at night, and most importantly, the people and sense of community that have been and will always be, a constant through the decades.

Lot 117 - Susanne and Michael Ferrie

Summers At The Cottage

(told by Susanne)

We bought our Piers Island property in the early 1960s and tented on the lot for the first few years. Howard Eckman (Lots 31 and 33) and Michael used to sail in the Swiftsure Yacht Race together, and they heard about Piers when Barb Eckman's parents (the Hams) bought Lot 23. Both families visited Piers on a number of occasions, and ended up buying properties themselves. Susanne remembers on her first visit to Piers getting 'the first degree' from one of the full-time residents (Paula Kent - Lot 32) as to who was she and why was she on Piers. They became good friends afterwards.

We spent months every summer clearing the property of broom and gorse and finally built a small 12'x12' cottage with a propane stove. We had plans to build a round house, but instead it has become sort of a 'House that Jack built' with all the add-ons. It still remains a cottage that our kids and grandkids enjoy part-time.

Older people always used to refer to Piers as 'that Doukhobor Island'. The imprisoned Doukhobors used to make their own pottery water pipes, and I still have a part of a pipe we dug up on our lot.

We have always been part-time on Piers, and every Friday night during the summer, we loved making the trek from Canoe Cove to our Piers cottage. I remember how a number of people wanted to get a tennis court built on the island, in the north meadow (next to Lot 135). However, everyone was so busy getting their properties cleared and their houses built, that it never happened.

A favourite memory for us is that every night at 7 p.m., all the children, especially the teenagers, would gather in the north meadow and play games such as 'Capture the Flag.' There was great camaraderie for all the kids on Piers those days. It is interesting how things have come 'full circle' with pots and pans being banged together at 7 p.m. in 2020 to acknowledge the caregivers during COVID times.

Susanne and Michael Ferrie

Lot 121 - Bill and Margaret Bender

Piers Island Early Reminiscences

(written by Elizabeth Parfitt/nee Bender)

In the spring of 1969, I asked my parents if three girlfriends and I could spend a few days at Piers over spring reading break from The University of Victoria. They agreed. I did not operate the boat, but my good friend Arden was an accomplished and experienced sailor and my father (Bill Bender) granted her permission to captain the family boat back and forth to Piers Island. At the time, the family boat was a wooden runabout with an outboard motor.

We arrived safely and enjoyed a pleasant day. After supper we decided to take a walk around the island. The wind came up while we were walking and when we returned to the cottage (Lot 121), we were dismayed to find the boat was missing. We quickly searched the beach in both directions but there was no sign of it anywhere. There was no choice, we must get to a telephone to contact the Coast Guard and also my father.

Back in those days there were very few phones on Piers Island. There was a payphone at the government dock, but I knew the nearest phone to us was at Bill and Belle Ham's house at Lot 23. By now it was fast growing dark. We did not have a flashlight, but we did have a coal oil lantern. So off we set, four girls on a windy dark road with a flickering pool of light. Back in those days there were very few full-time residents, so there were no lights from dwellings along the way - just the wind moaning in the trees and all the funny rustling noises from the bush. It seemed like a very long walk in the dark and we were so relieved to at last reach the warmth and light of the Hams' cottage, and see the carboys of Sake with their bubbling raisins sitting on the warm fireplace hearth.

We contacted the Coast Guard and my parents and then we had to retrace our steps along that long road home to Lot 121. We didn't sleep much that night, but in the morning we were very relieved to be advised that the boat had washed up unharmed on a nearby island. We were forgiven, but we never asked to go alone to the island again. I am still friends with Arden.

Doukhobor visit Summer 1992: In the spring of 1992 Mary Tucker (Lot 50) was contacted by a Doukhobor family regarding an elderly man who had been imprisoned on Piers Island in 1932. He wished to make a return visit. The contact came from Bill Barisoff, and the gentleman who wished to visit the island was Alex Barisoff, his father.

The Barisoff family, grandfather Alex, son Bill, and brothers Mike and Walter, came to Piers Island, where they were greeted by Mary Tucker. She took them on a walking tour, which culminated with a visit and tea with my parents, Bill and Margaret Bender at their cottage at Lot 121. This property sits on the site of what was the entrance to the Piers Island Penitentiary. There is still one piling from the old dock in front of the property. I have pictures of that visit and letters which were exchanged afterwards. Bill Barisoff went on to serve as Liberal MLA for the Okanagan riding from 1996 to 2013, and later as Speaker of the House in British Columbia from 2015 until his retirement.

Other special Piers memories:

Where have all the toads gone? Back in the days we were growing up on Piers, there were toads in abundance. A walk along the road after dark would invariably generate lots of rustling noises in the growth along the roadside. Shine the flashlight on the noise and you would discover a toad scuttling away through the dry leaves. Sometimes we would pick them up, and when our warm hands touched their cool bodies they would pee; it was endlessly amusing. I assure you no toads were harmed and we would put them back where they came from to continue their journey in peace. I have not seen a toad in many, many years.

Happy Hooker on the Rocks:

I remember one stormy night at my parents' cottage sometime in the early 1970s when my Dad's boat, the *Happy Hooker*, dragged its anchor and almost ended up on the beach. The *Happy Hooker* was our family boat; it had been built as a fishing boat but my Dad purchased it before it was finished and set it up as a cruiser. It was a big wooden boat and when we discovered it one night coming for the shore, it was all hands on deck, or in this case 'in the water.' I remember wading out into the sea with water up to my armpits trying to push it away from the rocks. Many hands were involved that night, including members of the Ferrie family (Lot 117) out there with us. Our efforts were successful and the *Happy Hooker* was unharmed.

Halloween costume parties at the firehall:

For several years when our kids were young we made the trek from Port Alberni to Piers Island to attend the Halloween costume party at the firehall. It was a highlight for our kids. There was lots of laughter, good food and fun. And the bonfire! I recently threw out the lovely ribbons we won as a family for our Little Red Riding Hood group costume one year.

Margaret and Bill Bender

Alex and Bill Barisoff, Mary Tucker, Mike and Walter Barisoff

Lots 123, 131 - Scott and Penny Denoon

The Japanese Style Cottage

In early 1969, we learned that the cottage at Lot 123 was owned by Jack MacIssac, a contractor for B.C. Hydro who had been installing the power pole grid on the island. When he bought the lot, he hauled in fill to raise the property level from the nearby vacant marsh. He also dug a deep trench above the high-tide mark to vertically install large fir and cedar tree sections to form a breakwater wall to protect the lot from erosion. His wife, an architect, designed an open rafter Japanese-style cottage with a wide surrounding deck. We pooled our resources and borrowed money from parents, who also became excited about the project. We made an offer but could not stretch it any further, so we walked away. Several months later they called to ask if our offer was still viable and it was then accepted. There followed many happy years as the kids grew up boating, sailing, and learning to drive with Dad's WW2 Willis Jeep from Calgary foothills. We became close friends with the neighbours; the kids with the Bender and Ferrie kids.

On a sunny day in 1989, an unusual event occurred on the south-east shore of Piers, when a property seller and buyer were moving. During a transfer of belongings at Lot 25, a Hammond organ fell out of a helicopter cargo net into the sea. Steve Cruise, the manager of the insurance company, decided to conduct the investigation himself given the unusual circumstances in the case. Noting the attractive surroundings, with his notes complete, he decided to walk around the island looking for possible properties. Our small cottage with a half sleeping loft above the living area was attractive. Steve and Pauline made an offer on Lot 123.

Penny had injured her leg after a ferry wave hit our boat on the beach several months before. She hobbled, was tired of the hassle, and hoped we might find a property with a wharf. We accepted the offer and started looking. But where? Distance and dollars were negative factors, but the dye was cast and we were leaving on June 30. As we introduced Steve and Pauline to the Annual General Meeting, I added, "We are missing Piers already, so if anyone knows of a possible alternative property on Piers let us know". Howie Eckman (Lot 31) who worked with my brother in Vancouver, suggested we contact the land surveyor who owned property next to the Youngs on Biscoe Beach. They seldom came to Piers and had been thinking of selling. We offered on the tidy rustic cabin. They accepted and with that happy transition we were able to continue our happy life on

Piers. I have great appreciation of the lovely additions, energy and artistic improvements made by Steve and Pauline on our former home at Lot 123.

A Touch of Old England and Perhaps the Himalayas:

When we moved in Victoria, we inherited a very mature protected cedar. This was believed to be an Atlas or Himalayan. Dr. Robertson, when returning from World War I with his wife a nurse, built the home beside the tree on the corner of Lansdowne and Dean. That tree is like a sister to the cedar standing above the statue of Emily Carr on the south-west corner of the Empress Hotel property. Penny and I took some of the unique cones (which stand upright on the branches instead of hanging) to Piers, as well as two saplings to plant. The cones are the size of hand grenades, the tops of which look like rosettes or wooden roses when they dry. Each seed looks like a petal. One of the nurses at my mother's Aberdeen nursing home in Victoria would collect them, dip them in varnish to fix the petals and make Christmas decorations with holly and fir. Unfortunately, it takes years before the tree actually starts producing cones.

When the English gentleman Sir Clive Phillips-Wolley purchased Piers Island in 1901, he established a rather upscale estate home close to where the Morson home now stands. He planted a fig tree sapling from Kew gardens close to the foundation of the original house. Wayne Morson and I decided to trade seedlings, in hopes that we could each see these rare species flourish on our respective properties at Lot 113 and Lot 131. My cedar seedling is surviving and still growing slowly, but the one traded to Wayne and Gloria appears thriving and is more than 40 feet high.

On another note, we brought ballast brick from ships from English sailing ships used to pave Wharf Street behind our office in Victoria. When Victoria repaved the street, we brought those bricks a few at a time to Piers, saving them from landfill. The return ships were refilled with timber and cargo, while some of those grooved paving bricks are now used for our fire pit and walkways on Piers.

Cougars:

We have had at least a couple of stories of cougars on Piers Island. In 2014, Bryce Young (Lot 133) was one of the first persons one morning to see a young cougar near his back gate, just outside our property. (Perhaps Gloria Morson was the first from her hot tub at 6 a.m.). He raised his arms and growled at it - no response. When conservation officers were called, the cougar was sent up a tree by dogs. Preparations were made on the ground with fir boughs to cushion his landing after a tranquilizer dart brought him down. The cougar was then removed by wheelbarrow to marine transport, and escorted off by excited and relieved admirers.

It was not so pleasant an experience for an earlier feline intruder. When we were recent newcomers on Piers in the mid-1970s, we trailered our runabout from Gordon Head in Victoria. An elderly neighbour asked where was I going with the boat on weekends. When I told him 'Piers Island', he became animated, explaining that he had been a guard (warder) on Piers during the internment of the Doukhobors in the 1930s. He told me that a cougar had made the swim to the island to hunt deer, and my neighbour was assigned the task of removing the cat, given the hazard to some of the Freedomites. Methods were much simpler and less sophisticated. He was able to shoot the big cat in the meadow near the Doukhobor bunk housing.

He had interesting stories about the camp and the passive resistance of the inhabitants/ internees. Their communication between separated men's and women's units was by singing during their orchard and farming activities. I was later to become more closely involved when I had the good fortune to supervise a young parolee released from B.C. Penitentiary in New Westminster. He was a hard-working stone mason who was related to a former Piers prisoner. There was a cohort of Freedomite inmates from the Kootenays who had been convicted of civil disobedience, but most of the children of the prisoners made the transition into society and became very productive members of society. A good book on the History of the movement is Simma Holt's 1964 book: *Terror in the Name of God: The Story of the Sons of Freedom Doukhobors.*

Flag Pole at the Firehall:

One spring day in the mid-1970s, riding past the Admirals Inn on Belleville Street on Victoria's harbourfront, I noticed their Navy style flag pole was in two sections on the ground behind the building undergoing renovations ahead of the tourist season. After several weeks, I saw the pole was still lying on the ground (I was expecting to see it painted and restored to its position on the corner near the Coho Ferry terminal). I got thinking that I would love to have it for our property at Piers (having been a young sea cadet in Calgary as a teenager). The owner said it was going for scrap so I offered $100 and we had a deal. Putting a mattress on the roof of my eight-passenger van, we were able to strap the two 18-foot sections to the roof and, during an amazingly quiet moment for highway traffic, we drove to the Dolphin Road boat-ramp. We used Fire Chief John Currie's larger boat to get to Harry Point, where I put the two sections on sawhorses and sanded and painted and added new pulleys and lines.

It soon became apparent that this was not practical for the size of our property, where a smaller straight tree would work as well and look more appropriate. I approached the Fire Department and suggested that I would donate the pole and build the cement base with two five-foot U-steel beam uprights with through bolts to hold the pole vertical. Several talented islanders, including Bob Clarke and Dave Poulsom, were great at assisting in the process. The morning for raising the flagpole was somewhat akin to a First Nations Totem Raising and came with sunshine and no wind. There were a few hands on deck to guide and hold the flag pole while the truck pulled from the meadow. We held our collective breaths as the pole neared the magic finish. Next it was celebration and success. I advised the Admirals Inn that their former flag pole is proudly home on a high mound in front of the Piers Island Volunteer Fire Department (PIVFD) and community hall. Our family has had a wonderful history on Piers. A cherry tree in the orchard is dedicated to Penny Denoon (passed away in 2006). We are delighted to have so many amazing experiences and lasting friendships.

Denoon Family

1970s
A BUZZ OF ACTIVITY

By the mid-to late 1970s, there were approximately 30 to 35 permanent residents on Piers. Six of them were a family with four children under age 10 (the Clarks at Lot 63), so 20 per cent of the full-timers came from that one home. Most of the other full-time people on the island were retired or semi-retired. Word was spreading about Piers and there were five oil-company families from Alberta, who bought separate part-time properties on the island. In addition, three professors from the University of Lethbridge, Alberta, and their families also decided to buy on Piers.

Many islanders were building smaller cottages but there were also some larger houses being built for year-round occupancy. There was a buzz of activity happening on the island. Neighbours helped each other a lot, and there was a continual exchange of 'odds and ends' to save islanders trips across the sea into Sidney and Victoria. Notices were posted on the wooden bulletin boards at the Piers public dock and the firehall. Word of month spread the news about needed articles - there was no BB (Bulletin Board) or Internet in those days.

Since the summer population was expanding quickly, water became a huge issue because the water smelled of sulphur, the water pressure was very poor, and the aging surface water line began to spring many leaks. In the 1970s, the water system progressed from deep-drilled wells with an auxiliary pool system for pressure to a totally new system. A clean water system was established with the building of the Piers water tower in 1973 (the foreman was Mike Siska, still at Lot 88) and the formation of the lower 'Kent' reservoir, named in honour of Charlie Kent (Lot 32). Charlie conceived the idea of the reservoir in 1970 and was in charge of its completion in 1978. He also put trout in that reservoir and he and others enjoyed fishing there. Many islanders volunteered endless hours for this important project of providing clean, safe water for Piers. Also, BC Hydro finally completed power installation for the whole island by the end of the decade.

In the early 1970s, the fire department was operating well, but it was not supported financially, since the focus on the island at that time was on the water improvements. The volunteer firemen were always holding fund-raising events to pay for fire-fighting equipment or they paid for it themselves. By 1975, although many islanders supported them, the Piers Island Volunteer Fire Department was the brunt of continuous criticism from the Piers Island Improvement District (PIID). Finally, after another request was denied for new fire equipment, according to one of the original fire crew, the firefighters said, "You look after it (the firehall and equipment), and we'll just be firemen." The PIID responded with: "Your services are no longer required."

The firemen were upset but they were all young people with young kids, so that gave them more time to enjoy family life. They remained dedicated to the cause and still dealt with emergencies. However, the fire equipment was no longer attended to and there were no more training practices. The fire department went into a real slump. For the next few years, a skeleton group of volunteers, especially Lionel Green (Lot 15), acted as caretakers of the fire department building and equipment. Without full fire protection, the island was at great risk of a serious fire.

There were a number of 'firsts' on the island during the 1970s. The first community dances were organized and paid for by the firefighters themselves and were held at the Sidney Hotel or at various dance halls in Victoria. In 1974, the first official dance on the island was held outdoors at the original firehall, and became known as 'Moonlight Madness.' The first fishing derby was held in 1970, a huge event for the island. Fish in the sea were plentiful during those years. The BC Sailing Association sponsored the first sailing lessons on Piers. The Rosses (Lot 28) built the first private swimming pool since there was no action happening to build a public pool.

Besides the idea of a public swimming pool, there was also talk about public tennis courts. However, those discussions were put aside because everyone was so busy building and, of course, not everyone was in favour of those ideas, especially because of the cost, the liability and the maintenance.

Lot 1 - Gordon, Audrey and Cam Russell

A Happy Life On Piers

(told by Cam)

September 1970, my parents purchased their Piers lot. Fraser (Reg) Biscoe, the realtor, and Dad phoned my mom from the public dock on the island after my dad had come to BC to view the property. Mother wanted a south- facing property, not too far from a town, and a larger lot. This lot was 1.26 acres and going for $10,000. Mother said not to come home without buying the lot. Dad said, "It sounds like we'll go ahead with the deal!" My mother called the shots in the family.

I visited Piers the first time in 1972 and the house was built in 1975. It was a Linwood home package. Dad was a pen-and-paper kind of guy, rather than hammer-and-nail, so it was a good choice.

I got into trouble within five minutes on Piers at age 4 ½ years. I started to climb a sapling and Dad had a talk with me about saving trees and that the baby fir tree needed to grow up big and strong. It is still there today. During the summers out here, it was mostly my Dad and me with a tent set up by the sea. One time Dad was napping, and I saw the biggest dog I had ever seen with horns out of his head. I screamed and Dad laughed explaining it was a deer. It was my first time, but certainly not the last time that I saw a deer. Whenever I came to Piers when I was young, I couldn't wait until I could get out to play with the other kids.

I was introduced to Mary Tucker (Lot 50) when I was eight or nine years old. She was selling a washer with two compartments, one for spin and one for dry, for $50. Mom had arranged the sale and sent me to Mary's house with a wheelbarrow. Mom said Mary was a force to be reckoned with. She told me, "Don't mess with Mary and just be polite." Mary was a force, but I grew to love her over the years. Her life experiences were incredible and she was good to me.

Berneice and Bob Archibald (Lot 66) were special people. Berneice often had her bright pink coat on, and always had a bag of candy with her. One day Dad found her wallet on top of the dock, and sent me to Berneice's door to deliver it back to her. At the door she yelled that she was undressed and asked me to wait. I waited over an hour! I got a hug and a big kiss on the cheek for my "good deed." She was very sweet and treated me well.

In the late 1970s, Norm Ayers and his wife (Lot 13) had two kids my age, so I used to play with them a lot. Norm built the house, but he had no skills. No measuring was done and he used a chainsaw to cut the wood for the frames. When Dad visited for first time, he asked, "Is this house level?" Dad kept putting balls or marbles down, and they always went straight to the corner. Frank Williams bought the house in 1983, and he tried to fix the levelling. In the end he gave up, enjoying it as it was.

In the early 1990s islanders would call Frank for permission to take down trees. Mike Scoones's dad (Lot 29) wanted some trees taken down and he asked Mike and me to do the job. Loaded up with beer and axes, we went to the Scoones property to take down trees. Frank got many complaints about two guys with beer and axes going to chop down trees in the centre of the island. Frank came to check on us. He was somewhat inebriated and stood there, rolling back and forth on a log. He kept saying, "That dammed gin," and he let us just do the job. He was a good guy. Frank looked after our house when my parents were away for awhile.

The beach was the most important thing to us kids. In the 1970s there was a couple who lived on their boat at the dock and my Dad hired them to do some work. One night four boys, including me, put a load of pilings into their boat and it nearly sank. We sure got into trouble about that.

The first owner of our neighbouring Lot 2 was Denis Langois, who built the original panabode house around a huge boulder. Denis had a plan to bring TNT and apply for a blasting permit, which would have destroyed many properties, including theirs. The permit, thankfully, was not granted. My dad was very nervous about all that. Eventually the panabode was torn down and the boulder was buried.

Joe Friendenthal (Lots 49 and 53) took me fishing when I was about 11 years old on his boat *Little Bit*, which was small but very sea-worthy. Joe said, "Be ready at 5." I thought it was supposed to be 5 p.m., but my Dad said it must be 5 a.m. It was pouring rain at 5 a.m. but we still went out. Joe said rain at the very early morning hours was the best time for fish, and the harder the rain, the better the fish catch. I caught my first fish that day, a 22-pound salmon. Joe took over and reeled it in. When we held up the fish on the dock, it was taller than I was.

Howie Sneade (Lot 41) and Harley Dyte (Lot 37) and some of the other older guys on the east side often loaded up their boats with beer from the city for a party on the weekends. One time they totally filled up a small 14-foot aluminum boat with more than 100 cases, piled up as high as they could. They figured the more beer they got the more money they saved. However, they lost a quarter of the cases; probably some are still under the sea. We teenagers rescued some of the beer and took it to the reservoir area in the centre of the island and had a good party ourselves.

We moved full-time from Alberta to Piers in 1997 and I drove the truck out to B.C. My parents didn't like to travel together, so it wasn't until 1997 that they were together on Piers. Full-time life turned out not to be as appealing as they had hoped because of the boating, but the shuttle helped a lot. Mom especially liked the peace and serenity of Piers. Dad had friends on the island, from his working days. In 1967, Harold Skolrood (Lot 92) and Dad were part of the University of Lethbridge founding faculty. Harold mentioned Piers Island to Dad and that's how we ended up here. Hal Weaver (Lot 39) and Dad were also fellow professors from the University of Lethridge and Hal came to Piers around 1983. My sister has only been here 10 days in 50 years. She is very urban. That's why this is my house.

I am very happy with my years on Piers, and I love it for what it is. I want to keep the peace and quiet. I don't like it when people clearcut and want all the urban comforts. I like keeping my property treed, and so did my parents. In the evening, I hear the frogs and toads right in my yard, and I love the nesting sounds.

** *Author's Note:* Sadly, Cam Russell passed away the end of January 2022. At a bonfire on Biscoe Beach with 50 islanders, many spoke fondly of his acerbic wit, his love of Piers and his willingness to help his fellow islanders.

Cam Russell

Lot 5 - Carol and Doug Peaker

Good Times On Piers

The first owners of Lot 5 on Piers were Stephen and Maureen Franks. The second owner was Tom Williams, who was a surveyor who worked with Reg Biscoe and built the original house on the property. The next owner before us was Dr. Nicholson and family who lived full-time in Klamath Falls, Oregon. The Nicholson family had a number of children and lived part-time on Piers until they sold and bought a cottage on Salt Spring Island.

We rented Phoebe Noble's place (Lot 40) the summer of 1970 when we bought our Lot 5, which was located right at the Piers government dock. At that time, my husband Doug paced off lots on Piers with the realtor, Reg Biscoe. The Biscoes were friends with the Smiths (Lot 7) and he found out from them that Lot 5 was for sale. We acted quickly and bought the place.

We lived in Victoria and later on the Saanich Peninsula, but for several years we also lived in Montreal, Quebec, and London, Ontario. We loved coming to Piers for the summers and on many weekends during the year. I would arrive on Piers with four kids and a cat and dog. Later in August, Doug arrived for his holidays and at the end of August we would all travel home together. I remember how wonderful it was that I could phone in my food order to Queen's Payless Grocery Store on Resthaven (next to the former Hylands Fish and Chips). They would deliver the groceries to Canoe Cove and even put the groceries in the boat for me. They did a good service and got a lot of business from Piers islanders.

I still remember the original water from the ponds in the centre of the island as being very sulpher-smelling. I would have to bring five-gallon jugs of water to Piers because the current baby couldn't tolerate the local supply. I also recall how the water pipe was on the top of the road around the island, and in the cooler weather the shower would suddenly stop because the water had frozen in the pipe. I often answered the phone at the government dock. We were the closest to the dock and that was the only phone on the whole island. After taking the call, I would run around delivering phone messages I had received.

Doug lived in the house fulltime for awhile in the 1990s. He died in 1994 after an 11 year battle with Hodgkin's disease. We owned the cottage until we sold in 2016. I still have wonderful memories of good times on Piers.

Lot 18 - Jim and Mary Strain

Many Fond Family Memories

(written by Sandra Donnelly - middle daughter)

Jim and Mary Strain purchased a cottage on Piers Island in 1979 at the recommendation of friends. The Strain children were grown, getting married and starting families of their own. Jim loved ocean fishing and Mary enjoyed cooking and entertaining guests. They loved having family and friends visit them on the island. Jim would take friends fishing and tour the many islands. Mary was a gracious hostess to the many visitors at the cottage. The Strain offspring and their children spent numerous weekends over the years at the cottage. Dad would often plan his never-ending deck and dock repairs to coincide with visits so that he could get the help he needed from his sons and sons-in-laws. Not to be left out, the daughters and daughters-in-law would clean the cottage and cook some pretty good meals for all to enjoy. The grandchildren loved the swings in the yard, riding their bikes around the island and finding never-ending treasures along the ocean shoreline.

The best memories that we have are of the fishing derbies, early morning fishing trips, walking the island pathway, berry-picking outings, Barb's wedding and Dad's 80th birthday party. About a year before my Dad passed away he invited me (his middle daughter) to visit him at his North Saanich home. Dad wanted me to accompany him to Piers Island and then go on a road trip up the island to visit relatives, a good friend Roy Kilpatrick, and then spend a couple of days with my brother Hugh and his wife Connie. This was a special time for us, as it is the only time I can remember having my Dad all to myself. We shared a lot of stories and I had the opportunity to ask my Dad a lot of questions like: "What makes you happy? What are your best memories? What would you do differently in your life if you had the chance for a do over?" This was a great opportunity to get to know my Dad as a person instead of a father. The day we spent on Piers Island was beautiful. We ate lunch together and then walked the island. We stopped in for coffee at the homes of several neighbors. The neighbours were welcoming and very hospitable. It was clear to me that there is a strong community on Piers.

The weather changed abruptly in the late afternoon. Dad and I had to make a hasty departure from the island in the middle of a sleet storm. I was confident my Dad knew his way to the Sidney dock and we would return to the mainland without incident. Unfortunately we hit the dock a bit too hard on landing and made a dent in Dad's boat. I was surprised at my Dad's relaxed attitude because in earlier years he would have been mad at doing damage in such a careless fashion. Live and learn, I guess! Piers Island continues to provide many fond memories of our time with our parents.

Mary and Jim Strain

Lot 24 - Don and Fran Gilley and Family

Piers Island Yacht Club

(written by Graham Giley)

Do you know the Gulf Islands Driftwood newspaper, published in Ganges, Salt Spring Island? Well, we do, and boy, did we get our money's worth with each issue back in the day before it became a respectable paper. Some of the noteworthy stories include:

- Boy hit by an errant hubcap flying off a car
- Man has flat tire on wheelbarrow but saves garbage
- New Principal at Fulford School should wear gumboots not a tie
- (Personal ad) Looking for a good woman who can clean and cook fish, dig worms and owns a boat with motor

But by far the biggest story for us was the June 1982 article about the Winter Cove Yacht Club (WCYC) Sailpast. I would challenge anyone to read the story and not fall over laughing. The Commodore's Sailpast involved participants ranging from rowboats to 30-foot cruisers. Some had to be towed. The display of seamanship was marred only when the tow-lines of two incapacitated boats entwined, requiring an impromptu exhibition of rescue and life-saving skills. Refreshments and dry clothes were provided on the Commodore's barge. A work-bee had to be scheduled to repair the dock, which was damaged by one of the boats. Another necessary repair was to a barn on nearby Samuel Island that was damaged by the live-round cannon that was fired to start the event.

This article was read and re-read over happy hours all around Piers Island in the first week of July, 1982. It even disrupted a fire practice to the point that nothing got done. Within hours, Don Gilley and Norm Ross (Lot 28) decided that if the WCYC could have a Sailpast, so could Piers Island! The **Piers Island Yacht Club** was duly formed over dinner with the sole purpose of holding a Sailpast. Not ones to sit around and wait, the date for the first Sailpast was set 72 hours hence, on Saturday, July 10, 1982 at the appointed time of 1500 hours on the Gilley/Ross dock at Lot 26, followed by a party on the deck of the Ross's pool (yes, we had a pool on Piers.)

The Sailpast, a sail-by salute, near-shore salute or 'review of the fleet' is steeped in more than 600 years of British Royal Navy tradition and history. It was introduced in yacht clubs around the world as a continuation of the naval habit of having Admirals (and/or Royalty) review the fleet on special occasions.

On Piers Island it looked more like the Beverly Hillbillies: Marine Edition. As befitting a yacht club of such distinction, there were rules. Of course there were rules:

- Boats had to be decorated using only what could be found on-island;
- Occupants had to be in thematic costumes of items found only on Piers Island;
- If you appeared to be taking it too seriously, you would be doused with sea water;
- No cannon was to be used as it might damage relations with our cross-passage neighbours.

Don Gilley was named Officiating Commodore, mainly because he was the only one with a navy blue blazer in his Piers closet and the dock was decorated to fit the occasion with leftover birthday streamers and Christmas tinsel. Approximately 30 boats participated in the event, including B.C.

Ferries, which slowed their vessels for passengers to watch and saluted the participants with a long horn blast. As each boat passed the dock they saluted Commodore Don Gilley, who was situated on a raised dais, and who would acknowledge each salute with a blast of his anaemic air horn and suitable wave of the arm. Costumes of note included:

- Diane Perry in a wetsuit, hardhat with large galvanized eye bolt out the top, floating by with an old tire inner tube under her arms - as a mooring buoy.
- Norm and Trish Ross as pirates in an aluminum boat decorated as a lifeboat.
- The Ross girls dressed only in beach shell bikinis in their Arabian Night Harem-themed boat.
- Graham Gilley as Popeye in a hand-made spinach can boat that promptly sank directly in front of the dock - requiring a marine rescue by the pirates who were halfway through a jug of "something".
- Barbara and Howie Eckman covered in twigs and moss in the forest fairies-themed boat.
- Fran and Bruce Gilley standing in flower pots with toilet seat flower petal masks, all the while trying to pilot the boat.
- Don Gardiner repurposing his hockey referee jersey to arrive as a historical Piers Island prisoner (thank goodness he was clothed).

After each boat had duly saluted Commodore Gilley, everyone retired to Ross's pool-side deck to enjoy a glass or eight of Norm Ross's Chainsaw Whiskey Punch, which helped keep things going until late in the evening. Rumour has it there was dinner as well, but no one can confirm that.

Lot 44 - Dennis and Joyce Wells

Pioneering On Piers

(written by son Rick Wells)

Around 1972, Dennis and Joyce Wells purchased Lot 44, the original log cabin on the south side of Piers Island directly across from the two red channel marker buoys. This log cabin was built by Maurice and Eleanor D'Estrube. Maurice and Eleanor (Sandeman) started their Piers Island log cabin adventure in the early 1960s, when Maurice was in his late seventies. First, they built a small one room A-frame 'Swiss Cottage,' as they called it, plus a tee-pee outhouse, both of which are still standing on the property. Later they built a one-room permanent log cabin, including a large stone fireplace with rocks from their beach at Piers Island. Afterwards, they added on and doubled the cabin size. Dennis and Joyce, along with Joyce's cousin and her husband added on another section to the log cabin in the late 1980s using logs from Bert Johnson's Saanich property which was close to the D'Estrube's home.

Dennis and Joyce (nee Clarke) were connected with Piers Island from the mid-1950s after Joyce's cousin Hilda (nee Gallop) and her husband George Doran built a large log cabin on Lands End Road (at that time Lands End Road was just a gravel road). During the 1960s, the two families would sometimes trade residences during the summer holidays and the Wells family often spent time boating and fishing around Piers and Arbutus Islands.

Dennis and Joyce visited Piers Island frequently around 1968, about the time Bert and Betty Johnson (Lot 83) began working on their property on Piers. Bert and Betty had known Dennis and Joyce since their early twenties. Dennis (and later Joyce) were lifelong close friends of Cecil and Sheila Gould (Lot 101). Dennis and younger son Richard occasionally helped Bert work on his original one room trailer and later on Bert's log cabin. Bert, often assisted by Dennis, did most of the plumbing work on the building of the new Piers Island firehall 1992 to 1993.

The D'Estrube (correct spelling according to Maurice; not to be spelled Destrube he'd tell us) family were pioneer farmers who built homesteads across Canada until they finally ended up in Victoria (close to where Bert and Betty Johnson lived). Maurice was also a banker. When Maurice was in his early 90s, he began looking for a particular person or family to take over their Piers Island cabin. It was around that time that Dennis and Joyce were interested in finding property on Piers Island - this was after unsuccessfuly searching for a special piece of land on Salt Spring Island.

The log cabin at Lot 44 was named *Notre Folie* by Maurice and Eleanor (his third wife, as he was a widower from his two previous marriages), which translated from French means 'our madness'. It's easy to understand why that name was applied. Stairs initially had to be carved into the side of an almost vertical shale bank by hand. Materials were hauled over by rowboat and other small craft, roof shingles were split by hand and a lot of cement was made at the end of a shovel. On the beach was a saltwater bath that filled near the high tide line and then heated in the sun all day to ease your muscles later in the day. The guest book at the cabin is interesting, and continues to record changes and people that visit and contribute to Lot 44 *Notre Folie.*

Maurice and Eleanor had a very specific set of criteria for the person or family who were going to purchase their cabin. There were many lunches, visits, and informal interviews both at Piers Island and at their Saanich home on Santa Clara Avenue. Dennis had to prove he was a good wood worker (he was), prove he knew all the strange tools Maurice and Eleanor had, and prove he could do things like row a boat to Dolphin Road and back, because that's what all the original Piers Islanders did - the likes of some of our good friends Mary Tucker, and Bill and Arthur Oldfield. Joyce had to know all the plants and all the pioneer stuff that a good old-fashioned farmer needed to know. The Wells boys spent time with the D'Estrubes to prove they could correctly chop and pile a good amount of firewood, clean gutters and roofs, and also chop down trees by hand. Most important, we all had to know the value of a good root cellar and how to make one.

Dennis and Joyce had three children - Susan, Robert and Richard. Susan was the oldest and didn't have as much to do with Piers Island as Robert and Richard. Robert has had various periods of close involvement with Piers Island, and Richard being the youngest, was initially stuck on Piers Island during the earlier years, hanging out with the parental unit and their older friends. Richard became the work horse for projects which included helping build many parts of Mary Tucker and Enid's pre-fab house (Lot 50), several projects at Bill Oldfield's house (Lot 46), and several stints being summer caretaker for the grounds of Mr. and Mrs. King's (Lot 42) house, plus helping Bert Johnson. The Wells's cabin is situated between Bill Oldfield's house and the house originally owned by the King family. Mr. King owned several pharmacies in Alberta and the family visited Piers Island each summer. The Wells family soon became good friends of the Oldfields along with Mary and Enid. Dennis and Joyce travelled abroad often with Bert and Betty Johnson and also camped various times with

Mary Tucker and Enid, travelling down the Oregon Coast. They all combined a road trip or two with Lionel and Deanna Green.

Bill Oldfield and his brother Arthur were connected with the Oldfield family in Saanich who are all connected to Oldfield Road. Bill was known to have worked in the Arctic on the DEW (Distant Early Warning) line during the Cold War. Bill was a bit of an eccentric. He loved electronics, gadgets and old cars. He later became a dentist in Vancouver. Arthur was reported to have been a nuclear physicist who became injured during an explosion of some sort. Arthur lived on and off with his brother Bill on Piers, and was also caretaker on several nearby private islands. Both men were very intelligent. Arthur was also a gifted painter of nature. He won $1 million on the lottery very late in life and eventually bought Wally Bains' former cabin (Lot 10) close to the government wharf.

The Piers Island Government wharf area originally housed a very old log-constructed sheep herder's shack. That shack also protected the only public payphone on the island at that time. Only a handful of cabins had phones in the early 1970s, so when the public phone failed you were seriously cut off from communicating with those back home on the 'big island'. It was often a nightly ritual to walk to the Piers Island public payphone and wait to try to get your call in privacy, without a lineup for it.

In the early days, a walk at night around Piers Island was truly magical, and thankfully the centre of the island has remained intact and basically undisturbed. There were incredible and varied natural smells and sounds. There was no human noise once the ferries shut down for the night - everything was dead still. There was a deep darkness but somehow you could still walk on the road without a flashlight just for fun once your eyes adjusted. The meadow was always full of deer, and had a deep almost alfalfa smell to it. Back in the 1960s and 1970s there were giant toads and frogs, particularly between the old firehall and the current water tower area. The frogs and toads could be so large and strong that an adult human could barely hold them with two hands. They would often escape your grasp. When the frogs and toads came out at night it was quite noisy on the road, but only in certain areas and times.

Maurice and Eleanor D'Estrube continued to come to Piers Island for a few years after they sold the property to the Wells family. Dennis transported the D'Estrubes and hauled equipment, plywood, logs and windows in his beloved Vogler Bros Seacraft, a 12-foot clinker built boat built in 1912. That ancient 1930s three-horsepower Briggs and Stratton engine did a lot of work over the years.

The 12-foot long cedar planked oak ribbed boat has a storied history. She had fished and been part of many marine communities around Saanich and Victoria. The boat has been part of the history of Saanich Inlet, Oak Bay Marina, Canoe Cove, Deep Cove, Brentwood Bay, Hall's Boat House and has seen a lot of time in and around Piers Island, Lands End Road, Salt Spring Island and Portland Island.

Dennis's clinker is restored and now residing on display in the Saanich Artifacts Museum. Robert also salvaged Mary Tucker's sad, abandoned 16-foot clinker 'Myrtle' off the beach and partially restored it, eventually donating that to the Cowichan Wooden Boat Society. They fully restored it for a new owner. Dennis completely re-designed and built a 20-foot cedar and hardwood cabin cruiser at his home in Saanich. In the mid 1980s that boat was launched and was used extensively for Piers Island travels. The boat ferried friends and family back and forth to the island and was used for fishing. That cedar boat has recently returned to Lot 44 and is being restored by Robert and Richard.

In the days before golf carts, everybody (young and old) walked, rode a bicycle, or used a wheelbarrow or a backpack. In the early days, the only memorable vehicles typically on the island were the original old fire truck, a red VW Beetle under a carport and the ancient Fire Department tractor. Occasionally a construction truck or two showed up, and a few other vehicles came and went. More hidden away were other gems, such as Bill Oldfield's giant 1947 Lincoln Continental convertible - cream yellow coloured with red leather upholstery. Apparently the Queen had sat in it so Bill said. Bill also had a 1950 Austin A-40 pickup truck that he bequeathed to Richard as long as Richard could get it running again. The Austin soon got an engine transplant from Robert's old Austin and the pickup was soon circling the island again picking up soil, firewood and hay, of course totally uninsured and with a 16- year-old driving it! A very young Len Gillespie (tree faller Len, a very close family friend of the Wells') almost put the Austin through the Ham's (Lot 23) meticulous fence trying to navigate the corner from the old firehall to the government dock. The Austin had no brakes. Len was about 13 years old, the tires were bad, and the steering was even worse. Those were the days!

Kids had speed boats back then, but no experience and definitely no boaters licence. At 12 years old, you could head off exploring for a good part of the day - taking your life jacket was the only requirement. Some lucky kids got to have a 9.8 horsepower on their 10-foot speed boat, but most seemed to be restricted to 7.5 horsepower. One lucky group of kids had a 20 horsepower on a light 10-foot plywood speedboat. It was not uncommon to be swamped by ferry waves and then get towed back in. Good fun - gas was cheap and it was exciting to head to Canoe Cove to get more.

Dennis and Joyce Wells lived for over 60 years in the house they built in Saanich. Almost all of the houses these families built or lived in are still standing today. Dennis was a mapper/photogrammetrist for the Province of BC. He worked on projects for the Ministry of Environment and the Forest Service.

Because of his knowledge of maps, surveying and of hydrology, Dennis was likely involved in discussions involving the upper reservoir and related Piers Island projects. Joyce held the fort at home and maintained the many projects she was involved with. Robert and Richard also worked in the Ministry of Environment and the Ministry of Forests, and Susan worked for the School Board.

Susan, Robert and Richard still live in the greater Victoria area. Richard married his wife Trish (nee Bruenen) on Piers Island in a small private ceremony on top of Summit Hill. Robert and Richard now own Lot 44 and are slowly restoring and upgrading the log cabin. Dennis and Joyce's six grandchildren - David, Brent, James, Stefanie, Russell and Angela - plus their great grandchildren, all grew up spending quality time on Piers Island.

Dennis and Joyce Wells

Lot 47 - Dewayne and Elizabeth Parfitt

Memories Of Piers Island

The Parfitt family of Dewayne and Elizabeth started out by visiting the Bender family cottage at Lot 121 (Elizabeth's family). In 1975, we decided to purchase Lot 47, owned by Hank and Tess O'Mara. It was a small 250 square foot cottage with a water tap outside and a kitchen table and small apartment-sized fridge inside. There was nothing else inside. So, we started from rustic roots and, while the cottage was enlarged to 500 square feet over the years, it is still very small but functional.

Over the past 45+ years we have had so many memorable moments. Even prior to getting married and purchasing the cottage, we had time on Piers at the Benders' cottage. One Sunday, Elizabeth and Dewayne went over to the Benders' cottage to help Bill with some projects. The plan was to pick up Margaret in the afternoon and bring her over. Unfortunately, a strong wind blew up and it was impossible to get to the Benders' boat that anchored in the bay in front of Lot 121. As a result, the three of us were marooned on Piers. That Sunday afternoon, we went for a walk around the island and stopped at Charlie Kent's place (Lot 32). He was a good wine maker and we were greeted with some of his makings. We had a good visit and consumed lots of wine, which helped us walk back to the Benders' place later in the afternoon. The wind blew all night and into the next day, which was a workday for Dewayne. Dewayne remembers calling his boss in Victoria and advising him that he was marooned on Piers Island with Elizabeth and her Dad and couldn't get to work. I don't think they believed Elizabeth and Dewayne were with her Dad, as they were only engaged at that time. Dewayne was ribbed about that for years.

We so remember the many picnics, fishing derbies, Moonlight Madness dances, Piers Pancake Breakfasts, Walkabouts, and all of the other activities that the islanders enjoyed. After adding two boys to our family, Robin and Ryan, they had lots of fun playing on the island with their many friends and acquaintances. In those days, we never worried about the boys, because they were on the island and couldn't get lost. They knew they had to be home for dinner and by dark. Otherwise, they were free to roam. Times were simpler then.

There are many ways to move on and off Piers Island. I remember one such move when Colleen Fitzgerald moved to Lot 25. It was all done by helicopter. Her furniture and goods arrived at Dolphin Road parking lot in the moving truck. Her possessions were placed in nets, and a helicopter would hook onto each net, one at a time, and take it to Colleen's. She had a crew at the parking lot and another on her deck; each crew loaded and unloaded on each end of the journey. During one of the trips over to the island, her organ was the single item on that particular trip, and unfortunately it fell into the ocean just off Clive Island. I am sure the fish are still playing that organ today.

Other remembrances include the single engine plane that landed in the north meadow when it was experiencing engine problems. Fortunately, the plane and passenger were unhurt. We also remember one of the small B.C. Ferries vessels lost its steerage in front of our place at Lot 47 and ended up grounding itself just off our dock. While it did not sink, it took awhile for it to be freed. This made an article in the *Victoria Times Colonist.*

Piers Island has always been our sanctuary where we could get away from life. Even living in Victoria, Vancouver, Prince George and now Port Alberni, we can always find Piers as a place where we can enjoy peace and serenity.

Bender and Parfitt families

Lot 63 - Fiona and Brian Clark

Wheelbarrow Life For A Family Of Six!

We moved to Piers Island in February 1976, with four children under the age of eight. There were only about 15 permanent residents, all older than us, so the kids had many surrogate grandparents and were well spoiled. We had arranged with the barge to move us but at the last minute that was cancelled. Brian had just come back from working with helicopters in the high Arctic so he and his buddy Tony, suggested using one. After a brief reconnaissance trip it was agreed; we all travelled to the island by helicopter. It was the easiest move we've ever done - a two-minute turnaround and everything landed on the deck and was moved into place. By the time Brian arrived on Piers, I had a load of laundry going, hamburgers for all, and the beds made and ready. People came out of the woodwork to see what was going on and later we heard there were bets as to how long we'd last. We lived on Piers for 11 ½ years!

Living there was a great experience and has left all four kids - Duncan, Janice, Andrew and Robert, very confident and able. We did not have a wharf, so we used the government dock and had a half mile walk home. We never had a dozen unbroken eggs because everything was moved by wheelbarrow - including Fiona after knee surgery. The kids missed the odd day of school due to weather, but basically it was life as normal.

Our youngest son's birthday is on Halloween, and trick-or-treating was difficult. So, we had a bonfire on Association (now Biscoe) Beach with hot chocolate and fireworks. Everyone came and "Robert's Bonfire" became a tradition.

One harrowing experience came during a bad storm. Janice was in the hospital and was supposed to come home. I couldn't go across to Vancouver Island, so a friend picked her up. Several people needed prescriptions filled and food, so Svend (Lot 56) who was a prawn fisherman and had a skookum boat, took Charlie Kent (Lot 32) and me across. Charlie took care of the shopping and I picked up Janice from my friend. Svend was unable to dock his boat due to the weather, so we threw Janice onto the boat and luckily Svend caught her. Charlie and I managed to get on board. We all arrived home safely.

Altogether, living on Piers was a great time. We had lottery parties, Midnight Madness dances, fishing derbies, association picnics, Terry Fox runs, fire practice, grass cutting, membership in local government and being with great friends.

Duncan was eight, Janice was seven, Andrew was four and Robert was two when we moved to Piers. The only vehicles on the island were an old VW beetle on the island (belonging to Joe Friendenthal at Lot 49) and the firehall tractor. What a difference. Three of our kids visited Piers in 2019, and had a tour of their old house. They said they found both the house and the island were a lot smaller than they remembered.

Clark family

Lot 83 - Bert and Betty Johnston

(written by good friend, Cec Gould, Lot 101)

Bert and Betty Johnston built the log home at Lot 83 with logs from their acreage in Cordova Bay. The house was designed with all of Bert's ideas, including the etched glass windows. Betty loved owls, and that theme was incorporated throughout the house. Betty died in the 1990s and Bert 'lost heart' to finish the house. However, another islander, Wayne Neidig (Lot 85) encouraged him to finish, and Bert was glad that he did.

Bert was a very quiet person and kept mostly to himself. He was close to his immediate neighbours - the Gaits (Lot 87), the Hoytes (Lot 81), and also Maurice Destrube and the Wells family (Lot 44). He and Dennis Wells did all of the plumbing for the firehall. I really got to know Bert when I asked him if I could use his truck and barge to pick up the prefabricated cabinet units for the kitchen and washrooms in the firehall. He had a small motorized barge and took the units from Barnacle Road dock to Piers.

Bert was a hard worker and did a lot of work on the 'new' Piers Island firehall in the early 1990s. Bert was a big supporter of the Piers shuttle after he sold his barge. He used the shuttle faithfully until the end of his life. He said, "The shuttle is the best way to meet people on the island."

Everyone on Piers knew Bert as 'Bert,' but his real name was Wilfert. Other friends (off island) knew him as 'Pete.' So, he appears to be a man of 'multiple identities'. Bert was a good friend, but he did have his definite ideas about things. We disagreed a number of times, but we remained friends to the end.

In the 1980s, both Bert and his friend Dennis Wells built their own 22-foot wooden boats. Bert was very proud of his boat, and he was a very meticulous craftsman. Since he and Betty had no children, he donated his boat to SALTS (Sail and Life Training Society).

Bert passed away in 2017 in Victoria, and the Piers property was subsequently sold to a young couple, Julien Bahain and Katie Steenman, who are also very fond of boats.

Bert and Betty Johnston

Lot 86 - John and Diane Currie

Volunteering And So Many Memories

(written by son, Gordon Currie)

I started going to Piers (age eight) in the early 1970s. I was the oldest of three boys (brother Doug was one year younger, and David five years younger). At the beginning, we couldn't afford to buy on Piers, so we rented the Skolroods's cottage (Lot 92) for a few summers. I remember so many boats tying up together on the moorage outside the cottage, with lots of friends visiting, including the Schaddelee family of the Dutch Bakery in Victoria. Dad and Diane finally bought their property at Lot 86. We camped in a tent until they built their full-time home in the mid-1980s.

Fishing is a big memory. We fished almost every night. Dad had a tide book that was his Bible. We always fished between Piers and Salt Spring in the 1970s and 1980s, before the big ferries came along. Dad was so proud when he caught a 23-pound Spring salmon right in front of Association Beach (Biscoe Beach). We used to watch people dive off Arbutus Island right in front of our home. They often dove for abalone. In early 1970s, one diver had a heart attack. He was given CPR, transferred to Piers, and then taken off-island to hospital by ambulance. We heard he survived.

My brothers and I built tree-houses on the island. We would sweep the leaves off the ground and built a lot of those forts. Dad never let us put any holes in trees; he was very much into protecting the environment. There were a lot of deer on Piers, and especially in the meadow near the beach and in the centre of the island. John and Diane always went on nightly walks after dinner and I liked going with them. We always saw lots of deer at dusk.

My brothers and I would take our best friends over to Piers. We always had a great time riding our bicycles around the island. In the early years, there were only one or two work trucks on the island. Bicycles and wheelbarrows were the common form of transportation on Piers in the 1970s and 1980s.

The biggest thing I remember about John and Diane was that they had lots of friends and were always volunteering. They supported each other with whatever they did. They worked hard together with lots of other islanders to get the new firehall built and in getting a new fire truck as well. Dad was real proud of that accomplishment. Dad scrounged up fire equipment from all over B.C. for the Piers Island Fire Department, everything from hats, to ropes to hoses. He was the Fire Chief on Piers and was also the Executive Director of the BC Fire Chiefs' Association.

I remember Diane was really big on preparing the Christmas decorations and handmade ornaments for the Piers Christmas Party. Yearly, every Piers Island firefighter received a gift of one Diane's handmade fire-department-themed Christmas ornaments. She was also great at sewing the costumes for the big Halloween and Christmas parties. Diane was quite a seamstress and sewed costumes for dozens of girls figure skating in Victoria. Diane's girls and grandchilden loved going to Piers over the years and had fond memories.

Volunteering was a huge part of John and Diane's lives. Besides volunteering for the fire department, Dad and Diane maintained their first aid certification and in the 1980s, they were the first to be called for medical emergencies for strokes and heart attacks. When an emergency occurred, they would go to homes on their bicycles, deal with the emergency, and then arrange for people with big boats, like Sven Mariager (Lot 56), to transport them to the ambulance on the other side. Sven and Grace Mariager were very kind to my brothers and me. It was Sven who built my Dad's first boat on Piers. He was an amazing builder from Scandanavia.

Dad and Diane were very involved with the community. They loved the people of the island and the community of Piers and its rich history. They wanted to stay on Piers forever, but they had to leave because of dad's medical problems. He was so protective of Diane and wanted to make sure that she was not overwhelmed with the home and boat and dock on her own if something happened to him. He survived his illness, only to lose Diane in 2008. Dad was sad that he lost a lot of their connections with the island.

Diane and John Currie

I started going to Piers when my brothers and I were kids, and if I wasn't living up north in Dawson Creek, I would have loved a property on Piers. Fifty years later, Piers still holds wonderful memories for all my family.

Lot 99 - Richard and Judy Zala

'Zala Zoo' Memories

(written by daughter Tracy Zala)

In the late 1970s, my parents, Richard and Judy Zala bought Lot 99 on Piers Island. This would become our home away from home for the next decade and more. We bought a boat, got organized, and began our adventures, heading to our cabin in the woods almost every weekend and all holidays. We promptly erected a log sign saying, 'Zala Zoo', to welcome fellow islanders jaunting around the ring road. This story is a quick look at my memories of getting to grow up adventuring freely on Piers Island.

As a young child, along with my two brothers, Jeff and Rob, our days of tide pool wading, playing in the woods, and making moss/tree forts, searching the island for Doukhobor artifacts like the abandoned buildings, water wells, and orchard fields, gave freedom for our imaginations to run wild. We were free range children who met many of the other Piers island children (Mike and Megan Jones, Alisha and Jennifer Dahl, Gillian Gray, Michael and Melanie Jarrott, the Denoons and Jennifer Stitt) and built life-long friendships. We would cavort about from cabin to cabin, play hide and seek in the middle of the forest areas, go beachcombing, bike ride around the island while feeling like we were the true adventurers of Piers.

When we got older, we would take the rowboats out on the ocean, build campfires, water ski, go shrimping at night down at the public dock, take the boat to Canoe Cove for gas and a treat, go island hopping to Princess Margaret Island (now called Portland Island) to see the wild sheep, zip across in the boat to Salt Spring Island for ice cream ventures without adults, and chase the B.C. Ferries vessels and jump the waves as they travelled back and forth. We really got to live our best lives.

I remember the pre-arranged activities, like the summer picnics at Association (Biscoe) Beach, with games galore spiced up with a bit of family rivalry to win. Everyone got excited by the fishing derby where I felt we spent hours and hours trolling slowly around Arbutus Island waiting for the perfect catch - usually a cod over the coveted salmon we wanted. You can't forget the firehall dances with harvest moons and late nights. To top it off, the excitement of getting to spend your allowance to walk or bike down to Mrs. Hoyte's stand with the honey bars for sale - oh, what a big treat!

There are so many Piers Island memories that I share and laugh about in my adult years now. Who would imagine that my mother could find outside chores for us to do on the island? She would have us clean up the forest debris of dropped branches and rake leaves for beach fires. We would comb the beaches for litter (and sometimes treasures) that washed ashore. We would take turns watching our boat that was moored out front, with hopes that it wouldn't come loose and float away during storms. In the fall and winter days inside, we would use binoculars to record tugboat information in a book my mother kept. Simple joys of checking the crab nets, seeing if our friends were on the island that weekend, or going blackberry picking for crumbles, pies and jam were part of our island life.

The best experience that Piers Island gave us as children was freedom and joy away from the hustle and bustle of organized activities, pressures, and expectations. It afforded us the opportunity to dream, adventure and build a love for the outdoors experiencing a simplistic way of life. During my growing up days on Piers Island, I was away from the phone, cars, and TVs. We played lots of board games, crafted and cooked. I can still create a great pancake because I got to make Saturday morning pancakes and bacon breakfasts. I was close with my siblings, Jeff and Rob, and we learned to love the land, water, and creatures that lived there. Eagles, seals, and whales were part of our daily life. Now that I live inland in Alberta, each trip I take on the B.C. Ferries, I go on the outer deck, peer longingly at Piers Island as we pass it and think how lucky I was to have such a fortunate childhood full of memories most only dream about. Thank you Piers Island for shaping my childhood and giving me nature's basic tools to love our land and water while embracing the beauty all around me.

'Zala Zoo' family

Lot 101 - Cec and Sheila Gould

The Best Time Of Our Lives!

In 1979, we bought the vacant lot at Lot 101 from the original owner, who was the brother of Doug Gate (Lot 87).

In the 1950s, while on a cruise in the Gulf Islands in a cousin's launch, we had moored in a bay and came ashore on Biscoe Beach for a stroll and a picnic. In the 1960s, I rented Miss Ojala's cottage (Lot 6) for three weeks and explored the island. In the early 1970s, I rented the Wells' log cabin (Lot 44) for my family, while I commuted to University of Victoria's summer school. I used the little cottage at Lot 44 as my study area. That was also our introduction to the well-attended Moonlight Madness dance.

In 1979, Sheila and I rented Miles and Fran Primrose's cottage (Lot 38) for three weeks. One day on a return from a trip to Portland Island, we spotted a 'For Sale' sign on Lot 101. We contacted Reg Biscoe who showed us several properties, including Lot 101. We were able to buy it and move our small travel trailer onto it. We lived in that trailer until 1984, when we framed the cottage with assistance from our son-in-law David Craven. Over the next nine years, Sheila and I finished the building. Sheila was new to building but was right into it. We love Piers Island, especially the fishing and various island events.

For both of us, the building of the 'new' firehall in the 1990s was the big highlight of our time on Piers. The response from everyone was amazing. Those who could, contributed labour and special skills. Those unable to do that, donated a lot of money. A core team of people organized the project at every stage. Fred Thompson (Lot 61) designed the floor plan and drew up the working drawings. Piers got the last B.C. Lottery Corporation (BCLC) matching grant for volunteer fire departments. George Hoyte (Lot 81) took on the herculean task of recording the hours every volunteer donated to give us 'sweat equity' because our contribution was matched dollar for dollar by the BCLC. Dave Poulsom (Lot 112), a retired land surveyor, surveyed the site boundaries after the location was chosen, following consultation with island residents. He laid out the siting of the hall and perfectly squared the cribbing forms. After the concrete was poured, he meticulously levelled the sand fill inside so the floor could be poured. Don Gait (Lot 87) used all of his own equipment to clear and excavate on the site. Bob Clarke (Lot 55) and his son framed the washrooms, kitchen and office spaces in the training area. Other people donated lots of time and money, which was used for materials we had to purchase. Many contractors commented on the excellent quality of the professional volunteer work that was done. It was my honour as Chair of the Piers Island Improvement District at the time to work with such generous, keen and talented people. I have only mentioned some of the many islanders involved. It was an amazing community effort.

A huge Piers memory for both of us is of the time a small plane made an emergency landing in the meadow behind Biscoe Beach. Sheila and I had walked counter-clockwise around the island and when we got to our path, I glanced toward the meadow. We were shocked to see a silver Cessna nose-down. We ran down to it and found it stuck in a rut parallel to the road. No one was around. The two people from the plane had left in search of a telephone for help. He was a very experienced pilot because when he had run out of fuel over Salt Spring Island, he glided into the only open space available. He and his elderly mother were taken to Swartz Bay by boat. The plane was picked up by a large helicopter a week later.

Emergency landing at Biscoe Beach 1992

In the 1990s, Barbara Watson saw a small business opportunity in establishing a ferry service to Piers. Previously, there had only been water taxi service. She worked hard trying everything she could to make it pay. She encountered a number of hurdles imposed by the Capital Regional District (CRD), which had taken over the government wharves. She was going to have to pay a fee every time she touched the government dock. So, for awhile, the ferry boarded at Canoe Cove marina and docked at Berneice Archibald's wharf (Lot 66), so that Barbara didn't have to pay that fee. At a Piers Island meeting, Henry Charlesworth (Lot 135) proposed that we form a shuttle co-op and buy two pontoon watercrafts. Too many opposed the idea, but the co-op was formed when a group met with Barbara and guaranteed her a monthly rate based on fares collected by the co-op. I collected the fares and kept the records and Sheila did the computer work. Barb eventually sold her pontoon boats and the business to the Smiley family and the co-op continued the collection of fares and monthly payments.

We loved our part-time adventure on Piers. As soon as Sheila and I came home from our schools on Friday, we got our bags (already packed), grabbed a burger in Sidney and spent nearly every single weekend on the island.

Sadly, Sheila died in 2016, but I know she would been happy that I sold our Piers 'get-away' to Conrad and Magdalene van der Kamp, who joined their relatives on the island - the Changs (Lot 95), Chris and Betty Muller (Lot 9) and Jackie Charlesworth (Lot 135). Building the cottage and taking part in all of the Piers events was the best time of our lives!

Cec and Sheila Gould

Lot 106 - Jim and Helen Currie

A Piers Island Saga

It was a beautiful July day in 1972 for our family of five and our dog Holly, to set up our camp on our newly purchased Piers Island lot. The tide was right for our boat launch. We took our supplies, including tenting equipment and our food, and were looking forward to an overnight stay. We had prefabricated the panels for our outhouse ready to raft over behind the boat. The going was slow because the rafted outhouse acted like a sea anchor; we arrived at the beach much later than expected and laden down with all our supplies. In the dusk and at high tide we trekked across the high banks of our neighbours' properties (the Duffies and Polsoms), possibly to their chagrin and to our embarrassment. We erected our tent by flashlight in the scrubby, uncleared bush.

We enjoyed our tent platform and cooking shelter for several years as we became familiar with the island and with our neighbours who were mostly at the same stage in temporary shelters. Below the bank and over the beach, we hung a swing supported by a willow tree. That swing was popular with our kids and with beach walkers as they passed by. We did many beach walks ourselves and with family friends and guests at low tide. In those days there were more paths at the edges of waterfront lots, where you could climb to escape the beach rocks and there were no fences to restrict access. Jim knew all the interior paths and history of the island and often went over the summit on his marathon training runs - always stopping to pull broom on the way. At this stage at our campsite, we were connected to the water line, which was a surface line that ran around the Island. We used lanterns for lighting and a wood-fired stove for cooking and heat.

In 1976, we began construction of the cabin with its location close to the bank to obtain the view. The cabin was framed by Jack Glover from Sidney, who had done previous work for us. Jim finished the inside with the occasional assistance of brother-in-law, Ernie Forsyth. Every summer for many years, our two to four-week holiday was spent installing cedar paneling both downstairs and up. We would go for a paddle in our canoe round the island or beyond at the end of the day. At that time, the island was not a place of delight for our two teenage daughters, since there were always endless work projects and few friends close by. Our son Ian was younger and happier with lots of opportunities to explore, usually in the company of other boys who became life-long friends.

As the cabin progressed with connection to water line, electricity and plumbing, Eileen and Lisa soon ran the boat on their own and brought their friends over for company. I was working as a home care nurse out of Sidney in the 1970s, and was on call on the weekends. However, having no phone at our cabin, I would hike across the middle of the island to the phone box at the government dock to check for messages. Usually, I was much relieved not to have any messages, because a message would involve a boat trip away from Piers.

Speaking of boats, we had our share of adventures with strong westerly winds and the boat on anchor. On two occasions we found the boat in the morning, beached up on Biscoe Beach. But usually Jim would be up in the storm in the dinghy hoping to secure the boat in the darkness.

At that time, we all shared experiences with neighbours as the need arose. If someone was finished with a sink or a window or door, we could use it to build or finish a shed. We even shared outdoor showers heated by the sun if someone had a functioning one. Logs from the beach were used for foundations and bridges. Having a colleague who was the public health inspector was fortuitous when the time came to install a septic field.

There were parties and dinners with late night walks home along the beach or on the road, which was then a country lane overgrown in parts with alders. We cleared a swampy alder grove from our lot to become a playground, useful for croquet, bocce ball, and Kubb, and endless fun for grand children as they grew up. The grandchildren invented countless games and found endless adventures with roving groups of island kids. They had complete freedom to explore the island and the ocean, where they have learned to fish. For many years there was a fishing derby in August. It was followed with prizes and a corn roast.

That sums up the 1970s into the 1980s. The Joys and the Challenges carry on.

Currie family

Lot 109 - Janis Dunning C.M. and Jacques Lemay C.M.

Piers Island - A Harbour for Our Souls

(written by Janis Dunning on behalf of Margery Piers/Dunning, and the Dunning/Lemay family)

In 1974, my mother, Margery Piers, began a journey of 40 years of adventure, nature, love, and refuge on the island namesake of her family. In turn, three generations brought our children to the island and eventually left it with abundant love. Now we harbour in our hearts the dreams and memories we formed on Piers Island.

Our first emotion each time we went to Piers Island, was exhilaration! The wind whistled though our hair as we bounced over the waves with eyes wide open, elated grins and sparkling energies. A new adventure was beginning!

For me, our little cottage was a creative hideaway:

- For writing dozens, even hundreds, of televised stories for children all across the nation.
- For creating pieces of theatre to celebrate all of Canada's bounty and to elevate the spirits of its peoples.
- For whittling wood, for painting shells.
- For savouring the aroma and thrilling the senses with the flavour of fresh-baked bread.
- For healing, bonding, guiding my children, and for helping my husband to relinquish the burdens of his escalating career.

For all of us it was a refuge:

- A place we could flee to from a life too big.
- A place to peel off layers of burdens.
- A place to bring our love, fears, and tears, sometimes flooding the cottage with tears, washing the mind and soul. Then, with no design, beginning afresh.

Eventually the island became a haven:

- For sacred evenings with newfound women friends where it was safe to share fears and courage and new ways to take steps forward into the unknown.
- For learning, and allowing healing.
- For rustic Friday evenings of sharing food, friendship, laughter, wisdom, experience, and glimpses of new horizons.

Piers Island gave us time:

- Time to hold on to those dearest in life.
- Time to watch the children spread their wings and find glee in the independence of running freely through the woods, smiling at every kind islander along the way.
- Time to be free from intrusions. No telephones, no TV, no one propelling our lives.
- Time for rejuvenating the soul: Drinking in the rain dripping from the leaves; feeling the gentle, caring earth on the paths. Sensing eternity taught by the wisdom of the tallest trees.

The trees remember us singing on the trails. They embraced our youngest, protected them and encouraged them to see the first glimpses of their own dreams, then gently guided them to the trails that led them home. Our hearts ache for the emotional journeys we travelled. When emotions and imagination were too big to fit into the worlds we lived in, it was time to shelter them at Piers Cottage and fold them into our stories, memories and poems. Now and forever Piers remains a harbour for our hearts and for our most tender memories. And we remain forever haunted, for now I know that we can leave Piers Island, but it will never leave us.

***Piers Island was named after Margery Piers' great-great uncle, Henry Piers.**

Janis Dunning, Genevieve, Matthew and Jacques Lemay

Lot 113 - Gloria and Wayne Morson

The Perfect Place To Raise A Family

Wayne rented a place on Piers for the summer for a month or two in the late 1960s. He knew Reg Biscoe through work meetings and asked him to let him know if a nice sunny property with a good beach access came up for sale. We bought Lot 113 sight unseen in 1976, and we didn't even own a boat. Robert Harvey was the seller of the property. His grandfather owned the whole island in the 1930s. The grandson bought this piece of land, but never built on it.

We borrowed a boat to view the property we had bought. We went to the neighbour's (Launers Lot 111) dock next door and had to pull broom just to get to our land. It was solid broom - we couldn't even step on our property. We started coming out for day trips in the summer for two more years. Every visit to Piers, we pulled broom to clear some land to get a small trailer on the property. By that time, Darren was three years old and Tylor had just been born. We put a trailer on the property in 1979 and for 12 years we came out to Piers for weekends and a two-week holiday in the summers. (Wayne only had two weeks of holiday each year). Every visit to Piers in those early days, we had to bring lots of supplies for camping in the trailer and we only had an outhouse.

Our property has the original foundation from when Clive Phillips-Wolley owned the land around 1900. I have a picture of the big dock that Phillips-Wooley built at that time. Because Sir Clive built the house on our property, the land on the north-west side was cleared for an orchard.

We built our cottage in 1991. The excavation had been done with the foundation forms in place before barge day. Then the first barge run brought over a cement truck and pumper. The second barge brought a second cement truck and the third barge brought over lumber. The last truck brought bricks for a fireplace. Wayne had it all precision-timed but it rained all day long, which presented challenges. When the last truck was leaving, it was sliding into the old house foundation until Wayne yelled for the guy to "boot it," and prevented the truck from sliding in. It was an eventful day that we will never forget.

Years ago, Fran and Miles Primrose (Lot 38) brought over some of the Doukhobors to see the area and Wayne was part of the visit that day. A Canada Film Board film was made of the Doukhobors in Canada, and that visit was featured in the film.

The fig tree near the foundation was the first fig tree in Canada. Sir Clive had a horticulturist who brought it over from England. That fig tree still produces fruit after over 100 years.

After barge day, the professional crew built the house to lock-up stage, working from dawn to dusk all through September. There wasn't a drop of rain during that construction. After that, it took four years to finish the inside of the house - all on weekends and holidays because we were still working. Then we added onto the house for retirement in 2002, and moved full-time to the island. That never was the plan, but when Wayne retired we didn't want two houses, and we didn't want to part with Piers. Almost all of those years, we spent most of our vacation time on Piers.

We didn't build the dock until 1998. Before the dock, the four of us would arrive by boat with a bird in a cage, a cat in another cage, and all the boys' worldly possessions, and make lots of trips from the mooring buoy to the property. I'm sure that provided lots of entertainment for the rest of the bay, when the Morsons arrived for the summer.

The big thing about Piers was doing things 'not cityish.' The boys built forts and rafts, and then swam out to the raft and spent hours in the water. Then, of course, there was also waterskiing and tubing. The boys always wanted to come and spend time on Piers instead of hanging out in Victoria. The kids enjoyed the simplicity of the 'old-fashioned picnic' and the dance at the old firehall - called 'Moonlight Madness' or 'Dancing in the Dirt' under the moonlight. We took the kids there and back in the wheelbarrow. The dance was so old-fashioned and unique.

We always felt that Piers had a positive influence on the boys' upbringing and we were so thankful we owned island property. What we appreciated the most, was that all ages of kids played together (not like in the city). They played flashlight tag, kick the can, and 'Ante Over' - just pure fun. The boys looked forward to seeing their island friends every summer and also loved bringing friends over from the city and sharing the Piers experience.

We used to have the beer and wine festival in the old firehall. Medals were even given out. Wayne was one of the original organizers of the event. It was well-attended and always so fun.

As teenagers, the boys wanted to spend their time on Piers, but always wanted to earn a bit of extra cash. They put up signs to work on the island, so they painted cottages, split wood, and did lots of odd jobs, including demolishing an outhouse. The boys always wanted to come to Piers. We didn't go through the stage that they wanted to stay in the city. We wanted the kids to enjoy the island outdoors, play on the beach, and just be creative in nature. I still want to keep the house so that the grandkids can experience what their daddies experienced - quality family time.

Wayne Morson

Morson family

Lot 115 - Gordon and Ros Alexander

That's My Island: A Piers Island Reflection

"That's my island there. Mine's that red and white cottage just behind Clive Island. Yup. It's that island just there. Got it? That's Piers Island. I'm at Lot 23, " said Bill Ham .

We were standing on the Queen of New Westminster ferry enroute to Vancouver, talking with Bill, who like all islanders we were to discover, considered that he owned the whole island, and in a way they do. A 4x8 plywood sign announced lots for sale and gave R. Fraser Biscoe's company name: Island Seafront Properties.

Thus, we discovered Piers Island by chance in the fall of 1978, after we had been invited by friends who had a cabin on Pender Island to spend the day with them. At that time there were only two ferry runs a day to Pender: 9:45 a.m. and 5:35 p.m. Having missed the morning ferry on the designated Saturday, we had no option but to go home, frustrated and determined to find recreational property for ourselves that did not rely on BC Ferries to get us there. Also, at that point our two-year-old daughter did not appreciate long car trips any more than we did, and reaching an island in one hour door-to-door was a bonus, in spite of the fact we needed to acquire a boat to do it. Another bonus was a community water supply from the wells, which filled the lower reservoir. We had explored some of the other Gulf Islands and realized that water was a major issue. We reasoned that if we had a water problem on Piers, it would be a problem for everyone else, and therefore the community would find a solution, not force us to drill deeper, carry in our own supply, or do without.

We bought our lot at 115 Mackenzie Crescent in May 1979 from the Britts, then of Thailand, for full price, against Gordon's wish to make a lower offer. Next was the purchase of a 14-foot Thornes open aluminum boat. The lot had been part of the original Phillips-Wolley homestead; we have most of the tennis court. When we bought, there were only three trees on it, all arbutus. Two have since succumbed to the disease that attacked most of the arbutus in the area. The huge older tree in the middle of the lot behind which we built our cabin, is still there, very reduced, but surviving. We chose to build 100 feet back from the water for the winter warmth and all-day sunshine, which proved to be a wise choice.

The first job, as every pioneer knows, is to clear the land. Since the lot was basically covered with what my father later described as 'virgin scrub', we had to clear a path from the beach to the building site so that we could get building materials up. We began building in the spring rain of 1980, and scoured demolition sites in Victoria for cheap, useable lumber. Building a reasonably sturdy cabin with only a small open boat for a conveyance, and a two-year old sitting on top of 4x8 sheets of reject plywood was a challenge, but Gordon said he was experienced, and he was motivated. The metal roofing came from a boat storage building in Vancouver, and consisted of 24 sheets 2.5 by 14 feet, $5 a sheet, shorter pieces thrown in if removed from the job site. It has been added to twice, but basically looks the same as it did when finished in 1981. Besides, there was no more roofing available in that colour and at that price. It has been our 'relaxation' place, where only the most essential 'work' was ever done (mowing the lawn, sometimes). The kids could run free and safe with friends and quiet walks were always available. The amenities were basic, but perfectly good for a few days and, barring bad weather, our little boat, now upgraded to an avocado green Starcraft runabout, could get us home quickly if necessary.

Only after two decades on the island, did Gordon realize he had heard of Piers Island before meeting Bill Ham. Mary Tucker (Lot 50) was the connection. Gordon realized that Mary had bought a Paneloc prefabricated cottage he had helped build in Vancouver for shipment to an island near Swartz Bay. For his summer job in 1963, he worked for a company developing a prefabricated circular cottage with 12 sides, which stood on a platform of pie-shaped wedges forming a floor with a tilted set of pie shaped wedges forming a roof. The walls were held in place by metal bands top and bottom, which tightened like a barrel. One of the first produced Paneloc homes went to Piers Island. It is still on Lot 50.

We have only ever been part-time Piers Islanders, rarely staying over for more than two nights over a weekend. When our children were young, staying for longer than that was rarely feasible, because supplies ran low and Gordon's job at Camosun College was demanding. There was a golden period in the late 1980s when our children were old enough to have friends on the island, and leave us in the cabin, blessedly alone. However, time passed, and too soon the cabin became 'boring'; they wanted to stay in town. So we, of necessity, were in town with them. Then, they grew, left home, and we had the place to ourselves again. Now, of course, with families of their own, all they want to do is get back to Piers - a very old, cyclical story.

We have had many highlights in our 40-year experience of Piers. John Currie, then on the Piers Island Association, asked Cheryl Eyres (another relative newcomer) and me to organize the food for the island picnic in the August following our arrival. We knew there would be between 200 and 300 people, and we had to choose a menu (spaghetti casserole), and organize volunteers to cook and serve it. Neither of us had ever done such a thing before, but it was a great way to meet islanders quickly and to integrate ourselves into a community with a very strong volunteer ethic. This was very necessary as the islanders could only look to themselves for entertainment (picnic and games, fishing derby, Moonlight Madness dance, and the Walkabout), safety (volunteer Fire Department and first responders), and many other volunteer aspects of running an island community.

The picnic was a huge highlight for our family, the children's games in particular. Wake-up time rivaled Christmas day in our small cabin. The various ribbons collected (mostly reading 'I participated') stayed on our small fridge for many years. Gordon participated in both the Piers Island Association and the Piers Island Improvement District. Also, his work on rejuvenating and maintaining the water system gave him not only a close circle of very talented and knowledgeable people to work with, but also an in-depth understanding of the infrastructure of the island and its history.

Of course, there are advantages and disadvantages to any living situation, especially one where you are only at a recreational home part-time, and must reach it by boat, subject to wind, tide, and fog. When we first bought our property, the old Queen ferries created an enormous wash, which we frequently underestimated or mistimed. In our third year on the island, when we should have known better, we left our one-year old son on the Dolphin Road ramp while we readied the boat. The next time I looked, he was bobbing out to sea - life jackets do work. We also had an accident-prone daughter, who necessitated a very large first aid kit, and frequently curtailed weekends. She has a healthy respect for ladders after a fall on her way up to the attic loft. However, most of our highlights were positive, centred around the beauty and tranquility of the place. How blessed we have been to be a part of it.

Piers Island has been a large part of our lives for over 40 years now. It has been the place we could get away on the weekends. Whatever needed to be fixed could usually be put off, and 'projects' were minimal. For example, we took a five-gallon hot water tank over to the cabin - its five-year guarantee expired in 1989 and it is yet to be installed. But who needed showers there when you could get home in an hour? Having recreational property, of course, does mean that you tend to go there rather than anywhere else. However, since we are not great travelers that was not really a problem, and we have had the best possible neighbours and friends in Wayne and Gloria

Morson, right next door. Since Gordon has been retired and we have not been tied to the weekends, our favourite time to go is mid-week in the winter (weather permitting), when most of the other part-timers have left, and our bay is almost empty aside from the gulls and the occasional heron on the dock.

Bill Ham was right. We too have thought of Piers as 'our island'. At the same time, we have been happy to share it with others.

Gordon and Ros Alexander

Lot 119 - Trevor and Donna Matthews

Five Decades Of Enjoyment

In 1972, two families, whose husbands were long time friends, bought Lot 119 for $8,000 total. The families were the Matthews (Trevor and Donna) and McQueens (Bob and Kay). For the first few years the two families tented on the island together. The McQueens and Matthews then decided to self-build a permanent structure, which was occupied in 1978. The structure accommodated both families at the same time. Bob McQueen's health became problematic, so the Matthews bought the McQueens interest in the home in the 1990s. This interest in the property was subsequently transferred to the Matthews' sons, Bruce and Terry.

In early days, the island was labelled as 'unorganized territory' under the jurisdiction of the provincial government until 1979 when the Capital Regional District was formally organized. As the house was built before 1978, it had a 'right to occupy' and was grandfathered in. When B.C. Hydro came to connect the hydro, an electrical inspection was requested. A provincial electrical inspection was reluctantly provided, but the electrical permit passed just fine.

Lot 119 has an interesting history in terms of the Doukhobors. It served as the centre of the Piers Island Penitentiary for over 500 male and females, as well as the warden and staff. Lot 119 was the site of the men's prison and a separate woman's prison facility. The entire island had been confiscated by the Federal Government to the chagrin of the owners. The prison lasted for four years until 1935, when the whole building was dismantled, including the penitentiary dock. One piling still remains and the odd artifact can still be found on Piers Island.

Amazingly, there were a number of babies born during the incarceration years on Piers, even though the men's and women's prisons were well separated. Perhaps, it was because once in awhile the warden allowed special visiting privileges between couples.

Tony Booker (Lot 137) brought the Victoria Doukhobor choir for a concert on Piers several years ago, including some descendants of those imprisoned on the island in the 1930s. After the concert, some of those descendants came to Lot 119 to personally view the former site of the prison. The Matthews shared information they had of the warden's report and some photos. This was a significant visit for both the Doukhobor descendants and the Matthews that brought back tragic memories.

Having good water to drink on Piers Island in 1972 was somewhat problematic. The water came from wells and had a sulphur taste (like rotten eggs). Water to individual lots was carried by a 1 ½" black plastic hose that traversed the middle of the lot. Connecting the plastic hose was the responsibility of each landowner. One of the permanent residents on Piers suggested that, if a line under the water was connected to North Saanich, Piers Island could have Sooke water. The resident was a competent, amiable 'jack of all trades.' With the assistance of others, this individual got permission for the underwater line to connect water from North Saanich to Piers Island. The resident asked me if I could round up a couple of friends and complete the job, which I did. It was a straightforward task. I asked the individual if he needed help to connect the line. He said, "No, I will do it myself!" which he apparently did. Islanders were happy to subsequently receive clean, clear water from North Saanich.

Lot 119 has become the Matthews family centre. It is a place that the Matthews seniors, Donna and Trevor, have always enjoyed, as well as their children and grandchildren. They all grew up in the part-time home on Piers and loved exploring the surrounding natural lands and ocean. From time to time the family have participated in the activities and missions of the PIA and the PIID regarding the upkeep of the island. For five decades, three generations of the Matthews have enjoyed their place on Piers.

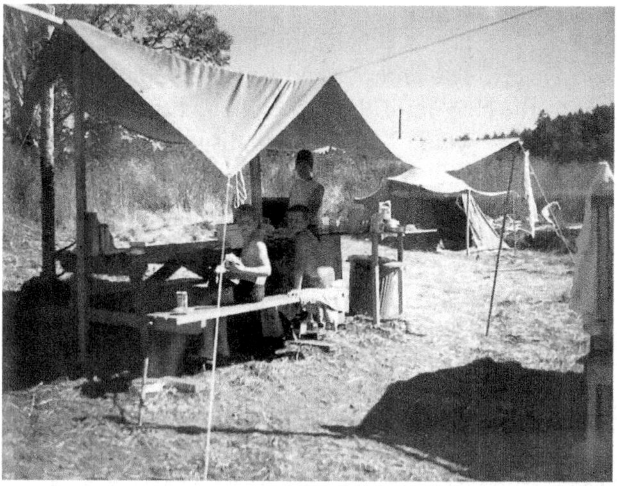

Matthews family early days camping on Piers

Donna and Trevor Matthews

Lot 137 - Tony and Barb Booker

A Little Corner Of Paradise

I 'discovered' Piers Island one day when I was out sailing. As so often happens, the winds in the Gulf Islands can be very fickle, often not showing up at all. Being becalmed, I decided to tie up at the Piers Island dock and have a look around. I was immediately smitten.

The property that our wonderful neighbour Jackie Charlesworth now occupies was for sale. We discovered that it was owned by friends of Barb's parents. While I was in negotiation with them, I happened to be chatting with some of my fellow students at the Slavonic Department at the University of Victoria and it turned out that one of them had relatives who were trying to sell their property on Piers. Not only were they asking less money, they were willing to reduce it for the "right" prospective buyer. To find out whether I was the "right" person, I had to go to the Scoones' home on Galiano Island for an interview. Partly because I was obviously not a speculator and possibly because I, like Barbara Scoones, was a pianist and serenaded them during the 'interview', I was deemed suitable. Not only that, but they offered to let me pay off a portion of the purchase price to them over a 10-year period. Such kind people!

Unfortunately, my bank manager was not so kind. Even though, or perhaps because I was a musician working five part-time jobs, he didn't consider me the "right" person to lend money to. Fortunately with the help of friends and family, I was eventually able to raise the balance that I owed the Scoones.

We spent the next 10 years clearing the building site. We brought the building materials over on the sailboat. Then Frank Williams (Lot 13) would meet us with a tractor and trailer, and we would haul load after load up 'cardiac' hill to Lot 137.

Out of consideration to our neighbour Philippa (Lot 139) we even checked with her to make sure we sited our cottage in a location that would not block her view of Salt Spring Island (a courtesy later extended to us by Jackie). Out of consideration for our neighbours, we also did all the work with hand tools.

Initially we lived in the gazebo that the Scoones had built at Lot 137. Then we purchased a trailer from Kim and Robert (Lot 97), our artist neighbours from across the road on McKenzie Crescent. The year before my Dad died, he and my Mum came all the way from Manchester, England to help with the finishing touches. Since we didn't have an occupancy permit, they stayed at Lot 109, which we rented from the Lemays. During that hectic 10 years of working in town AND building a cottage, Barb and I ended up being really fit and at least 20 pounds lighter than we are now! We also added another 20 trees to the walnut and apple tree grove that the Scoones had planted.

We eventually had to sell the sailboat to cover our mortgage payments. We graduated to a much smaller dinghy powered by a Seagull outboard, then to Joe Friedenthal's (Lot 49) *Little Bit* and finally to kayaks. The latter is our preferred means of transport, though now with some health problems, we often use both the shuttle and the golf cart, which our super neighbours Steve and Philippa leave near the dock for our use.

Not only our immediate neighbours, but so many islanders have been helpful and supportive - Bert Johnson and his successors the Bahains, the Neidigs, the Gates, the Bryces , the Trogers and all of you who attend the concerts I have put on over the years and donate so generously to whatever charity we are supporting. Many thanks to all the volunteers who have kept this little corner of paradise running smoothly over the years.

I've always been intrigued by the Doukhobors and have read extensively about them. One of my Russian professors at the University of Victoria was a Doukhobor from Grand Forks. I visited him there and he introduced me to his friends and took me to see their museum. Several of the students in the School of Music at University of Victoria, where I also studied, were of Doukhobor descent and started a Doukhobor Choir in Victoria. In line with tradition, the choir sang without notes and in a quasi-improvisational manner. Later, I discovered that Piers had been a penitentiary for the more anarchist of them known as the 'Sons of Freedom' and that the women and men, though separated, were able to communicate by singing to each other over the separating fence. Apparently the singing could be heard on Salt Spring Island.

It seemed that the Victoria Doukhobor Choir was a natural choice to come and visit their ancestors' place of imprisonment, so in 2013, I invited them to perform on Piers. It was a lovely concert and very moving not just because of the tragic history, but also because of the powerful music.

Barb and Tony Booker

1980s
A TIME OF TRANSITION

During the 1980s, more people were moving full-time on the island. By the end of the decade, there were around 95 residents occupying 40 full-time homes. As usual, the summer population doubled with the return of 'part-time' owners.

Many people were completing their home-building projects and were able to enjoy the amenities of the island more. Building still continued for others, and the need for building permits through the Capital Regional District (CRD) became a requirement. Many part-time families with teenagers spent the entire summer months on Piers and long weekends during the rest of the year. There was no shuttle service on Piers at this time, but Captain Ted Aubrey from Sidney was the guy to call if your boat wasn't working or you needed transportation. He would charge $25 a trip to or from Piers on his 18-foot Double Eagle.

The Piers water system was transitioning from the reservoir in the centre of the island to a joint system with the CRD. Water conservation was highly encouraged with garden-watering being limited to hand-held hoses; sprinklers were not allowed. The Piers Island Volunteer Fire Department (PIVFD) remained sadly eroded down to a 'maintenance only' group. In the early 1980s, interest was expressed by the growing community that a formal fire department be established again, to deal with potential disasters. Slowly, the fire department started up again, some summer fire practices were held and cottagers were informed of basic safety measures to prevent fires.

In 1988, John Currie (Lot 86) became Piers Fire Chief and he initiated training programs and upgraded equipment for the fire department. Once again there was an active fire force on the island. Discussions were happening regarding the building of a new firehall to meet the growing needs of the community. There was considerable dissention as to the necessity of this new building and its location. A community consensus was finally reached where property owners would pay one-third of the cost of the new firehall, while the rest of the monies would come from volunteer labour and a government grant.

Piers Island became part of Islands Trust in 1980 with a meeting of residents in Sansha Hall in Sidney (now Mary Winspear Centre). Piers Island's first official community plan was established with Bylaw 51 that same year. The number one of six goals voted by islanders was "To preserve Piers Island's rural unspoiled character, natural beauty and views, and to protect its foreshores and surrounding waters."

Some special events occurred in the 1980s. The Terry Fox run was organized on Piers during the summers of 1981-1985, with great community participation, spearheaded by the Clarkes (Lot 55) and the Clarks (Lot 63). The summer annual picnic/races continued with the addition of the magic of Professor Whimsey (Hal Weaver, Lot 39) and Moonlight Madness carried on as an enthusiastic 'dance in the dust' for islanders. The fishing derby remained well attended each year and most islanders enjoyed fishing throughout the year.

Lots 2, 135 - Margot Fitz-Gerald

An Idyllic Life On Piers

Around 1986, Mom and Dad phoned me in Colwood to invite me to see a house with them on Piers Island. They had lived in Manitoba for years and had returned from sailing to New Zealand and were renting in Victoria. The house they looked at on Lot 2 was too small for them, but perfect for me so I bought it. They later bought Sibleys' house (Lot 27). A helicopter move had Mom and Dad moving onto the island and the Sibleys moving off the same day. It was a symphony of coordination that took amazingly little time.

I continued working as a nurse at Gorge Road Hospital and Saanich Peninsula Hospital and commuted initially to Dolphin Road Government dock. When my boat was stolen from there, a slip at Canoe Cove seemed the most sensible thing to do. Stormy weather necessitated improvising some nights. For example, sometimes I would sleep in the car or when the great snowfall hit late December 1996, I ended up staying at a cousin's home in North Saanich. Once I recall after a night shift, I returned when the waves were crashing on the bow and freezing on the windshield. It wasn't pretty. Many boats sank that year from the weight of the ice.

I appreciated so many of the unique Islanders. My sister Colleen, Mom and I had bought a property (the farm at Lot 135) on the inside of the island from the Primroses. Arthur Oldfield rented a cottage on the property from us for awhile. He planted charming bunches of daffodils around, and mowed paths through the wonderful orchard of heritage Gravenstein and King apple trees which were planted by the Doukhobors who had been imprisoned on Piers. Then Arthur moved to the Cronin's waterfront house (Lot 10) where he grew orchids and ginger and lived with his dog. The house he was renting came for sale, and by a miracle Arthur ended up winning big in the lottery. So, instead of renting, he was finally able to buy the Piers house for himself.

Like many Piers Islanders, serving on the PIID (Piers Island Improvement District) and the PIVD (Piers Volunteer Fire Department) was part of everyday life. Highlights for me on Piers were the Moonlight Madness dances at the old firehall and the picnic with all the great games - egg toss, sack races, and many more. The races were always well attended by current and past Piers Islanders and friends.

My recollections are mainly of going back and forth to work. One day a mink hitchhiked a ride with me on my way to work. He got more than he bargained for when he scooted onto the front deck of the boat and we hit ferry wash. It would think that was his first flying lesson!

It was an idyllic life on Piers - the peace and wonder of the forest, the tempestuous sea and the amazing community.

Margot Fitz-Gerald and sister Colleen

Lot 13 - Frank Williams and Ingeborg

A Piers Island Legend

First Sighting

A first sighting of Frank and Ingeborg mid 1980s:

Frank wearing his made-by-Ingeborg zip up sweater with 'PIERS ISLAND' knitted across the back
his baseball hat, his glasses, his jeans, his work boots
driving the tractor or attending an island function.

Ingeborg wearing her visor, her glasses, her hair tightly bunned, her bright pink lipstick, a cardigan over her shoulders held on by sweater clips, a pressed blouse and trousers, her white cotton work-gloves and a pair of clippers........
riding behind Frank on the tractor, holding his shoulders.
as if going to an island function,
adding a white naval hat and epauletted navy jacket.

Riding together up the road,
careful not to cross the daisy strewn mid-line unless necessary

What is remembered, lives
Lynn Pritchett (Lot 23)

Biscoe Was Wrong

The realtor Reg Biscoe always wanted people to fit into Piers. Reg was dubious that Frank Williams wasn't going to be suitable to be a Piers Islander - boy, was he ever wrong about that!
Hal Weaver (Lot 39)

Altruism

Frank gave his talents and time to the island for over 30 years and all agree that he is a Piers Island legend to be preserved. When ill health forced him to leave the island, an impromptu presentation was made - Frank didn't like a fuss, never needed a pat on the back for doing things, he just did them. *Pauline Olesen and Steve Cruise (Lot 123)*

** *Author's Note:* Since Frank and Ingeborg had passed away before the writing of this book, the above islanders have granted permission to include previous dedications to Frank and Ingeborg. Due to Frank's incredible long-term dedication to volunteering on Piers, the Piers Island Fire Department has dedicated the Old Firehall to him - Semper in Memoria'.

Remembering Frank

"Today, 34 UVic Alumni can thank Frank for their degree.

Fortunately for Frank Williams, born in 1927, his grandfather, Frank V. Hobbs a.k.a. "the Grand Old Man of Saanich", believed strongly in providing and increasing educational opportunities. Hobbs sat on the Saanich School Board for over 17 years and helped Frank financially to attend college. This, combined with Frank's saving from working weekends while attending high school, enabled him to attend the Victoria Normal School and Victoria College. Later, Frank attended UBC and then obtained his Master's degree at McGill University in Montreal.

Frank's studies concentrated on the sciences. He decided to specialize in meteorology after he noticed a job posting while attending McGill.

Although Frank was employed by the Federal Government, he worked with the United States Navy. He was stationed in Frobisher Bay, Nunavut and Gander, Newfoundland as well as other northern parts. Eventually he was assigned to HMCS Bonaventure as a Lieutenant Commander.

Frank never had children of his own, but followed his grandfather's example of helping others access post-secondary education by contributing to Registered Education Funds for family and friends. Frank passed away in 2016, but through a gift in his will to the University of Victoria, his and his grandfather's legacy will continue to encourage and support future generations of students through the Frank Hobbs Educational Bursary."

* Printed with permission of the Times Colonist Spring/2022 Edition

Frank left us on the evening of April 2nd, 2016. He would have been 89 on his birthday, May 6, 2016. A group gathered at Biscoe Beach the following evening and toasted him with 'Gin and Tonics,' as did other friends around the world.

Frank Williams

Dedication to Frank at the old firehall

Lot 16 - Isabel and Charlie Stewart

An Incredible Place Of Peace

(written by Susie Todd, daughter)

In the early 1960s, James and Edna Megson of Oak Bay, Victoria purchased 16 McKenzie Crescent on Piers Island from the owner/developer of Piers. They built the modest two-bedroom cabin which would become the much loved home of four generations.

James and Edna sold the cabin in 1987 to Charlie and Isabel Stewart of Sidney. Charlie and Isabel had grown up in Scotland and always loved the sea. They knew that as they grew older they would not be able to sail their sailboat *Sheena* for very much longer. However, they did not want to lose their connection to the ocean. The oceanfront cabin was perfect for them to sit and watch the ever-changing views of boats and ferries gliding past.

For more than 30 years, Lot 16 would host the craziest parties with a huge number of neighbours and friends from around the globe. Pirates, ghosts, bank robbers, Santa, and Robbie Burns all showed up on the deck for merriment over the years. Isabel had a deep and lasting love of Piers. She visited all around the island, enjoyed the Red Hat get-togethers with other Piers women and always had a positive funny story to tell any audience. Isabel was true to her calling as a representative for Revlon Company. She strolled around Piers always immaculately dressed and coiffed. Susie heard someone refer to her as the Meringue. Always that fluffy white hair!

Son Charlie and his wife Christine from Calgary made their annual trip to Piers with their two girls in tow for many years. The girls spent happy summers with Granny with the white hair, exploring the forest and beaches and engaging in craft-making of all sorts. There were very few full-timers on Piers in the beginning years, so visits were real vacations with the kids catching up with other children that visited annually, too.

Daughter Susie and her husband Cal Todd continue to spend time on Piers today, enjoying a home that is packed with the memories of a lifetime. Memories include stories of a ferry that lost power and almost hit Piers; a piano that was being airlifted by helicopter to Piers but was dropped into the ocean; and our stairs to the beach disappearing and then being found at the government dock on Piers, neatly secured to allow access to the beach from the walkway.

There are not too many places left on this planet that offer such an incredible place of peace and safety. On the island you can engage with the community as much or as little as feels right at the moment. Piers Island offers so much for anyone who is lucky enough to call it theirs.

Isabel Stewart

Lot 20 - Roy and Joan Allen

Fond Memories Of Piers

(told by Roy)

I was good friends with Jim Strain (Lot 18) from the 'old days' in the oil business in Calgary. In the late 1980s, the Strains invited us over to Piers for the weekend. We loved the island so much, we bought the cottage that was for sale right next door to him. We saw it and decided to buy it that weekend! We then bought a boat and suddenly we were 'Islanders'.

Joan and I always loved going out to Piers, although Joan wasn't so keen on having to spend hours going to and from Sidney, just to buy a quart of milk. But we got used to that.

We really enjoyed the Moonlight Madness Dance in July, and liked climbing the Piers 'mountain,' which was funny considering we were from Alberta! We liked the Piers people and we always had a good time there for about 25 years.

The only reason we moved from Piers was when we had a chance in to buy a place in Mexico. Many fond memories remain of Piers Island.

Joan and Roy Allen

Lots 25, 27 - Colleen Fitz-Gerald Earla and Conrad Fitz-Gerald

Many Wild Adventures!

Everyone in our family loved Piers. As ex-Manitobans, it wasn't only the escape from the cold winters, but also the exciting seaside adventures. My son and his friends, as young teens, wore 'camo-clothing' and armed with squirt-bazooka water-guns used dusk and the forest paths as the perfect water-stalking game site. They stalked each other, in their pre-teen and teen years, returning exhausted and famished (and wet), ready for food and a good sleep.

I remember the *Peregrine* at the mooring buoy in front of Mom's house just between Clive Island and our passageway, breaking away during a November's fierce southeasterly blow. The shock as Mom, talking to me mid-morning (coffee-break for me at Resources Branch in Esquimalt) said, "The boat is just fine, I just checked it... Oh-my-gawd... It just broke away...I gotta go..." The call went dead. I packed up and took leave from work to head back to Piers. Mom grabbed rubber boots and jacket and flagged down Hal and Barbara Weaver (Lot 39), who were heading past in their 'tinny' from their early A.M. grocery shop in Sidney. Mom got aboard the tinny with Hal. Barbara and the groceries were left at the dock. Barbara got to the house and immediately called the Coast Guard.

The 'tinny' was a 'David' 16-foot aluminum skiff compared to the *Peregrine's* 25-ton 'Goliath' ferrocement schooner. Hal and Earla valiantly chased the *Peregrine*, heaving at the currents and waves. The *Peregrine* gained momentum in the seas, pushed by the wind and the Clive-Piers channel current. They all progressed into the narrowing of the seas and towards the reef, drawn towards its black square signage.

The seas were feisty as they ever get. Seeing them with rollers five feet and more in height was daunting. Hal and Earla, adrenaline-fueled and fearless, approached the rolling schooner and came alongside. Somehow, Mom hoisted herself six feet onto the *Peregrine's* heaving deck, an impossible task for the youthful, never mind Mom being in her early 70s. (Her memories of sailing in the South Pacific in the 1980s with husband Con flooded back to her.) She dropped the anchor… it held!

I arrived at Canoe Cove, just as my brother Tom did. I shouted, "*Peregrine* has broken free!" He said, "No she didn't. I told Mom I would pick up this swivel because I was worried about *Peregrine* in this weather at the mooring without it". "No, Tom, it actually HAS just BROKEN FREE! It happened while I was talking to Mom about 45 minutes ago. She was watching it!"

We decided to take my smaller, more-manoeuvrable open-boat Hourston, instead of the bigger, beamier cabin-sporting Hustler powerboat. We headed together towards Piers. Tom was dressed for business with a suit and tie and Florsheim shoes. In the rain, he shed the suit jacket and tie, but the leather shoes had to do. The boat was open to the weather and with wind and sea spray, we were getting drenched.

The site we beheld was the Coast Guard 'standing off' and *Peregrine* heaving at anchor just off the reef. Mom had managed, single-handedly, to get aboard and drop the anchor, and it held.

My outboard kept conking out as waves slapped over the back end of my boat, but each time it restarted and we were able to get in the lee of the schooner. Tom climbed aboard the heaving vessel and joined mom. Together they made sure the anchor had enough scope, but not too much to have the boat engage with the reef.

The Coast Guard sent a dinghy over to hail the boat, but stood it off because it appeared Tom and Mom had things in control. Almost in control: the engine hadn't been started in several weeks and that would be the next test. True to form the old Lister diesel turned over and the engine began to run smoothly. Now the boat could be put in gear and the engine used to keep her off the rocks. With the Coast Guard standing by, Tom and Earla aboard *Peregrine*, put the motor in gear and lifted the anchor. They motored her over to a sheltered spot near the Dolphin Road dock.

Beside the ferry terminal and behind buttresses and out of the wind, we dropped anchor and spent the weekend in that bay. We toasted Hal and Mom and their saving of our beloved schooner *Peregrine*. Just one more 'adventure aboard' notched in Earla's belt.

We all loved our days on Piers.

Conrad Fitz-Gerald, a friend and Earla Fitz-Gerald

Peregrine

Lot 39 - Hal and Barb Weaver

Our Piers Story

We were getting close to retirement and Barb and I wanted to come west and get a home close to the water. We looked from Port Hardy to Victoria, and on several northern Gulf Islands, but we wanted to be closer to civilization.

I was working with Gordon Russell at the University of Lethbridge and he told us about Piers. We stayed with Gordon and Audrey on the island (Lot 1) during spring break. We walked around the whole island, and the realtor Reg Biscoe introduced us to all the residents he could. He wanted to make sure that people would be involved in the island community. In 1983, one of the lots Reg showed us was Lot 68 (now 68A). I thought there was a ball in the water, but it turned out to be a seal. I saw that as a sign, so we bought that lot. We camped in a tent on that property for two years.

Reg Biscoe was the first realtor on Piers, and would show up at the annual meetings. He and his family owned the house at Lot 2. He was kind of like the Godfather of Piers. Reg was saving Lot 68B for himself, but then he got cancer and died. We rented the Skolroods' cottage (Lot 92) for a month in 1985, and then we rented the Doug and Carol Couch's house on Lot 60 (He was the caretaker on Knapp Island and a fireman). We decided we would rent there while we would build our house.

The Couchs decided to move back to Piers, so when we were moving our furniture from Lethbridge, we found out Lot 39 was for rent and we started renting it in 1986. I had taken an early retirement at that point, at 59 years old, since I had been diagnosed with melanoma three years earlier. We used our little McGregor boat to take everything (an eight-foot couch, appliances and all our possessions) across to Piers. We piled it all onto the Piers red tractor (at that time, anyone with a driver's license could drive it) and drove it all to our new house. The Reeses still had lots of things in their house when we rented their place, so we moved some things across in our small boat. For the big items, such as a player piano, Dave Rees hired a helicopter. Things were loaded into a big net and then lifted off to the other side.

We brought a canoe, which we planned to use to commute with. Our first time over, Sven and Grace Mariager (Lot 56) thought he'd have to call 911 to rescue us - that was the last time we used the canoe. Sven was a Dane and had sailed on sailing ships carrying cargo in the 1930s or so. He was a real sailor, in the old sense of the word. He hand-made and manufactured so many things. Their living room ceiling was high with lots of windows so that he could watch the ferries. When the ferries were going too fast, he would call up the captain, and chastised him for their speed; he actually measured from point to point and calculated their speed. A guy (who had a boat called Storm King) would round up logs out of the water, since he had a license to collect logs for money. Sven got into arguments with him as he tried to take logs that himself Sven had saved. That Storm King guy figured he was the only one who could collect logs, but Sven set him straight.

Dave Rees, the owner of our rental house at Lot 39, suggested that he and Harley Dyte (Lot 37) build the dock together, with an easement on it. They couldn't build it straight because of the bedrock, so they put an angle on the dock and it became part of the Reeses' foreshore. When Barb and I moved in, there was no ramp and no float, so we used the Piers public wharf for our first three or four years of living at Lot 39. There was a piling that was too close to the dock, so they got TNT and blew up it up under the water. We all celebrated. I wasn't good at building so Barb and I decided that we would buy the house from the Reeses. The foreshore lease was put in the Dytes' name, but the Reeses put in the float. We each gave up part of our land to gain access to the dock.

One of the things we noticed when we were first camping on Piers, was that the deer used to come around the tent. At one point, Barb was walking in the dark and kept bumping into a herd of deer on the road. Living with the deer in the community of Piers used to be a wonderful part of Piers - there are hardly any now. There was a whole area of salal near our neighbour's at Lot 37 where the deer used to munch on a daily basis.

Barb got involved in the fire department in the early 1990s and helped with the old truck and fire hoses for about a year. Then they started formalizing things, so she left. Barb also got interested in the broom infestation and gathered people together to deal with the situation. People would collect the broom in a big truck and deposit it along a sand pile. Frank Williams used the tractor to transport the broom in truckloads to the bonfire area. Then we all had a big bonfire to burn the broom. One time, the fire got too aggressive and started to scorch some of the nearby trees.

We got people interested in pulling the broom around the island and it became a semi-professional endeavour with six or seven of us volunteers. We pulled all the broom roots up from the firehall along the east side and onto the south side. Some people were against pulling broom (Mary Tucker and Bill Oldfield loved the yellow flowers), but we believed in it because of the invasiveness issue and for fire prevention. That was a great job, and our biggest contribution to the island, especially on the east side. Even harder to get out is the prickly purple thistle and we were involved with that too. I got welders gloves to do that job.

My dad was a doctor in the US Navy and we moved around a lot. I was in China for a couple of years, moving there when I was two months old. Because of my dad's career, I never lived in a place more than a couple years. After Barb and I got married, we lived in Hawaii, and Oregon, California, and Lethbridge for 17 years. We've now been part of the Piers community for over 35 years. It has been good to know so many people, although lately there have been so many changes. People now build big houses and the main road is being ruined by all the big trucks. People used to build houses themselves with lumber they hauled behind their boats, but you can't do that now.

Our neighbours, the Sneades (Lot 41) had chickens for years, and a peacock. They had lots of laying chickens that came to visit us, and they used to be really messy around our place too. I have mellowed now and don't let things bother me too much anymore.

When Henry Charlesworth drew up the map of Piers, I helped in a minor way to clean up some things. I came up with the idea of laminating the maps and that became a real money-raiser for the Piers Island Improvement District. I was also Emergency Co-ordinator for a couple years.

I got really interested in magic, after working in a magic shop called *Hollywood Magic* in Hollywood, Los Angeles. Then, I got seriously involved in magic in New York (in my late teens), and I met some big magicians. In 1953, I worked in a magic shop in New York and dropped out of school at the time. Years later, when I had my melanoma, I got back to playing the saxophone, and someone found out I knew magic, so they asked me to perform at the Piers Picnic and then kids' birthday parties. I performed in Victoria and Sidney, and I needed a name, and came up with 'Professor Whimsey.' I really enjoyed doing the Moonlight Madness shows, and doing senior shows in the Victoria area. I got thinking there were a lot of senior homes out there, and I actually went out and did a lot of solo shows. A few years ago, I was asked to perform at the Piers Christmas party and I really enjoyed that.

Hal and Barb Weaver

Professor Whimsey

Lots 54,64,72 - Ray and Betty Byers Gail Byers, Bob Byers, Barb Baker

The Byers Family On Piers Island

Our family's adventure on Piers Island started in the fall of 1974, when our Mum and Dad (Ray and Betty Byers) bought Lot 54 from Joe Friedenthal. Actually this wasn't the family's first involvement with Piers Island. Our grandfather, Captain William D. Byers, ran a boat charter service from Sidney to the island from 1932 to 1934, during the Doukhobor period.

For the first couple of years, we had family picnics on the site at Lot 54. Then came the building of the cottage. Dad hired people to do the framing and drywalling. They started in the summer of 1977. Most of the construction was done by family and friends and several weekends were spent putting the siding on the house. Barb's father-in-law built the stairs to the deck. It took a couple of years to complete the house. Gail's husband, Peter, widened the deck in 1982.

Our parents tied up their boat at the neighbours, Grace and Svend Mariager (Lot 56). Dad knew Grace from boyhood and he was in her Dad's (Freeman King) Scout troop. The dock was put in at Lot 54 in April 1990. Mum and Dad spent much of the summer on Piers hosting friends and extended family. Many 'Happy Hours' were spent with Grace and Svend, and with Mary Tucker and Enid Houghland (Lot 50).

In 1990, Bob and his partner Nancy Brown bought the property at Lot 64 and improved the small cabin that was on the lot. They lived there with sons Taylor and Riley during the summers and moved to Lot 54 for the winter. They sold the property in 1994.

Bob's story: One of the Piers Island characters that I fondly remember is Berneice Archibald (Lot 66). When Nancy and I lived on the island with Taylor and Riley, Berneice was our next-door neighbour. Although Taylor and Riley were only two and five years old, Berneice was intent on teaching them proper manners. One of her lessons was that when dining at someone's home and the meal has been served, you do not pick up your own fork until 'the hostess has lifted her fork.' To this day when we are having a big family meal, we will often start by saying 'the hostess has lifted her fork.' Although Berneice is gone now, she still lives in our memories.

Gail's story: In 1992, my husband Peter Johnson and I bought Lot 72. We camped for a year and then built a deck by the water. The next year we bought a small one-room cabin that had been built by a class of students taking construction at a high school in Langford. Peter and a friend dismantled the structure and it was brought over in pieces to Piers in our 14-foot aluminum boat. Peter cleared a spot for the building and put in concrete pads for the foundation. Another friend helped rebuild the cabin. Later an outdoor kitchen was added. Many weekends were spent on the island. We always brought our cat who stayed close by until one day she wandered off. Peter had to stay an extra day on Piers looking for her and finally found her in the middle of the island. She didn't wander after that.

In 2000, Dad died. Mum continued to come to Piers but not as often anymore. Peter and Gail sold Lot 72 in 2002. The family shared the Lot 54 cabin in the following years. Mum died in 2010. Barb spent a month on Piers in 2011 recovering from chemotherapy and took part in all the island activities. She and her husband Rick and their children Stephanie and Jordan visited the island when they came to Victoria. Peter died in 2013. Bob and his partner, Kelly Sprackett, spent many weekends at the cabin in the later years that the family owned it. Kelly particularly loved it because it reminded her of her childhood summers spent at the lakeside cottage in Ontario. Taylor lived in the cabin at Lot 54 for a couple of years. Riley also lived on Piers when he worked on the mail boat, delivering mail to the other Gulf Islands with Steve Barnes (Lot 139). We sold the Lot 54 property in 2015.

Over the years Betty, Peter, Gail and Nancy all served on the Piers Island Association and Ray served on the Piers Island Improvement District. Taylor served with the Fire Department. We all remember the good times on Piers - sitting on the deck reading a book, listening to the water, the boats going by, and the ferry keeping time for us. We also remember the fun of the annual picnic, the Midnight Madness Dance and the Walkabout. Our time on Piers taught us how much we could accomplish if we set our minds to it. It showed us how to relax and take time for ourselves and afforded us an opportunity to be part of an interesting and friendly community

Gail, Barb, Bob
Betty, Ray

Riley, Taylor Byers with Berneice Archibald

Lots 67, 69 - Gerry and Diana Kristianson

The Kristiansons On Piers

October 1980, one of Reg Biscoe's ads in the Times Colonist drew our attention to Piers Island. Reg transported us to the island from Canoe Cove on a Thursday afternoon and showed us the Barrett property (Lot 67). He then took us for a walk around the island, extolling the virtues of various property owners.

We liked what we saw and returned to Piers in our own boat the following Saturday. We tied up at the public wharf and revisited the property. Despite being accosted on the road by an angry permanent resident who accused us of occupying 'their' spot on the public wharf, we returned to our home in Cordova Bay, called Reg, and made an offer.

Biscoe prided himself on screening his clients to ensure only the right sort of people became Piers owners. We must have passed his test because he presented our offer to the Barretts and we became the new owners of 67 McKenzie Crescent. Frank Williams (Lot 13) used to take great pleasure in telling us how Reg Biscoe originally deflected his offer on the property, because he didn't think Frank would make a suitable Piers Islander. Ironically, Frank became one of the island's most amazing volunteers, devoting hours of volunteer work.

Like many other newcomers, we went through a lengthy period when we were defined in terms of the previous owners. Lot numbers meant little in those days. Ours was "The Barrett property" and it was clear we were being judged as to whether we were an improvement or disappointment compared to the previous owners.

At first, we were typical Piers Island cottagers. It was a 20-minute drive with our trailered 14-foot Double Eagle from our home in Cordova Bay to the Dolphin ramp. We unloaded on the beach and left our boat on a mooring inherited from the Barrett's. However, leaving Piers on Sunday afternoon to return 'home' became increasingly hard to accept. By 1985, we had decided that Piers would be home. That winter we began deconstructing the original cottage and using the materials to finish the partially built guest cottage. This became our weekend place as the house disappeared, along with numerous trees and stumps. With help from five gallons of diesel fuel and several old tires, the different rules of the day allowed us to use the meadow burn pile to eliminate a 20-foot high pile of stumps during the winter of 1986/1987.

Construction of a new house, designed by my architect brother John, began in the summer of 1987. We still remember the early morning phone call from John Herbert (Lot 69) to ask whether the carpenters could be more respectful of his holiday on Piers and not start hammering until after 8 a.m. We quickly acquiesced to John's request both as good neighbours and because his driveway was essential access for the trucks bringing 70 yards of concrete for the full basement foundation. Perhaps the most stressful moment of the build was at noon the day of the pour when the barge carrying the concrete pumper, three 13-yard trucks and the building crew would have been stranded until the next tide if the barge hadn't been carrying a small bulldozer capable of pushing it off the ramp.

The new house was 'locked up' in early fall. We finished the interior work during the winter of 1987/88 and moved in the following summer. By good fortune, this coincided with Lot 71 neighbour Ron McLeod finishing a new wharf, which we have shared with Lot 71 neighbours ever since.

It is fortunate, from our perspective, that the lots on both sides became available over the years. The Johnsons, original owners of Lot 65, had demolished the old bus that used to serve as their cottage, and in 1980 sold the lot to the Hanna family just before we bought Lot 67. As it turned out, the Hannas were not boaters and eventually decided they would be better off with a vacation property they could reach by car. They agreed to sell to us their lot in 1991, and we have since transferred ownership to our son's family.

In 2015, long-time Piers neighbours, John and Ann Herbert, decided it was time to give up their cottage. We are grateful that they have allowed us to take over their property at Lot 69 and rename it "Kate's Cottage" after our granddaughter. In the Covid 2020-2021 school year, it also became the Piers Island School for eight school children from Kindergarten to Grade 4. That made for very special neighbours.

It is our hope to remain Piers residents so long as health allows.

Gerry and Diana Kristianson

Lot 68B - Don and Lone Gardner

Our Piers Island Story

Our love affair with the Gulf Islands began in 1971, when we were living in North Vancouver. Our son's pre-school teacher suggested we consider the Cedar Beach Resort on St. Mary Lake, Salt Spring Island for a holiday. It was a wonderful place to enjoy time with our three children and we returned each summer until 1985.

In September 1975, our family moved to Calgary to create a financial subsidiary for a successful industrial real estate builder. Then in 1978, Don began working with Don Gilley at Dome Petroleum Limited. In August 1981, shortly after Don and Fran Gilley had purchased their property (Lot 24) on Piers Island, they met us with their boat in Ganges and brought us back to Piers for a visit. With foresight, the Gilleys introduced us to a real estate agent, Reg Biscoe, and that began our search for our 'dream' property on the Gulf Islands.

Biscoe's company, Island Seafront Properties Ltd. had recently subdivided his Lot 68 into five properties with Lots 68A, C, D and E for sale. Biscoe planned to build on Lot 68B, and his vision was to dredge the low area on Lot 68C to form a protected moorage site for himself and the purchasers of his other Lots. From 1981 to 1986, Fraser introduced us to numerous properties on Piers, Salt Spring and other Gulf Islands as well as North Saanich. We made an unsuccessful offer to Bill Daniels of Shell Canada for the undeveloped Piers Lot 100 in 1984.

In July 1985, we expressed our continuing interest in Fraser's Lot 68B since, to that date, Reg Biscoe had made no effort to begin building on the site. That resulted in a discussion of various sharing and financing arrangements whereby we would acquire and build on Lot 68B, and Fraser and his family could use the property in our absence. The discussions did not lead to any conclusion but on April 4, 1987 we made Fraser an offer for Lot 68B, subject to certain conditions, including the approval of the Archeological Branch, BC Ministry of Tourism, Recreation and Culture. Most of the original Lot 68 was and still is a registered heritage site subject to the provisions of the Heritage Conservation Act. Initially, we were discouraged because we received no response from Biscoe. However, on a Tuesday in early June, he called to say that, if we could make a deposit by Friday, he would accept our offer. We booked a flight the same day! On June 8, 1987, our offer was accepted and on July 17, 1987, following approval by the Archeological Branch, we took title to our Gulf Island 'dream'.

So began a search for a building design that would complement the unique southwest exposure of Lot 68B. Several suppliers were considered, with Lindal Cedar Homes represented by Dean Developments Ltd. in Sidney being selected. The contract for the supply of all building materials from Lindal was signed December 31, 1987. Bill Maxwell and John Gibbons of Dean Developments were great to work with and made the process seamless. A Lindal Cedar Homes design was modified with Lone's practical sense and the able assistance of Don's brother, Alan, an architect in Calgary. For a general contractor, we selected Altype Construction Services Ltd. operated by Chris Williams and his wife Susan. We selected Altype due to Chris's island construction experience on Pym Island and the fact that they had all the necessary equipment to construct a dock at our newly acquired property. The contract with Altype was signed December 29, 1987. Construction of the dock began on February 9, 1988.

The Lindal building materials were delivered to Sidney in April 1988, with barging and construction commencing shortly thereafter. One of the early highlights was the pouring of the concrete basement in the middle of the night to accommodate a favourable high tide. Several cement trucks and a pumper-truck were barged to Piers on the Georgia Transporter (Shield's Navigation Ltd.) and the basement walls were poured in record time. We were fortunate because Chris was able to attract excellent local trades to work on our project. A neighbour, Bob Archibald (Lot 66), became the unofficial supervisor of the house construction and, we believe, ensured the quality of the work being performed. Everything was on schedule and on budget during the early stages of construction, but by June, Altype had taken on several other contracts, resulting in less supervision of our project. By August, we had reached the 'lock-up' stage and had exhausted our budget, so the decision was made to suspend construction until we had sufficient funds to complete the project without incurring any debt.

From August 1988 to the summer of 1992, our Piers home sat empty and dark. However, we continued to visit Piers in the summer during those years, renting a cabin from Dr. Siddoo (Lot 51) one year and a guest cottage from John and Diane Currie (Lot 86) for another couple of summers.

During September 1989, we met Ward and Gill Stephens (Lot 79), owners of Madrona Bay Contracting and retained them to install our septic system and electrical service (using M. Twamley Contracting). These projects were completed in December 1989 and January 1990, respectively.

In 1992, we visited an artist friend of Lone's who had recently built a home in North Saanich on the bluff overlooking the Pat Bay Highway and the North Saanich Marina. During our visit, their contractor, Frank Jacobsen, came by to fix an outstanding item and we had the opportunity to discuss our Piers Island project with him. Frank and his family lived on Lands End Road and could see Piers Island from their property. That meeting led to a contract with Frank to complete the interior of our *Hytten* (a Danish word meaning 'The Cabin in the Woods'). The understanding was that Frank and his helper would work to complete *Hytten* between his housing projects. Between 1992 and 1994, work progressed periodically as Frank's time permitted; the workmanship was outstanding and worth the wait. Frank used his own boat to get to Piers and, we learned, would use the opportunity to catch a few salmon.

On August 10, 1994, the District of North Saanich granted us an occupancy permit and we began assembling furniture to make *Hytten* our 'home away from home'. In late August, Willis Rooke barged over a rental truck with our initial load of furniture and in true Piers Island spirit, several neighbours appeared to help bring the furniture up to the house. So began our family's time on the island.

Water transportation is a necessary part of the island living experience. During the early days, we used Ted Aubrey's water taxi service, Aubrey Boat Charters, to get back and forth. In July 1993, we purchased a 14-foot Sea Nymph aluminum boat and 9.9 hp outboard motor from Sherwood Marine to access our property. We kept the boat under the deck on Piers between visits and continued to use Ted Aubrey's water taxi when we first arrived and upon departure. Ted would kindly pick us up and drop us off at the airport and even wait at Thrifty Foods while we purchased our groceries.

Launching the boat on the beach following arrival was easy - bringing it uphill from the beach to the house was a huge effort requiring the coordinated skills and strength of both of us. Using an open 14-foot boat was a wonderful experience in calm, sunny weather, but a serious challenge in the rough and wet conditions of a normal winter. So, on August 5, 2003, we flew to Vancouver to attend the Vancouver Boat Show in search of a more weather-friendly form of transportation. After considering several options, we purchased an 18-foot aluminum hardtop 'Runabout' model from Andy Barry of Silver Streak Boats in Sooke, B.C. On November 8, 2003, after arranging for moorage at Canoe Cove, we took delivery of our shiny new boat *Kattegat* at the Piers Island compound launching ramp. *Kattegat* is named after the body of water separating northern Denmark from Sweden.

About 1996, John Currie, as Fire Chief thought it would be a good idea to have a 'Piers flag' to fly at the new firehall. He solicited design submissions from islanders and received numerous designs, including one from Lone.

However, the project was controversial for several reasons and the planned selection process was cancelled with all designs being returned. Don and Lone discussed using the flag design on a t-shirt to be sold at the new Walkabout event. So, in August 1998, Lone created the first Piers Island T-shirt with a Blue Heron illustration and she has offered a t-shirt with a new design each year, except during the coronavirus pandemic of 2020.

Piers Island has been a huge part of our family's experience. We have memories too numerous to mention. Dinners and conversation around the kitchen table, celebrations on the deck, swimming off the dock, kayaking along the shore, walks around the island, ribbons from the annual picnic, community events at the firehalls and entertaining our friends and neighbours. We miss the friends who have left Piers but are delighted with the evolution to younger, permanent families on the island. We have benefited from the volunteer contributions of islanders over more than a half-century to make Piers Island the wonderful community that it is today. Our heartfelt thank you to those both past and present.

Don and Lone Gardner

Lot 71 - Ron MacLeod

Life On Piers Island

I first found Piers Island in the early 1980s. I was working on a pile driver building private docks. We had been called over to the island to put a dock in for Brian and Joanne Sibley (Lot 27). I had been over a few times after completing the Sibley's dock, to dive on various mooring buoys around the island. Shortly afterwards, we moved to the island. We bought Lot 71 on Piers September 15, 1983 when I was 24 years old.

My first plan of action was to rebuild an old wood boat that was on the property. Once I had completed it, we called it the *Pierless One.* This seemed fitting since I hadn't built our dock yet. Next was to rebuild the existing cabin, construct a retaining wall and a dock for the *Pierless One.* As time went on, I built a number of docks and floats all around the island, along with installing mooring buoys and anchor systems.

There were 35 permanent residents on the island at the time we moved onto Piers. We enjoyed the dusty Moonlight Madness dances at the old firehall; a good time was had by all. The annual fishing derby was always a fun weekend as well.

Winter storms were always interesting. A few of us would gather in our boats in the lee of Biscoe Beach Bay. This, of course, would turn into an overnight storm party. The odd night, I would be called upon, for broken chains on floats. I would put on my diving suit and dive for the broken chain, tie come-a-long ends together to add a shackle to keep the float off the beach.

In a freak accident, I broke my neck on the island and was transported by our local fire department crew by tractor down to Biscoe Beach to be airlifted to Victoria.

In the day, we would all get together doing various projects on the island. Whether moving someone's belongings in by helicopter nets or flying over trusses for a new house, it usually meant a big homemade meal served by somebody. I got to know who the best cooks on the island were, because when I was hurt, many would bring home-made meals for me, which were always delicious. I have many fond memories of Piers and the friends who lived there. So many stories and such a fantastic place to live. We left the island on my 40th birthday. Our last large party on the island was my 40th and our 'Going Away Party' all in one! Cheers Piers!

Ron MacLeod

Lot 77 - Lynne and John Armstrong

"Those Armstrongs"

We lived in a big rambling house off Durrance Road in Central Saanich. I was working for a small firm with offices at the Institute of Ocean Sciences, with children in middle and high school and one at the University of Victoria. Incurable romanticism had previously driven Johnny and me from our home in California to a remote island (Read Island) north of Quadra Island, and a life centred around boats. Home, school, work - all accomplished in an environment of no roads.

We had moved to Victoria when the kids outgrew the local one-room school. We saw an ad in the paper for the property on McKenzie Crescent and borrowed a boat to go out there. We couldn't believe it. It was our dream house! Big enough for all of us, and the only access by BOAT! Johnny and I thought living on an island would put a moat around our teenagers. In order to get there or to leave, we would have to drive them in a boat. Seemed a great idea.

For our first boat, I bought an old 30-foot Monk design built in Kitimat by the father of a man I knew from work. I wanted a cabin with full living facilities because I thought we might get stranded by the weather. Since we needed to get to school and work every day, the boat would need to stay at the dock. I never learned to dock it by myself and although we had some great trips aboard in the early years, we finally gladly sold the *Tyro*. By the end of our 10 years on Piers Island we had five boats, all built by our sons – *Armstrong* boats.

We made such wonderful friends on the island. Ronnie and Debbie MacLeod (Lot 71) were our nearest neighbours and we became very close. Howie and Diane Sneade, Jill and Ward Stevens, Phillip and Lydia Chang and family, Earla Fitzgerald and her daughters, Wendy and Mike Smart, among many others whose names I can't recall, although their faces are vivid in my memory. We hosted our 25th wedding celebration that first year. I remember Mike Smart made us a cake decorated with the story of our journey together, starting in New York City and San Francisco, and then getting married in Italy. Mike went on to help our sons develop their boat-building skills by letting them build in his shop. There was a boat for Knapp Island and a little one for Bryce and Charl Young. It was the start of what became our sons' life's work, building aluminum boats.

There were many neighbour folks who had Virgo as their zodiac sign. It inspired a huge Virgo birthday party every year. I particularly remember Earla Fitzgerald coming down our driveway with a wheelbarrow full of champagne. We hosted a lot of teenage gatherings and John and I would stay with the MacLeods overnight, only returning to our house after our children had hired the carpet cleaner. Johnny and I moved a foam mattress out onto our upper back deck every summer so we could sleep outside. We bought vegetables from the horse-driven farm cart. With such wonderful produce, it made Piers my only residence not to include a big vegetable garden. I joined the island book club and met more interesting people.

Josh liked to waterski around the island on New Year's Day. We had rowing races from our dock, out around the white rock marker we called 'The White Lady,' and back. For better or for worse, we became known as 'Those Armstrongs'!

Our son Josh brought home a Vietnamese potbellied pig, which he named Windsor. Windsor thought he was a dog and would follow us on walks around the island. He was very popular with our neighbours who would come to visit him, not us. That is unless he had happened to practice his snout digging skills in their gardens on our evening walks.

The many long years we spent on Piers are now a mosaic of wonderful memories. The kids grew up, married and left home. We held on to the hope it would become full of family every summer, to replicate my childhood memories of my grandparents' cottage on Lake Erie. But just before the wedding of our youngest daughter, we decided to sell the house and move back to the 'big island', Vancouver Island. I thought I could never be as happy as I had been on Piers. However, it was great to be able to order a pizza for delivery, and not to have to carry the garbage into and out of the boat. It is true that I have lived happily in several other wonderful places since. Nonetheless, Piers Island remains for me a vivid, unique environment in which to have lived and raised a family.

Written by Lynne Armstrong - On behalf of John, Annie, Josh, Cory, Faith and Victoria Armstrong, and their spouses, and the 16 amazing grandchildren who have joined our family.

Lynne and John Armstrong

A young Josh Armstrong of future 'Armstrong Marine'

Lot 91 - Lydia and Philip Chang

Thoughts about the Piers Community

(told by Lydia, June 2019)

I have a lot of things I can say about Piers. To begin with, I love the centre of the island as much as anyone else, because of its peace and tranquility. However, let's not get too crazy about it. It is lovely and we all want to protect it. The stones in the centre of the island are not a religious site. I like the history they represent - the Stonehenge we call it - where the old Doukhobor water tower was located. Some people feel it has religious meaning, but it doesn't. Places like that are simply to be respected and enjoyed for what they represent.

Most of the time, we islanders get along with each other in the community; however, there are times we don't. Years ago, when we put in new trees, we had one of the islanders lie down in front of Don Gait's backhoe. That is what happens on the island and sometimes we can get ourselves very worked up. If we just calm down and talk about it reasonably, it doesn't have to reach the crescendo that it often does.

Most of us would like to keep things as they are because life is so special on Piers. Sometimes we don't realize things until they affect us personally. I didn't realize until I couldn't walk how important it was for me to drive down to Biscoe Beach in my golf cart, so I could visit one of my favourite spots. I got chewed out by a Piers islander saying that I shouldn't be there with my golf cart. It made me realize that there are some people who would really appreciate being able to just get down to the beach to enjoy it. It's not a sacred place. We are not destroying anything. I realize now that there is space for something like that if all just listen to each other.

I have a suggestion that could work for the centre of the island. Maybe someone from the fire department or the Piers Island Association could perhaps take a person up to see the beauty of the middle of the island, if it was really important to them. It would be good that there is at least space for something like that. It would be good to have that as an option. Some people are being told that they do not have the ability to go to that area of the island; I think it could be valid to talk about this more. If people say no, then so be it. I don't want everyone going everywhere through the centre of the island. It would be nice for people to be able to go for a quiet visit if it is important to them.

I got thinking that it would be perfect to set up a little care home on Piers. People like Mary Tucker who want to stay here on the island surrounded by friends, but who also need care in their older years. Neidig's place (Lot 85) would have been perfect - four bedrooms, four bathrooms all on the same level, with a big living room where islanders could drop in and visit. It would be a good home for four to five people. Of course, you would have to get funding and have to ask the authorities. Friends of ours (six women in their sixties) bought a house together on Salt Spring Island (Vesuvius area). They are all independent women and love to travel, so it works great for them. I believe the option to stay in one's community is vital.

Let's think progressively. Why not have a windmill in the centre of the island? Let's be self-sustaining. We have so much wind that it would be great to create energy. This island has the potential to do so many incredible things. I know Jackie Charlesworth (Lot 135) is thinking about inviting people to her large property to put in their own gardens. The water is right there; the place is fenced and it would give her lots of company. Not to mention, it would be a wonderful community project.

For me, the best part of Piers Island (besides the wonderful sea) are the people, especially family. I love the sound of the little ones in the house. It does get kind of crazy noisy here sometimes, but I love it. At times, I just want to be quiet and read a good book. The kids used to bring all their friends to the Moonlight Madness dance at the old firehall. It was chaotic, but great to have all of us together.

What is most important to me is having all the family together. I loved that we could do that on Piers.

** *Author's Note:* Lydia passed away July 2019. She was the first person that I spoke to about the book, and Lydia wanted to make sure her story was included.

Steve, Lilien, Lydia, Philip and Tony Chang

Lots 94, 8 - Rebekah and Steve Gawne

Home Schooling And Island Fun

My life on Piers Island started 35 years ago. In 1987, my husband-to-be Steve Gawne, brought me over to the island with my girlfriend. We came back and stayed at his house when he was away. Years ago Mike Smart built my boat, the *Gregoire*. We lived at Lot 94 for years. Steve was Piers co-fire chief in the late 1980s.

I home-schooled all three of our kids, Adolina, Edward and Mathew. It was kind of crazy but it was a lot of fun. We all loved the fact that Barry Tate gave us art classes. I think I learned as much as my kids did art-wise. I learned the importance of persistence to do what I desired. The kids loved animals and I taught them a lot about the creatures around Piers. We had lots of mink at our place and they were always under the house. We couldn't get rid of them, but the kids loved them. Kelly Stevenson (Lot 96) once brought me an octopus to show the kids. Home-schooling was a lot of fun, especially when focusing on all the animals.

I remember when we finally built the stairs down to the beach. Take the kids to the beach, take them off the beach - that was my life and I loved it. I carried one kid on my back, one on my front, and one on a leash down to the beach every day. My kids would astonish me -- they were wild children on the boat. Even when young, with life jackets on, they loved to swim from the boat to the shore. No fear in those children!

A treehouse was built in the centre of the island on a cliff. My kids used to play on that - it would drive me nuts. I got worried about them when they hung over the cliff. Kenny Sneade (Lot 41) would join us - he built the tree house. We all rediscovered the orchard and we explored the middle of the island all the time. All the kids would come to play on our yard, especially on the tire swing. We hung the fishing net between the trees. Our back door was always open for a visit, especially for the kids to get cookies and cinnamon buns.

Philippa (Lot 137) gave me chickens and I kept them in the house. Then they got so big and jumped over the baby gate, so I had to move them outside. The dog was really good and he never chased the chickens. Then I built the chicken coop - apparently the mink knew how to get into the coop and they killed all the chickens but one. The mink only killed for the livers, which was so sad. On another occasion, three otters chased me off the beach, up the stairs, and right up to the house. I picked up all three of the kids and ran up the stairs and quickly shut the back door behind us. Piers always was full of adventures.

Living on Piers brought a lot of experiences that were different from city life. We would go to Genoa Bay just to have dinner and the restaurant would always give us a treat to bring home. We would go to Salt Spring Island and find foxgloves. On Piers, I only asked for practical unique things: a chainsaw, a wood splitter, and a guy to go with it to do the work with me.

I had 14 years of making cinnamon buns for the Fire Department. They seemed to appreciate that, and I enjoyed contributing for the Firefighters - they are so dedicated. I looked after many octogenarians, including Mary Tucker. The kids and I would clean out her closets and make sure she had good food to eat. I looked after both the Oldfields, too. We were just volunteers and the kids learned a lot helping. Before I became a health care assistant, I was doing picnic baskets for the old people - all part of the community. Our island is an incredible place and we have such an amazing community.

Piers neighbours are great. One day, I phoned the Barbers (Lot 21) for an idea of something to eat for a cold day. Tammy gave me the best chicken soup recipe ever, and I have made it many times. The Barber girls were the first babysitters for my kids. The kids collected slugs, and they followed me all around the island with their slugs. When I had the Kubota, I pulled Frank Williams out of the ditch with his tractor. He was a character. He really wouldn't accept help, but he finally accepted help from me that day.

The Piers community is incredible. I know the ladies (Monique and Wynn) have Lot 94 now. They let me go down to take a look at the place, which brought back a lot of memories. I have held on to the property on my own at Lot 8, and share the dock with Mike and Wende Smart. It's great to have good neighbours.

** *Author's Note:* Rebekah wants to pass on something to all islanders that she said to her children every morning on Piers: 'Do what you can. Be who you are. Glow like a glowworm, if you can't be a star."

Rebekah Gawne

Gawne family

Lot 95 - Donna and Don McNeely

A Special Place In Our Hearts

In the spring of 1988, Don and I saw a small ad in the local Sidney paper for a cabin for sale on Piers Island. It was a 525-sq. ft. cabin that needed a lot of TLC, but more importantly to Don, it had a very large, well-built workshop ideal for his projects. We bought it and lived there weekends only for three years until we sold the sailboat we lived on and moved full-time to the island. By that time, we had put a lot of hard work into the cabin and it had become a cozy little cottage.

The new firehall was being constructed during our time on the island. I had an idea for a library located in the hall and asked all the islanders for donations of their 'gently used' books. In no time we had bags and boxes of books delivered to our door. Someone said I should get approval from the council for the library, but I followed the advice of another islander to go ahead with it and ask for forgiveness later. The library took shape with three tall bookshelves and a large round table where visitors could gather while looking over their selections. It ran beautifully with the help of a few ladies taking turns opening and closing the firehall on Saturday mornings. I understand the library has grown and been relocated to another part of the building, and that a lovely fireplace has been installed to make it even cozier. It is wonderful that it is still going strong.

The firehall was, and still is, a perfect gathering place for all islanders. My favourite memories are the Halloween parties where competition was fierce for the best costume. Diana and Gerry Kristianson usually won with their incredible costumes. One year they didn't attend and Don and I were able to get a nod for our costumes of Don as a dog-catcher and me as a dog. It was with great amusement that I offered my homemade dark chocolate fudge on a platter with a small card that read "doggy-do-do fudge...made it myself." I said not a word because, of course, dogs can't talk. Kids, who like anything gross, loved it while most of the adults politely declined. Those pieces of fudge were quite realistic looking.

One summer I organized an 'arts and crafts' fair, which we held in the firehall. That first year showcased the talents of a small number of residents. The fair was well attended and seemed to generate a lot of interest. The number of exhibitors doubled the next year. By the third year it was obvious we couldn't accommodate all the exhibitors in the hall and the idea of a 'walkabout' was born. It was great fun to see everyone set up their tables on the side of the road with everything from lemonade and cookie stands set up by kids, to the adults with an amazing variety of crafts, sewing, knitting, homemade jams, fresh breads and baking, beautiful paintings and fine stone carvings. The talent pool was incredible. Everyone met old friends and new neighbours and the sense of community was strong and happy.

All the islanders looked out for each other, whether they were next door or across the island. Mary Tucker (Lot 50) and Enid Houghland came to my rescue early one morning. Somehow they heard that my dinghy had upset and dumped me in the water beside my moored powerboat. Luckily, I was able to haul myself aboard at the transom. I don't recall all these years later if I called out for help or if my neighbours, the Changs, saw me and came to take me to shore. When I had finished warming up in a hot shower, I could hear someone in the cottage. There in my kitchen were Mary and Enid heating up a can of soup for me. They had walked all the way from the other side of the island to help me. I still think fondly of those two dear ladies.

I am so happy to have been able to spend 10 years living on Piers Island. There is no other place like it. It will always hold a special place in my heart.

Donna and Don McNeely

Lot 98 - Anne and Bob Bell

Our Family Cabin On Piers

We began visiting Piers in the 1970s, staying with Trevor and Donna Matthews (Lot 119). In 1988, I was the commanding officer of the RCMP Depot Division in Regina, and Anne and I were looking forward to retiring and getting back to B.C. We were staying with the Matthews when Trevor took us to see Lot 98, which had just come up for sale. Back to Regina and in the middle of some social event, I got a call from the realtor telling us that if we wanted the lot he needed a reply right away. Back to the social party, I told a shocked but thrilled Anne that we now owned a lot on Piers Island.

When we started to work on the lot, it was overgrown with so many shrubs and trees that we got lost trying to find our way from the road to the front of the lot. After a great deal of preliminary work clearing our chosen site, we were ready to think of building a home in 1991. We had always liked the Pan-Abode structures, so that is what we chose. Delivering and shipping to an island is always a problem, but with lots of family help and advice from our great neighbour, Bob Crooks (Lot 100) we were able to do most of the work ourselves. We laid the first log on August 12, and had all the windows, doors and roof finished by September 14.

Our intention in building this cabin on Piers was to create a place for our family. Our daughter Elizabeth and her husband Scott, and our son Stewart with his wife Laura, helped with building and love the place. We now have six grandchildren, all of whom have been coming to Piers since they were born. We all love our family cabin on Piers.

Anne and Bob Bell

Lot 100 - Bob and Maureen Crooks

We Thank Our Lucky Stars To Be Piers Islanders!

Piers Island has been our full-time home since 2005 and our special place for 33 years. Our first visit to the island was by invitation from a neighbourhood girl that Bob had chummed with during elementary and junior high school in Victoria. Laurene moved to Calgary and they lost touch, but then 20 years later, out of the blue, Laurene called to tell us that she and her husband, Jim Strain (Lot 18), had a cottage on a little island off Sidney called Piers Island. They wondered if we would like to renew an old friendship by joining them for the annual Piers Island Fishing Derby.

We soon became close friends and spent many good times with them and their neighbours on the south side. At that time, several 'Oil Patch' families from Calgary owned properties on Piers and it was that workplace camaraderie that brought them to the island. The group included the Strains (Lot 18), Allens (Lot 20), Gilleys (Lot 24), Walkers (Lot 48), Gardners (Lot 68B), Daniels (Lots 98 and 100), Forseths (Lots 102 and 104), Poulsoms (Lot 112), and the Gabilles (Lot 129).

Laurene Strain and Joan Allen were amazing cooks and both couples were excellent Bridge mentors to us. When their cabins filled with summer visitors, it was instant Bridge tournament time, with loads of laughter, liquor and sumptuous potluck meals. They were a fun-loving group, so creativity never waned in the entertainment-arena. There was JP's July 4th 'Bastille Day,' replete with a costumed and condemned King Louis, nuns and priests and of course, 'Madame Guillotine.' We can't forget Ray Forseth's 'Calgary Olympic Drinking Team,' whose dead-on potato gun accuracy waned directly as the beer count rose. In those years, fishing was good, which meant there was always a salmon on the BBQ somewhere, along with a cold beer, bottle of wine and maybe even…a bottle of rum.

Heading home from this idyllic paradise back to downtown Victoria on a Sunday evening was only made bearable by knowing we would be likely be back soon.

When our interest in the island grew to a serious level, Jim 'negotiated' a deal with Bill Daniels, another petroleum colleague, to sell us his property at Lot 100 (he also owned Lot 98) in late 1988, and we became the proud owners of our own property.

With our first projects, we cleared out years of forest debris and installed our water and hydro services. Infrastructure was very basic - a pole and poly shelter over our picnic table, and a small tool shed complete with a luxury Porta potty. For the next eight years, our 13-foot aluminum boat was our only mode of transportation, and over the years it did yeoman's duty moving tons of materials.

In the early 1990s, we started building our retaining walls, beach stairs and pier, by hand, which is the way almost all of our building was done. The walls and stairs, made from rocks and stones scavenged from several other island beaches, took a full year of work on weekends and vacations. Building materials were shipped over in or towed behind the tin boat. For the pier alone, eight creosote pilings, 6"x12"x22' creosote beams, bundles of lumber, 300 buckets of gravel, 25 90-lb bags of Portland cement, a cement mixer, rebar, shackles, bolts and fasteners were all ferried from the compound to our beach in countless trips, sometimes with so little freeboard that a badly timed wave could mean disaster.

Once started, we just didn't know when to stop. So, with lots of welcome help from family, friends and neighbours we carried on and built our float, main residence, workshop and, finally, the guest cottage. By 2005, we had both retired and became full-time residents in the Piers Island community. It remains our home still, complete with two staples of island life - our trusty golf cart and Bob's treasured Kubota tractor.

So many years and so many stories, but one of our most cherished events was the marriage on Piers Island in 1996 of our younger son, Ken, and Ami, our 'daughter by marriage.' A last minute change of venue meant a half-finished residence and float had to be built or made usable in short order, but with only scant minutes to spare all was made ready. Eighty guests and family members were shuttled over and along with the groom's party, we eagerly awaited the bride's arrival by boat. Our freshly painted pier served as the aisle, and dolphin balloons formed the archway beneath which the couple read their vows.

Our brand new firehall was transformed into a reception hall for its very first wedding and a wonderful dinner of two 25-pound 'Alberta beef' barbequed roasts was prepared and served by the Strains and Allens as their wedding present to the newlyweds. They completed the occasion with their serenade to the new couple with an original wedding song, accompanied by Joan's renowned guitar playing. Dancing and partying were followed by a beach fire for the guys and a sleeping bag party for the gals. More than 40 guests and family spent the night, many in the tent city newly erected in the back yard. Ami wore her wedding dress for the entire evening with the comment, "Why not? I'm never wearing it again!" This was just as well as the bottom of the dress had wrapped itself around the wheel of the small trailer that served as her carriage to the hall, so it had to be 're-engineered' by Roy Allen using the miniature scissors of his Swiss Army Knife while the bride stood perched on a chair!

We love to tell people that the Crooks family has a multi-generational history on Piers Island. Bob's paternal grandfather was a Piers Island Penitentiary warder (guard) during the federal government's island incarceration of the Doukhobors in 1932 to 1935. As a result of some of the warders becoming friends with the inmates, we still have hand-made mementos given to his grandfather - an embroidered handkerchief and hand-whittled utensils - as well as Warder Crooks' 1932 annual wage statement from the 'PEN.'

More recently, three generations of Crooks men - Bob, our son Ken, and our grandson Kevin - have their names carved into the plaque that Gerry Kristianson crafted for the new beach cabana to acknowledge the volunteers who worked on the beach shelter construction.

There is no denying that living on Piers has presented many challenges over the years, but the island's lifestyle has never lost its appeal for us and the rewards are too many to mention. Soon forgotten are the 40-knot storms, the boat problems, that constant carrying, and those laden Costco trips home - always at low tide. Instead, it is the wonderful memories and the valued friendships that remain freshly imprinted and cherished. Scarcely a day goes by that we don't thank our lucky stars to be Piers Islanders!

Bob and Maureen Crooks

The Crooks' all-weather golf cart

Ken and Ami's wedding

Lot 125 - Colin and Meredith Robertson

Amazing Service From BC Hydro

We purchased our cottage in the winter of 1987. One of the first changes would be the old Kelvinator fridge with the rounded corners and small freezer compartment. We kept it for five years and decided to finally upgrade to a new fridge in 1992. At the time, we could take advantage of a BC Hydro buy-back program for fridges that were older and inefficient but still working.

We contacted BC Hydro to ensure that we were eligible for the rebate offer and explained that we were on Piers Island. We also let them know the logistics of getting to and from the island with vehicles, but were assured that would not be a problem and that they would contact us to make the arrangements. After numerous phone calls with BC Hydro, we discussed barging the load, vehicles and contractor pick-up. A decision was made by them to use a helicopter to remove our fridge. They let us know the date and time we were to pick up a contractor and cargo net at Canoe Cove Marina, and to then return to Piers Island to await the arrival of the helicopter. Our instructions were to get the fridge out to the field behind our property (Lot 125) in the enclosed cargo net, by 1 p.m. on the designated date. We did as instructed, wheeled it out on a dolly and waited.

The helicopter approached from the west at exactly 1p.m. It flew over the old picnic shelter and hovered over us at approximately 40 feet. A rope was lowered down with a snap hook attached. We grabbed the hook, snapped it into the cargo net ring and gave the pilot the 'all good' signal to raise it up. The fridge lifted off gently and slowly, the helicopter gained altitude, executed a 180 degree turn, and off it went. The time for this whole exercise was about four minutes and we watched as our fridge drifted away in the net. We took the contractor back to Canoe Cove and signed off on the removal of our fridge.

Within two weeks we received a cheque in the mail from BC Hydro. True to their word, we received a Refrigerator Buy-Back rebate cheque in the amount of $50.00.

Colin and Meredith Robertson

Lot 129 - Evey and Jean-Pierre (JP) Gabille

Our Discovery Of Piers

In 1986, JP worked for Dome Petroleum in Calgary with Ray Forseth and Don Gilley. Ray had often invited us to visit him on Piers Island on their many trips to Japan, so that year we finally made it. We stayed with the Forseths in their tiny cabin and, needless to say, we fell in love with the island and the sea. After looking at what was for sale with Mr. Biscoe, we decided on Lot 129, though we couldn't see much of it since it was covered with trees and prickly brambles.

When back in Calgary, a secretary who received the Victoria Colonist, told JP there was a lot for sale where the price was being reduced by $500 every week until it was sold. He called and found it was the lot we wanted, so Evey told him to go and negotiate, but don't come back without it! He did, in spite of a treacherous boat ride in the fog. And here we are still, 34 years later. Our grandchildren would disown us if we ever sold it.

What do we do on Piers Island? JP grows beautiful roses and herbs. Evey oil paints, volunteers for Emergency Services, is a first responder, and alternate library commissioner. We kayak, watch birds, read, hike in the forest, boat over to interesting places, and enjoy Happy Hours with our friends. Life is good here.

JP and Evey Gabille

Lot 133 - Charl and Bryce Young

Piers Adventures And Misadventures

1983 was a big year. Bryce and I got married in March, and shortly afterwards a lawyer friend of ours told us about Piers Island. Realtor Reg Biscoe walked us around the island, and strategically introduced us to five families, in part to see what life on Piers Island was about. Also, it seemed, the intros were to have islanders see what we were like and check us out. In September 1983, I started my new job at the Arthritis Centre and we also moved full-time to Piers. The original owners were Bob and Faith Scholefield, and our house was always known for decades as the 'Scholefield house'. We learnt this has happened to many islanders whose house was known for the original owner for a long time.

On moving day, the previous owner Bob Scholefield suggested that because the access to our property was tight, the moving van could back through the meadow towards the picnic shelter to have better access. That area is very marshy, as we all know now. We had hundreds of pounds of Bryce's books, and the truck sank up to its axle at some distance from the house. Just as we were wondering what to do, a group of eight to 10 island men suddenly appeared and created a human convoy, emptied the moving van and brought all the boxes into the house. Once the weight was out, the van got out easier. At the end of moving all the boxes inside, cases of beer and chili and other food miraculously appeared. The guys sat around eating and drinking, and we all celebrated the occasion. Then we never saw a soul again for two weeks. We loved the fact that we were in the middle of this incredibly supportive community, who also respected our privacy to let us sort ourselves out for a couple of weeks before getting into island life.

Slowly people came to visit. Two women arrived to welcome us to the island and to coach me. One of them said, "Make sure you learn how to drive the boat, because you never know when you will find the need for a new tube of lipstick." That made me laugh, but brought out the importance of the need to feel and be independent. Because I followed her advice, I took every opportunity to learn to drive the boat and to this day, I am very thankful I did. Bryce and I truly enjoyed our first three years living full-time on Piers trying to figure out island living and becoming more independent. That was before golf carts.

We learnt how to tell Piers Islanders by a toque, gumboots and a wheelbarrow. Everyone had a wheelbarrow. Our son, Brodie was born on Piers in 1986, and we used to take him everywhere in the wheelbarrow. I remember going to the outdoor Moonlight Madness party for the island. As a babe, we took him to the party in the wheelbarrow and he was held by lots of islanders all evening. At the end of the party, we wheeled him home in the wheelbarrow. That's just the way things were done then.

At that time we didn't have a year-round dock. The neighbours (the Carrieres) had built a summer dock that we shared; it was low to the water. This dock emulated the lakeside docks of northern Ontario, where the wife was from, so this was an emotional attachment to them. Every winter we would take the ramp and float out of the water, to protect the dock from the crashing winter logs. During the winters, we would tie to a mooring buoy and row to shore. After spending our first winter here of rowing back and forth from the buoy, the following year I decided to do a huge stock up on large heavy and bulky items in the autumn before the dock was taken off. At that point we were running a 10' open fiberglass dingy.

One day, I picked up Bryce, and he sat in the bow with all the groceries. It was a beautiful sunshiny day, and on the way home, a strong westerly came up. It increased all the way home. Unfortunately, I decided to take the east side of the island, rather than the south that time. Whenever I saw the waves coming across the bow, the look of alarm on my face would cause Bryce to turn to see what was coming. He got totally drenched each time. Just as we rounded the corner at Steve and Pauline's place (Lot 135), Bryce yelled, "Head to shore or we're going to sink!" I was so concentrated on driving that I didn't realize how much water was in the boat. Water had easily risen to our knees and the toilet paper was beginning to float. I headed to shore and landed on the shore only to realize that neighbours from the other side (George Hoyte and Joe Friedenthal) had witnessed our predicament, and were following our journey, running along the shore to help us when we beached. They helped us unload everything.

The next day, George appeared with a wheelbarrow and 10 kilos of sugar in it, and offered to take my soggy 10 kilos of sugar because his bees would not mind. It turned out the Hoytes raised bees and sold honey suckers and other honey items to islanders. I could not believe the kindness.

In the 1990s, I sent out the original notice for a ukelele group. I was inspired when watching a Youtube video of the British Ukelele Orchestra. My message read "Anyone interested in the Piers Island Ukelele Orchestra? Didn't know we had one? Call Charl." I was so happy when Philippa called first, and within a couple of weeks the Piers Ukelele Orchestra was founded. Five women (Charl, Philippa, Uta, Wendy Eden, and Marg Jesson) hired a music teacher from the Academy of Music in Sidney to come to Piers to give us two lessons, so we could all be at the same knowledge level.

Marg Jesson (Lot 68C) was the feisty one who was so bored of just playing Row Row Your Boat. She said, "Why don't we learn to play something more exciting like Leonard Cohen's Hallelujah?" Within a week that was our favourite song. Marg Jesson passed away two years later, and as a tribute to her, Wendy Eden (Lot 78) and I played the ukelele, and Kaia Bryce (Lot 42) sang Hallelujah at her Celebration of Life.

Charl and Bryce Young

1990s
A NEW FIREHALL AND A SHUTTLE

The biggest event of the 1990s was when the 'new' firehall was built in 1992-1993. There was initially much controversy about it, but in the end islanders came together to build and celebrate the new facility. There were grants for the project, but the costs were kept down substantially with so many islanders volunteering in whatever way they could. Some worked on the initial plans and funding for grants, others coordinated professional services, and many worked on the actual construction and finishing touches. Others contributed money. It was definitely an island project.

The new building attracted many volunteer fire fighters with John Currie remaining as Fire Chief for many more years. It had a large training room, and this led to other exciting developments. A volunteer group of first responders was formed in 1993 with Gerry Kristianson (Lot 67) becoming certified as an official instructor, so that all first responders could be trained right on Piers. Although the new firehall was not technically a community centre, it did serve as a room for large gatherings such as a summer art show and incredible dress-up Halloween celebrations (along with the yearly Halloween bonfire, just outside the door). September long weekend, an island pancake breakfast was held in the firehall as a fundraiser for the fire department. The building was now able to accommodate an annual huge Christmas potluck dinner for islanders.

In 1992, a 911 Emergency system had been set up on Piers to handle all emergencies through the CRD central system. The timing fit in well with the new facility and the first responder program. This 911 system was a huge improvement for the island, although the telephone-tree still remains a more informal basis for emergencies and other situations. There was discussion about dismantling the old firehall, but fortunately that was kept standing. It was still used for years for social events such as Moonlight Madness dances, Piers Octoberfest, and storage for island machinery.

During the 1990s, the population on Piers grew to more than 100 full-timers. A few full-timers worked off-island, but amendments to the Piers Community Plan in 1993, allowed home-based businesses such as artists, marine biologists and translators. Short-term B&B rentals (under a month) were not allowed. Although this was legally challenged on a few occasions, this rental bylaw has been upheld over the years.

There were very few full-time families with children during the 1990s. When they were school-aged, children were usually home-schooled by their parents. Some parents, who worked off-island, dropped their children at public school in the morning and took them home at the end of their work day. When the kids became older and involved in lots of extra-curricular activities, some parents drove their kids back and forth, while others moved back to permanent homes in the city. They kept their cottages as seasonal retreats or rented them out until the children left home.

Piers homes were getting bigger and more permanent. A number of part-timers were retiring and enjoying their cottages throughout the year; others were adding to their cottage to make a permanent home on the island. As the population of Piers was getting older, some sold because of poor health, although owners often passed their homes on to their children. With the age of the Internet, Piers was becoming more accessible to the world. A number of Americans, mostly from Arizona and similar hot-weather places, bought vacation homes to escape from the heat down south, especially with the US dollar being strong compared to the Canadian dollar at that time.

In the mid-1990s Barbara Watson, a certified merchant Marine Master, started a full-time shuttle service on Piers. She had huge aspirations for the service to run seven days a week and seven times a day (only five times a day during the winter). For $2.00 a trip, she tried to accommodate everyone - people working off-island, kids going to school, the working trades and all islanders needing to shop or attend appointments. According to Cec and Sheila Gould (Lot 101), who ended up selling their Piers boat because of the cheap shuttle, "Barbara was a tireless worker who even arranged with local grocery stores to take grocery orders for Piers Islanders." Unfortunately, the CRD threw a lot of hurdles Barb's way, charging her each time she touched the public docks to pick up or drop off passengers. After a few hard years of not making enough money, she sold the shuttle business (minus the *Ugly Duckling*, her winter boat) to Brian and Roxy Smiley, who continued the service for years.

1990s A New Firehall And Shuttle

In the 1990s, the community thrived, as it always has, with lots of volunteers on the PIA, the PIID and numerous day-to-day island activities.

Building the new firehall

Fire Chiefs Bob Clarke and John Currie in 1993

Lot 7 - Vicki and Derek Morrison

Many Piers Roots

(written by Vicki)

My connection to Piers began long before we started coming in 1991. During the time of the historic internment of the Doukhobors, my Great-Uncle George Savinkov, was interned on the island for its duration as a camp. My maiden name is Hlookoff.

Piers Island Angel: Some of my most wonderful memories of Piers involve John and Diane Currie (Lot 86). Diane was, I am sure, an Angel sent from above, always so very kind and generous of the heart and deed. Diane was always doing something special for someone, from making baby quilts for newborns to the island, to preparing meals and leaving them on doorsteps for those of us who worked full-time, to making Christmas tree ornaments for fire fighters for the Piers fire department Christmas party. She was so very creative and could make something from anything at all. Diane was always involved in either planning and organizing or helping out at most events on the island. I so enjoyed helping her organize the annual Halloween costume parties at the new firehall. We had many old-fashioned activities, such as bobbing for apples, pin-the-tail-on-the-donkey, and prizes for the best costumes. We had so much fun!

On another occasion, Diane, Derek and I set the stage for an 'Ole Fashioned Spring Country Hoe-Down' at the new firehall in 1995. We brought in bales of hay, kindly provided by Philippa (Lot 139) and the trailer that set the stage for Stuart Hemings, one of my former colleagues and friend, a square dance caller who would patiently try to teach the basic steps to enthusiastic Piers cowboys. It's too bad we didn't have 'Tiktok' in those days because a video of a bunch Islanders in their best cobbled-together western wear all trying to learn their left foot from their right may have gone viral. John Currie was very instrumental in securing the funding for the new firehall and setting the foundation for what it is today. As Executive Director of the BC Fire Chiefs' Association, John had many connections that helped set the stage for what is an amazing fire department, especially when you consider the size of our community. Thank you John.

Saga of Boats: I don't think many of us Islanders have gone unscathed from our winter storms. On two occasions we have lost boats. In the first storm, a giant log punctured a hole in the bottom of our boat and sank her. On the second occasion, a south-west wind came in and flipped our boat while it was tied to our dock - unbelievable! Luckily in that instance only the motor was destroyed. One very dark and stormy night, we arrived at Canoe Cove to find the boathouses rocking and rolling. Derek and his Mom, Pam (Lot 45), were waiting for me to come from work. Because it was so incredibly stormy, we borrowed Lorne Andres's 18-foot Hourston to come home. I doubt that Bill Hourston ever imagined his boats would safely go through such wild seas. That little boat would get buried in green water to the windshield and kept on going. While most islanders are converting to new-style aluminum boats, the old Hourstons were long seen as the 'gold standard' for Piers islanders.

Some of my fondest memories of first moving to Piers were of our old neighbour and friend Chris Greentree (Lot 9). Chris absolutely loved and looked forward to visiting Piers. He travelled all over the world with his work and Piers was the only constant in his life. He and his children always called Piers 'home.' I remember coming home from my very busy work life in Victoria to be greeted by his big warm welcoming smile, saying, "How is the hard-working girl today? Looks like you need to pop over and put your feet up for awhile." My time spent sitting on his deck was always most enjoyable, listening to tales of travel and earlier days on Piers. Derek and I very quickly became part of his family - hosting family reunions and parties through the summer. Because golfing was a passion for Chris, he would host an annual golf tournament in his front yard, putting up a bottle of 'Dom' for the winner, setting up a driving box and using our little tin boat *Ferry Food*, painted bright yellow, as the hole in one; so much fun. During one of the golf tournaments, we left *Ferry Food* anchored out in its spot, only to find in the morning he had disappeared. Chris and Derek hunted high and low, but poor little *Ferry Food* was never to be seen again. While not seen as environmentally friendly today, it was amazing that nearly all the golf balls driven into the sea would make their way back up the rocky shore to be collected each day. That same old bucket of balls was still around years later, although a few may still linger in the depths of the sea. Chris was a very kind and generous man who made a significant donation towards the purchase of the island's tractor.

Shortly after we moved to Piers, around 1993/1994, we were alerted by the sound of squawking crows coming from the property at Lot 11. What we saw was a falcon hanging upside down by one leg. It appeared to be tied to a tree limb, 25 to 30 feet above the ground. The poor bird was valiantly trying to defend itself, while being mercilessly attacked by a murder of crows. While looking for a ladder or trying to think of some way to come to the aid of this poor bird, the cacophony of crows moved to our backyard. Going to investigate, Derek found that the falcon had managed to break free of the tree and was now huddled in our backyard, still being hassled relentlessly by the crows. Thinking it would be best to remove this traumatized bird from the area, Derek was able to bundle it up in his jean jacket without too much resistance. Once safely protected under Derek's arm, we headed to his parents house at Lot 45 with the crows eventually giving up pursuit. As the falcon finally began to relax, we were able to examine him and found only a few puncture wounds and missing feathers. It was content to sit on Derek's shoulder but now what to do with him? It turned out what caused him to be hanging from the tree was his leather thong tether, which indicated that this bird was trained and belonged to a falconer. Derek remembered that a man named Mr. Bebe was a well-known falconer on the Saanich Peninsula. We found his phone number and called him to seek his advice. It turned out the bird was his and he was delighted at its recovery. It seemed that the bird had been 'borrowed' without permission from Mr. Bebe's farm by the then-bartender at the Stonehouse Pub. The bartender thought the bird would make a great addition to a medieval-theme night, but he had failed to properly secure it to its perch. After a quick boat ride to Canoe Cove, the bird and owner were happily reunited. Just another example of those quirky, once in a lifetime experiences that come to those who are fortunate to live on Piers Island.

Together with our neighbours, Carin and Kevin Elder (Lot 9), Derek and I hosted the very first and second annual Poker Paddle in approximately 2011 and 2012. Prizes for the best hands, worst hands and simply no hands at all were given out, followed by a gala front yard barbeque at Lots 7 and 9 - so much fun. This event set the stage for future Poker Paddles.

The Blizzard of 1996: What a wonderful place to be stranded. We woke up on a late December morning to find three and a half feet of snow. We were stranded on paradise for four days without power, but in true island fashion, we all came together to help each other out. It was a total winter wonderland without a mark in the snow. I remember walking up to Derek's parents' place (Lot 45), taking over half an hour to get up the hill as we sank up to our waists with every step in. A total winter wonderland, truly, incredibly beautiful.

Another shining example of Piers islanders' love to gather over a glass or two of their favourite tipple was the annual Oktoberfest organized by the 'Piers Island Vintners and Brewers Association' at the old firehall. Back in the early days of u-brew joints and 'just add the yeast wineries,' a group of islanders, in the spirit of friendly competition, thought it would be fun to gather at the old firehall to compare the finer points of each other's plastic-bucket plonk. In the theme of Octoberfest, smokies were barbequed along with generous portions of fried onions and sauerkraut. All stood around enthusiastically and boisterously comparing colour and clarity, hoppyness and body, until all was consumed regardless of quality. At the end of the evening, custom-made medals were awarded to proud recipients and a good time was had by all. I don't really know why this great tradition ended, but it could be happily revived if some were so inclined.

Moonlight Madness Dance under the stars.... it truly was. I so very much looked forward to our summer dance under the moon and stars at the old firehall. We would string lights across the road and set up the bandstand for the live band that would set the stage for an evening of fun. Islanders brought their lawn chairs and set them up in a large circle surrounding the dance floor. Prizes were donated and awarded for spot dances. At midnight, there was always a feast of different types of chili served with buns, salads and snack food. A truly magical evening dancing under the stars. Maybe, one day again at the old firehall?

Vicki and Derek Morrison

Lot 41 - Barry Tate and Patti L-L

Our Utopia

Whoever thinks they'll find Utopia? We did - on Piers Island! Barry originally came in the mid-1990s from an ad describing a waterfront rental, "5 minutes from Sidney." He had no idea that rental was on an island. He came to take a look at the place with the owner (Kelly Karr, Lot 53) and ended up joining a party at Al and Uta Bryce's house (Lot 42). He met so many interesting people, that he was immediately hooked and moved to Piers the next weekend. Patti joined him two years later.

We bought our house at Lot 41 from Howie and Diane Sneade, two of the original long-timers on Piers. Howie was an incredible workman and built a wonderful eclectic home. We still love the house with its many unique features, including artistic stained glass windows and the special turret-shaped, sit-around breakfast nook. We were both busy professionals when we bought the house so couldn't do justice to the amazing garden area. Over the years, we have brought the garden back to most of its former glory, complete with its artistic dry-stone walls hand-built by the Sneades, similar to the stone walls we later saw in Ireland.

One of our favourite joys on Piers has been the Moonlight Madness dance every July, especially in the early years at the old firehall. In those days, everyone brought lawn chairs and danced the night away on the dusty road, to the music of a live band perched on top of an old wooden cart. A 'midnight' chili dinner completed the evening. Other great times include the Red Hat/Black Hat get-togethers the third Friday of each month for the last 16 years. We love having our family (children Steve, Dan, David and Stacey, and our six grandkids) and friends visit us on the island, especially for the Piers family picnic and other special events. For 20 years, we hosted a 'Piers Day' for Patti's Toastmasters group, with a potluck meal, of course.

Our biggest highlight was our wedding, 'Barefoot on Biscoe Beach,' September 2, 2001. We had only been on the island a few years, so initially we invited a few of our close Piers friends, in addition to three boatloads of friends and family from 'the big island.' We said "no gifts" and, in true Piers tradition, we asked that guests bring their favourite potluck dish to go along with the main courses and beverages. We kept hearing rumblings like, "Did you hear that Patti and Barry are getting married?" Many of our island friends were feeling left out, so we finally decided to put up posters (pre BB 'Bulletin Board') and invited the entire island to our 'Potluck' wedding. About 70 people showed up, which turned out to be perfect for the celebration. People sat on logs on the beach for the ceremony and then came to the new firehall for an amazing 20-course dinner and dance. It was wonderful to share our special day with our entire community.

We love living on the waterfront, and gazing at the ever-changing seascapes and the stunning all-colour sunrises and unbelieveable tangerine full-moon rises on our east side. Barry says he has "never seen the sky or the sea ever look the same twice." A favourite thing for us to do during the summer is to take a day off and boat to three or more surrounding islands. We would have breakfast on Salt Spring Island, a lunch and hike on Portland Island, and then dinner on Mayne or Galiano Island. When we returned home 12 hours later, it felt like we'd been away an entire weekend.

Being a former Winnipegger, Patti was shocked to discover when she moved to Piers, that nearly half the full-timers on the island, were either born or had lived in Winnipeg. There are still quite a number of people on the island with Winnipeg roots. Patti was also the resident island realtor for nearly 20 years until retiring in 2015, and feels fortunate to have assisted so many people in finding their own Utopia in this incredible community.

Patti has appreciated so many independent women who have lived on the island. One islander, Mary Tucker (Lot 50) was a real rugged woman, who built her own house in the 1960s, and stayed on the island living in her own house until she was 95 years old. Her memory was so sharp, that when Patti watched tennis tournaments on TV with her, Mary knew the statistics and qualities of all the players, much better than Patti or anyone else on the island. Another islander, Berneice Archibald (Lot 66) lived on Piers into her 80s, despite people thinking she would leave after her husband died. She laughed and said, "Why would I leave? All my friends are here and where else could I walk the dog at midnight and not worry about getting mugged?" Piers remains a safe haven for independent women on their own.

We used to see many more orcas frolicking in front of our home in the 1990s. Although their numbers have dwindled, it is still a thrill to see pods of orcas displaying their acrobatics. Our biggest 'seaside' surprise occurred in the late 1990s, when Barry was in his home-studio and Patti was, of course, working in town. Barry heard a huge crash and looked out the window. He was staring eye-to-eye at the wheelhouse of a B.C. Ferries ship, grounded right in front of our home at low tide. It was the Salt Spring ferry with a newer captain, who, after an embarrassing couple of hours of waiting for the tide to rise, was finally able to hit the seas again. The incident even made the B.C. news. There were no casualties, except for Barry the photographer, who in all the excitement, sprained his foot racing down the stairs to photograph the event.

Volunteering has been an important part of Piers for us. Barry was a volunteer fire fighter for over 20 years and is often involved in different island projects. Patti was a fire fighter in the beginning years, and has been involved with other projects, such as the library and emergency groups.

One of our favourite activities on Piers is being part of the 'ukulele-playing, scotch-drinking, chocolate-eating group.' We have a repertoire of over 100 songs from Joan Baez to Bruno Mars. During COVID, we improvised by using a combination of Zoom and ChordU apps so we could still gather as a virtual musical get-together. On warm summer evenings the group meets at Biscoe Beach, and on rare occasions, we have been the 'opening act' for more famous groups, at house concerts on the island.

Living next-door to our neighbours, Manon and Michael Hobbis (Lot 37) and their historical 83-year-old Norwegian tall ship, the *Duen,* is so special. Last year (2021) we celebrated our 20th wedding anniversary with a wonderful private sailing on the *Duen* with their trained crew and our family. Also, Patti was fortunate to go on an unforgettable eight-day sail from Piers to Haida Gwaii in 2014 on the *Duen* with other islanders. She will never forget crossing the wild Hecate Strait with its 20-foot waves and the awe-inspiring whale sightings! We also experience wonderful sailing adventures on the *Nala* with Vicki and Derek Morrison (Lot 7).

We love our community of friends on Piers Island. Our off-island friends often ask, "What happens if you run out of something? The store is so far away!" A favourite memory from a few years ago, was when we had a major power outage and called neighbor Pam Morrison (Lot 45) in a panic: "We have an emergency. We're out of chocolate!" Within three minutes, Pam was at our door with a 70% Lindt chocoate bar. Now THAT is community!

Barry and Barry's 20th anniversary on the Duen

Lot 42 - Uta and Alan Bryce

Dilemma

A bracing, early spring day it was, and Uta and I - despite the stiffening gusts and waves barreling out of the west - were determined to head into Sidney with Kaia (seven) and Keito (four). This was before our youngest son Taise was born. In preparation for the voyage we donned the works - winter coats, toques, gloves, and lifejackets, and trundled out the door with Keito in the lead.

Darting ahead and down the long set of stairs that slither across the bank to our lanky gangway, Keito seemed determined to be the first at our bucking bronc of a beater boat. Partway down the gangway however, his pace slackened as he battled the wooly westerlies. He then stopped entirely and lowered his scrawny frame onto the gangway deck to get relief from the elements. "Good idea," I thought, chuckling away. At the time, what neither of us appreciated was that he had positioned his reedy body perpendicular to the gusts, one of which soon slammed into his slab-sided lifejacket and rolled him over the edge into the water or onto the beach.

Upon witnessing Keito's spectacular drift from view and uttering a few short Anglo-Saxon words, I quickly made my way to his point of departure. Casting my eyes below I saw that at least he'd hit the water, upon which he was bobbing up and down on his back, hollering away. Seemed like a reasonable response to me.

In cat-like fashion (as I recall), I sprang into action, running back along the gangway to a short set of stairs leading down to the beach. Not fatigued by the initial leg of my heroic response, I continued my dash to water's edge. "Looks bloody cold," I thought. "Perhaps he'll drift ashore; he's wearing a lifejacket . . ."

Ever valiant, I prepared for a launch into the surf. Realizing that my pockets contained my keys and wallet, I fished them out and tossed them down on the beach. Bad move! Upon contact with the sand the wallet opened and spilled its content: driver's license, credit cards and bills all the way up to $20. My identity and fortune immediately flew down the beach with reckless abandon, prompting a few more short Anglo-Saxon words.

I now faced a dilemma. Keito seemed to be doing OK. Better than my cards and bills. The hollering told me that he had a lot of life left in him. The optics of letting him possibly drift to shore however, had to factor into my decision-making. After all, "What kind of a role model would I be for Kaia and Keito if I chased after the money . . .?"

With newly found resolve, I took off my jacket, slipped out of my shoes and plunged into the surf, swimming at least 10 meters from shore to grab onto Keito's lifejacket strap and drag him to the beach where I propped him up and said, "Keito, are you ready for a treasure hunt?"

** *Author's Note:* Alan and Uta Bryce and their family have hosted many amazing house concerts on Piers. These included such notables as the 'Bills' and of course their own talented Kaia (piano and voice) and Keito (violin and voice). These events have been enjoyed by all who have attended.

Uta and Taise Bryce

Kaia, Alan and Keito Bryce

Lot 45 - Pam and Allan Morrison

The Best 20 Years Of Our Lives

(told by Pam Morrison)

It was 1991. We had a big house in Victoria and were thinking of moving. Grant, our son, had been to Piers many times and suggested it for us. We ended up buying Lot 49. It had been a party house for the son of the previous owner, a woman from the States. Before we moved in, we had friends and family come over to help and we took out tons of garbage. Allan and the boys and Sandra did a lot of work on the house.

Before we moved to Piers, Allan had had two open-heart surgeries and a heart attack. After we had been on Piers for awhile, Allan's cardologist said, "I don't know what you are doing, but keep it up." It was a wonderful peaceful place for someone with health issues to live.

We used to go Howie and Diane Sneade's (Lot 41) a lot. I loved to be in the hot tub with Diane after we gardened all day. Howie and Di had great times and good parties. Howie was known for his once-a-year 'guy' parties - horseshoeing and Ron MacLeod (Lot 71) getting a barge for the guys to go fishing. On the barge the guys fished in style, on lean-back chairs with umbrellas. That event was for boys only. The guys got up early in the morning, and then they would jump in the boat and go fishing. They would also stand on the green of the yard, and drive golf balls into a moored dingy. Amazingly, they were able to retrieve the golf balls on the seashore at low tide. Howie was a bit of a real wild guy, but fun.

Walking in the centre of the island was wonderful. Allan and I liked that a lot. And getting the new firehall built was such an amazing community effort. Everyone helped. At first people said, "We don't want that" (a new firehall), but it was so exciting when it started. I have a lot of photos when the ground was broken. One of the things that stands out for me is that a lot of the island women dug a ditch to bury the line for the 911 system, that went up to the old water tower. Berneice Archibald (Lot 66) was too old to dig, but she brought lots of food for the group picnic for all the women.

All the men helped with anything they could when the new firehall was built. Dave Poulsom (Lot 112) did a lot. Allan helped with whatever he could, but was limited because of his heart problems. It was a great community effort. There were people at the top who were the planners, but everyone pitched in, and everyone was so proud of it when it was finished. Everyone did a lot of work and it was also a lot of fun.

I went on my kayak around the island whenever I could - almost every night. I loved exploring Princess (Portland) Island. There was a group of Piers women who all kayaked. Once, we went on a long day trip. We were having lunch and had pulled our kayaks way up on the beach. We thought they were out of the way, but when the wake came after the ferry went by, most of our kayaks and paddles got swamped with water. We were laughing and had such a great time. There were about 10 of us and it was amazing.

Everybody was on foot travelling around Piers in those days. In the early 1990s, there were no golf carts. My dad bought a little red jeep called *Georgie* and Allan used to drive it to get to fire practice. Frank Williams (Lot 13) had the old tractor and he always worked and did so many unseen jobs for the island.

The Christmas parties were always wonderful, as were the Halloween dress-up parties. Margo Fitzgerald once went as a carrot, and Diana and Gerry Kristianson went as slugs. One year my daughter-in-law Vicki Morrison (Lot 7) and I went as firehouse dogs (spotted Dalmations). Moonlight Madness Dance was so much fun and we managed great outside the old firehall, dancing on the dusty road. Some islanders would take their wheelbarrows, and young children would fall asleep in them. When the party ended, the parents would simply wheelbarrow the sleeping children home.

There were so many storms during the winter. One bad storm, Earla Fitzgerald's (Lot 27) boat sank, and islanders, including my son Derek bailed it out. Afterwards, we all went inside her place for hot apple cider. During long-lasting, four-to five-day power outages, often only one side of the island was out. That meant volunteers from the other side made suppers for the side without electricity. Allan and I had a wood-burning fireplace with a flat top, and we cooked great meals on top of it during power outages.

Living on Piers was the best 20 years of our lives. We enjoyed every minute of it. We hated to leave, but we didn't want to have people to have to look after us.

Al and Pam Morrison

Lot 51 - Chris MacKay and Colleen Bryden

Thirty Years Of Rescues And Good Times

(written by Chris MacKay)

The first time I came to Piers was in the early 1990s, when I was in a race with another boat off Swartz Bay. We stopped to chat and he was going to a party on Piers and invited us along. It was Ron Macleod's (Lot 71) annual bash! A few months later, when I was renting a waterfront house on Ardmore (in North Saanich) and it went up for sale, the realtor left an MLS (multiple listings service) book and I saw a place for sale on Piers. I went to see it and made a full-price offer, but the listing had expired so I didn't get it. However, a year later I was able to buy Lot 51 and lived there full-time for 30 years.

My most memorable times on Piers involved rescues. I was sitting outside in the hot tub one night about 11 p.m. when I saw a flare come up from the water towards an airplane above. I phoned Search and Rescue with details of what I saw. They phoned me back at 2 a.m. and said they had rescued the guy who was sitting in a life raft in the middle of the sea. Two years later, in February, I saw another flare over the sea and called Search and Rescue. They asked for general directions and found a fisherman out at sea. He had been transiting to Vancouver and barbequing in his boat when the barbecue set fire to the boat and then the boat sank. He was found in the water. The flare I had seen was his last one. They said no one else called in. Even though I wasn't sure about what I saw, I still called. It made me realize how important it is to call for help, even if you're not sure what you're seeing.

One more rescue happened when Susan Hutchinson (Lot 127) and a friend of hers and I were going out boating to Port Browning on Pender Island. We saw three guys in kayaks frantically waving. One of the guys was in a kayak that was sinking and he was getting hypothermic. We quickly got him into our boat and towed his kayak. The guy was not doing well, so we dropped Susan's friend off on Knapp Island with the kayak, so we could get home faster. We called for medical advice, got him warmed in a shower, and took him over to Barnacle Road on Vancouver Island, where he was taken to hospital. He was a Canadian soldier who had just gotten home from a tour in Croatia and was kicking himself that he survived the war in Croatia, but nearly died on his first week back in Canada. He had stuffed some things in the kayak, and damaged the flotation tank, so the kayak was filling with water.

Crazy winter storms on Piers were always a highlight. During one bad storm, one of the chains failed on the shared dock at Lots 43,45,47 and 49. I went into Sidney for rope. We secured the dock to a large tree on shore. I used that rope on the dock a few more times over the years. I passed the 'dock rescuing rope' on to Aaron de Jong at Lot 49.

Fondly, I remember Earla Fitzgerald (Lot 27) who in her 70s, loved a good time. I had a very fast boat those days, and invited Earla, Susan and Barry Tate for a quick ride to Port Browning. In the middle of the 70 mph trip, I looked back to see how Earla was doing. She had such a great smile on her face. She loved the trip. A few days later, while browsing through some old records in a thrift shop in Sidney, Earla recounted her wonderful dinner/ boating adventure to a volunteer at the shop. By coincidence, that volunteer was my mother - what a small world.

Earla was always one for fun. One New Year's Eve, she spontaneously invited everyone on the island who wasn't doing anything, to come to her place for a party. I put on my coat and headed over. There was a bucket of party noise-makers at the door and there were lots of people to welcome the New Year in - Piers Island style!

Chris MacKay and Colleen Bryden

Lot 56 - Karen Chong and Steve Davis

Our Life On Piers

We moved from Edmonton and lived full-time on Piers from 1994 to 2002. We loved the island. People must have thought we were crazy for picking up all the driftwood on the beach. We used it for building our unique artistic gates and fences for our goats.

I especially loved so many of the amazing people on Piers. One of my favourites was my buddy Bill Oldfield (Lot 46). I remember when Bill fell off his roof and broke his leg. He was in his 80s. His foot was in a cast, and the whole island got together and helped him in whatever way they could. Some brought him meals, some helped with his yard, and of course, he also needed care-giving at times. I was quite amazed how the whole island pitched in. That was an amazing part of Piers. Bill loved Piers Island and he loved his dog, Rex. When Rex died, I came to comfort Bill and found him crying as he was building Rex a small coffin. His brother Arthur Oldfield loved Piers, too. Arthur rented Lot 10 for years, and then it was put up for sale. At the same time, Arthur ended up winning the 649 Lottery and bought the house. It was quite an amazing coincidence.

Bill Oldfield was an astonishing gardener and I learnt so much about gardening from him. He knew about all the plants and he even had a huge cactus on his deck that he was so proud of. He kept it inside the house during the winter, and it grew up to the ceiling. In the summer, he would take the cactus outside to the deck and it would bloom for one day a year, and it was a big celebration for him. One day, Bill came to our house so upset that someone was cutting up a pear tree along his road. I sheepishly had to admit to him that it was me. I thought I was helping Bill by pruning his pear tree for him. Once in awhile, Bill would get upset about something. He was old fashioned (before email) and would hand-write very eloquent letters about the situation to the P.I.A. or P.I.I.D.

Another person who had a big influence on my kids and me, was Rebekah Gawne (Lot 94, now Lot 8). I was such a 'city slicker' and Rebekah was this amazing 'pioneer woman'. There wasn't anything that Rebekah couldn't do. One night we were going across the water back to Piers in the dark in her boat, and we hit a log, bang on. It didn't even faze her. We just kept right on going. Rebekah did amazing baking for so many islanders, in pretty primitive conditions, with her three kids running around.

It was interesting for me to think that I was on the fire department. Just being around the guys and having a lot of laughs was great.

Berneice Archibald (Lot 66) was such a character. She was from Edmonton too and was always singing opera and playing the piano. She must have had at least 400 pairs of shoes. Pauline Olesen was a good friend and took me to her Friday AM exercise group. She and her husband Steve were always doing so many things for so many people on Piers.

I know my husband Steve would say that his favourite thing was that he could jump into his boat and go fishing whenever he wanted. One year, he caught so many salmon and prawns (still within our limit) that we had to buy a freezer. Steve still loves telling that story about Piers.

We had two goats, Hannah and Squeak. We got the goats for $50 each when we took our kids to Beacon Hill Park to see the baby goats one Spring. I have a strange story about those goats. They actually inspired me to quit smoking. I found myself on my knees weeding in the garden, and holding my cigarette to the side, so the smoke didn't bother the goats. The craziness of how that must have looked was so insane to me that I decided at that moment to quit smoking.

Lynn Pritchett (Lot 23) knew plants well. She told me to take Lobelia and that helped me quit smoking. We had lots of chickens and a very friendly rooster. Pauline made us an amazing glass plate of our rooster when we moved away. Most islanders loved our animals, but the chickens and rooster bothered the next-door neighbours 'who only came weekends.' When we moved to our farm in Mill Bay, we piled the goats into our little boat. It must have been quite a sight!

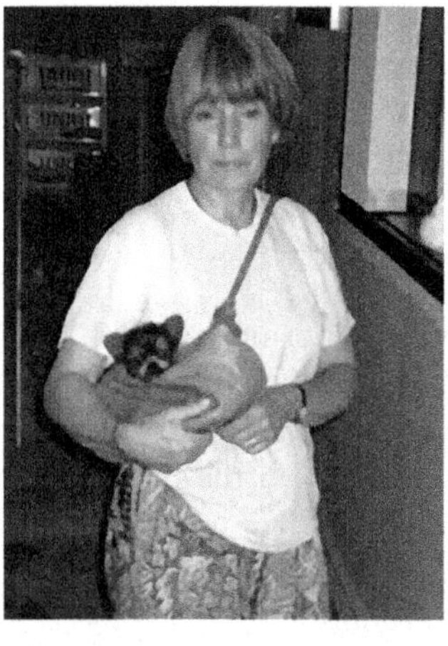

Piers was like a big family. People gossiped and talked and got together for all sorts of occasions, big and small. Someone would be mad at their neighbour one day, and then a few days later they were all eating smoked salmon together. It was just like family.

Karen Chong

Steve Davis

Bill Oldfield

Lot 59 - Joanna and Jim Mackenzie

Piers Island: A Sense Of Place

As soon as I saw the advertisement for our prospective home on Piers Island, I knew it was for me. The picture of a hammock strung across a deck laden with flower-filled planters said it all. My husband Jim and I had moved from Kitimat in northern B.C. and wanted to relocate somewhere on Vancouver Island. Not only was our new home by the sea, but being an avid sailor and lover of the water, I felt this was a dream come true. Having to travel by boat added to my joy, and I arrived with six cats and two dogs in our 17-foot runabout, not to mention all my favourite indoor plants.

On an early visit in the fall after we moved to Piers, one of my daughters and I came down from Kitimat to receive some of our household goods. These arrived across the water on a small barge. As soon as all the items were landed on our shared dock it began to rain. We had quite a distance to cover carrying all our gear, but miraculously Karen Davies' (Lot 56) son appeared out of nowhere and helped us move everything uphill into our place. To add to this warm welcome, we found bread baked by Rebecca and champagne given by our realtor, Patti L-L, awaiting us. Patti and her husband Barry soon became such wonderful friends and I could soon relate to their enthusiasm for the island.

Looking out east to Portland Island in the evening, we watched the breathtaking sunsets bathe her shores. The mornings heralded the sunrise as we had our breakfast. I enjoyed seeing the lights of the ferries at night, and often the moon lighting a path to the island. Seals and otters frequented our shared dock, and many mornings as I left for work I would disturb a couple of seals snoozing at the end of the wharf. A whale once came right into the shallows by our place, to the surprise and delight of a neighbour and me.

We were blessed with wonderful neighbours with whom we shared many meals and good laughs. Jean and Fred Thompson (Lot 61) were intrepid boaters, but Jean had never kayaked. I offered to lend her a kayak and this, being accepted, off we went. Fred was not too happy with Jean doing this, but she was amazing and tackled waves like a pro as we paddled around the island. As we entered our small bay, I went ashore and commented that we would impress Fred arriving home completely dry. At this, Jean did one big scoop with her paddle and went under. We were only in five feet of water. At least her hat was dry since she had left it on the beach.

The events on the island were as special as the people we got to know. I know very little about beer and rarely drink it, but won a prize at the beer tasting and dance at the old firehall. Bonfire night, dress-up parties, musical evenings, picking blackberries and apples, enjoying the home produce sold at the end of islanders' driveways, wandering to friends' houses with our trusty flashlights and our old red cat following behind, are some of the great memories etched in my mind.

The joy of being able to kayak daily and having adventures with friends on the water, were among the many riches experienced on our shared island. Never coming or going up and down the dock without carrying some commodity, whether it be a Christmas tree, parcels to post, garbage, or transporting our dogs, it all became part of the daily ritual.

Ferrying excited family and friends over to visit was so much a part of Piers Island life. There was always something happening and island celebrations were so unique and well attended. Attending Patti and Barry's wedding on the beach was one of those highlights. The party at the new firehall had all the women dancing to "Girls Just Want to Have Fun". Chocolate also featured pretty prominently.

I loved the feeling of living outdoors, but indoors. The garden path always started at our Canoe Cove moorage or at the government dock at Barnacle road. We loved breakfast at the Canoe Cove cafe, even though our dogs caused chaos getting wrapped up in the chain-link fence.

So many memories: watching the fog roll in and knowing I had 20 minutes to get across to shore for work before I lost visibility; being distracted and looking at the Christmas light display on a nearby island and ending up in Fulford Harbour; sucking kelp into the motor on my way home one night and drifting back towards Sidney; watching our boat bob around on its whips in a rough sea from our deck with our spot lamp. These experiences all added to life on a small island.

I am filled with gratitude for those few years that I lived in such an idyllic place enjoying the lifestyle that I so embraced. Two of my dogs and cats have their ashes scattered by Biscoe Beach because they too loved the island and its free spiritedness and natural beauty.

I love to visit and catch up with old Piers Island friends, and a few years ago I had the good fortune to be part of an adventure sailing up to Haida Gwaii with an all Piers Island crew on the magnificent wooden sailboat, the *Duen*.

Recently it has been fun to make music and meet new faces via Zoom with the Piers ukulele group. I am blessed to be living on another beautiful island (Gabriola), but Piers Island and its people will always have a special happy place in my heart.

Joanna MacKenzie

Lot 60 - Jim and Karen Boyette

Our Paradise On Piers

While dreaming of owning our own home in the Pacific Northwest one summer in the late 1990s, we were on Vancouver Island looking through real estate magazines when an ad for a home for sale on Piers Island caught our attention. We were taken to the island and fell in love with it. We made up our minds almost immediately that Piers was where we wanted to spend as much of our time as possible. The beauty of the island and the graciousness and spirit of the people we met that day truly touched our hearts.

The renovation of the house that we bought at Lot 60 took longer than we had thought because so much work was required to make it truly our home. The end result was so worth it. Our home and the island were like a paradise for us and for friends from the States who visited us. My memories of our lives there seem almost magical to me. Since my husband's death, I have longed to be back on the island with the wonderful people and to be surrounded by the beauty of the place.

So many happy memories. Wonderful, multi-talented friends whom I will never forget, the beautiful scenery (not to mention the peace, calm and tranquility of the place), fabulous dinners and parties at the homes of friends, Canada Day, eagles flying, hummingbirds, amazing children, watching falling stars from our deck in the summertime. I could go on and on. For me it truly seemed like Camelot.

I loved gardening on the island, even with the deer continually nibbling at our plants. Gardening there was like meditation for me. Oh, and the red rock crab - catching them, cooking them on the grill and savouring each bite. So yummy! I haven't had that type of crab since leaving the island.

I'll never forget living along the coast on one of the B.C. Gulf Islands. At times, being able to see seals swim past, as well as the occasional whale, was wonderful. I truly liked traveling to Vancouver Island for supplies, eating out, and seeing the sights there which entailed traveling by boat each time. It all seemed idyllic to me. My one regret is that I didn't take up kayaking while living there.

Very special memories include the 60th birthday party we gave for my husband, my own 60th given by friends, and the special farewell party given for Jim and me when we were leaving the island (sadly).

I will close by giving tribute to a very special longtime resident of the island: the queen of the island - Mary Tucker (Lot 50). Mary was an amazing woman who truly lived life fully. In my eyes she was a brave, totally independent, funny and feisty human being who inspires me to this day. I feel so fortunate to have known her.

Jim and Karen Boyette

Lot 64 - Sandy and Bob Brunham

A Sense Of Community

"No, no, dear, that's not how to hug! You have to put your heart against mine. Let me show you! "

It was 1995. We were having our first summer on Piers at our recently purchased property at Lot 64. The person trying to teach me the correct way to hug was our new neighbour, Berneice Archibald (Lot 66). Berneice was a delightful octogenarian, although she would never tell us her actual age. She would sing opera and we could hear her melodies waft over the deer fence. She welcomed us warmly to the island and told us the way of things.

We were here for the summer from our then-home in Winnipeg, where we both worked full-time. We were spending the summer with our 16-year-old son, Liam, and his cousin Wade. We were new to all things 'Piers' and lapped up all the experiences. We had bought the property from Bob Byers and Nancy Brown, who were moving back to the city. The property had a very rustic one-bedroom cabin, a claw-foot bathtub on a raised platform, no indoor water, but a tap outside the door and an outhouse. We loved it. We couldn't believe that we owned our own cabin on the ocean. The place also came with a 12-foot leaky aluminum boat with about an inch of free board, and rivets that had popped. We had to bail as we motored back and forth. We had limited boating experience from summers in Lake of the Woods, but we were keen and adventurous.

That first summer was a wonderful introduction to the magic of Piers. Liam and Wade would take off for hours to explore the forest or fish from the boat. They were both aspiring young magicians, and they couldn't believe their fortune when they met islander, Hal Weaver, aka 'Professor Whimsey the Magician.' Hal took the boys under his wing, taking them to the magic stores in Victoria, going to magician meetings, and spending hours with them to teach them the craft.

The main road on Piers was a little lane with two wheel tracks and grass in the middle. We would walk the island and marvel at how quiet and lovely and natural it was. Our beach was one of the best on the island. A huge ball-swing had been erected on a leaning fir tree on the neighbour's property. Every evening, kids from all around the island swarmed to our beach to play on that swing. We listened to and watched the delighted squeals of kids flying out over the ocean and falling in. We all did it. Every family member or guest who visited us had to ride that ball swing. It was a well-known fixture on the island until the tree became rotten and was taken down over 10 years ago.

After that first summer, we made all our work and holiday plans around Piers, coming out from Winnipeg several times a year. We loved our little cottage and the rusticness and simplicity of our life here. In 1999, we moved back to B.C. and could access Piers more frequently. We began to dream of retirement on Piers. We had realized that our little Piers community was exactly where we wanted to live full time. The sense of community on Piers, the friendships, the shared vision of living in nature was what appealed to us. In 2007 we tore down the little cabin, and with the help of our good friends and fellow islanders, Denis and Marge Jesson (Lot 68C), we began to build our dream home. The rest, they say, is history.

Sandy and Bob Brunham

Lot 68C - Denis and Marge Jesson

Living In Harmony With Nature

In 1996, we moved to Piers Island from Winnipeg. We had wanted to return to the West Coast and had made feeble efforts since the mid-eighties to find a suitable location and site that met our expectations for retirement, and that we could afford. Both were difficult. We wanted water access and a rural environment away from the mainland, with access to an airport. This we found on Piers Island, near Sidney, British Columbia.

I had every confidence in our ability to build the house from scratch by ourselves, with my being an architect and Marge having managed about 100 building projects. She was credited as being Winnipeg's first female contractor. We were under a severe time constraint. After clearing the land of fallen trees, we had only a month to excavate, build and occupy the house. We hired a carpenter and two 15-year- old boys to help us. An islander had a small bobcat front-end loader and Marge's brother, Chris, joined us for 10 days and installed the rough-in for the plumbing system.

We had anticipated a strong sense of community due to the relatively low numbers living on the island. However, we didn't imagine the degree of cooperation that made strong bonds between most Piers Islanders. As students of real and imaginary utopian communities, we both knew that strong communal relations only occur at certain scales, and when there is a common belief system or activity or common history to foster the bond. To our surprise there was, and is, an intensely strong bond that attracts people to such a place. It is one of an independent attitude and lifestyle, yet an understanding that everyone in the group must function interdependently when the situation requires it. Piers Island or places like it, do not suit everybody, but for those that it does, it can be paradise.

Our site was beachfront on 7/8 of an acre of forest and marsh on the southwest corner of the island. There are views on both sides of the point, west and south. We oriented the house along the north property line to benefit from selected views, solar gain, and to maximize the land available for other purposes.

Many architects who have identified with the natural landscape have found a special environment in the forest edge. Fields are lovely but are overly exposed to the elements, and to wildlife offer no protection from predators. Moving to the forest edge offered us protection from the north winds and maximal exposure to the sun for our gardens and passive solar gain.

Most important to us in the development of this land was the fragile natural environment that needed to be protected. The last thing we wanted was to bring concrete trucks to the island and drive them from the beach to the location of the house. The same was true for heavy timber, so I installed a pressure treated insulated wood foundation around a heated crawlspace, and devised a framing system which was made up of standard nominal dimension spruce, pine, and fir. This meant that all the material in the building was delivered by barge or by our outboard commuter, to the beach and then carried or wheelbarrowed to the house site. Though we had electrical power and therefore, power hand tools, we had access to no other powered equipment other than the bobcat used to dig the excavation.

Our life became one of constant hands-on building. I put together a temporary workshop where I built most of the cabinetwork, and extensive book shelving and built-ins. That winter when we weren't travelling around the country to see family, we had our own assembly line where Marge and I prepared the materials, built the units, sanded, painted and finished them.

This was a particularly satisfying process for me because encumbered only by budget, I was able to bring together most of my considerations about building. For this project there were few drawings. Decisions were made with the top priority always being to tread softly on the land, and ease the transition between manmade elements and nature. Even the deer were allocated their own place (the herb garden which they didn't eat).

Our relationships with the community intensified. Marge became the first Administrator for the island, and I became a Trustee of the Improvement District, a member of the fire department, and a first responder, roles that kept us busy for 10 years, along with doing small projects to help our island neighbours. The new freedom our lifestyle offered was a chance not so much to think in abstract terms about what we were doing, but to fully engage in the processes of living on an island, interacting with the land and sea, providing for our daily needs, and responding to nature's rhythms.

Marge and Denis Jesson

Lot 73 - Murray and Jeanette Elsom

Piers Island Memories

It was September 1995. Murray and I were newlyweds in search of a new and special place to start our lives together, when the opportunity to move to Piers Island presented itself. Moving from Vancouver Island to a smaller Gulf island comes with its bits of culture shock. There were learning curves, starting with the purchase of a boat to get us from Sidney (where our fish and chips shop was located) to our little Island paradise. Murray, who was confident in his one-time experience steering his uncle's boat as a child, set out on finding us the perfect boat. This was the start of our seven year honeymoon, waves and all.

We moved in just in time for Thanksgiving. Family arrived to help us winterize the cottage, and I had a whole traditional dinner planned. As Murphy's Law would have it, the oven didn't work. Fortunately, we had a barbeque and a good mind for improvising the cooking process. Ah yes, island life. It's not like you can just order a pizza (or fish 'n chips).

When my daughter, Kelly, visited from Toronto, we planned a day trip to Salt Spring Island on our new, perfect boat. Before setting sail on our three-hour cruise, we took some steaks out of the freezer, setup the breadmaker, and brought along a couple of crab traps. After dropping our traps, we continued on to Ganges Harbour, Salt Spring Island, for lunch. Such a lovely day, and it was going to culminate in a surf-and-turf dinner later than evening. But as we were making our way home, Murphy's Law showed up again in the form of a small fire on the boat. It was contained, but we were powerless and had to limp home with the assistance of the kicker motor. We passed by our crab traps, all the while trying to avoid the ferry path. Good thing Murray had all that boating experience.

We finally made it home, and as Murray was lining up the boat on the government dock, I jumped onto the bow through the cockpit. Before I could grab the rope, I slipped on the wet surface and ended up knocked out on the dock. The PIVFD (Piers Island Volunteer Fire Department) and first responders were there in no time. They checked my vitals and prepped me for transport to the ambulance that was waiting with its flashing lights on the North Saanich shore. As the volunteers were keeping me verbally engaged, Kelly leaned into my ear and said, "Mom, next time you want to meet your new neighbours, just invite them over for coffee."

The grandkids came the following summer. It was time for us all to meet and it was going to be a big change from the busy cities for them. Finally, they arrived. After the plane ride, it was a car and then a (first) boat ride to Piers Island! All arrived open- mouthed, tired and excited.

The next day after breakfast, we announced they could go anywhere on the Island alone, with the exception of private properties. The youngest, Jake, had never gone anywhere alone in Toronto. I gave him my whistle and explained how he couldn't get lost - the road circled the forest. Before I knew it, he was running back to me to show me something on the main road. There was a fawn, standing still, looking his way. Jake was so overwhelmed, he could barely speak; it was a wonder to witness his first time of 'freedom' and that he met up with a wild fawn.

The grandkids learned how to cook cabbage rolls, to eat spaghetti with chopsticks and to keep the fireplace replenished with freshly chopped wood. We would have filmed our major water fight but had too much fun to stop. They even entertained us by pantomiming commercials. We had a wonderful time.

And then the day before leaving came. There were long faces and complaining about each other. We suggested a last walk together on the beach. About 15 minutes later, Kevin spotted an unbroken bottle in the rocks. Then he helped. Yelp! There was a piece of paper in the bottle. We rushed back to the cottage, put the bottle in a plastic bag and smashed it carefully. It was a map on old parchment paper and dated 1763. (Grandpa was very creative.) We were directed through the centre forest and ended up on the beach next to the Clarkes' big summer home at Lot 55. The map directed them to pace the distance between a particular rock (it's still there) and the spot. They tried, with the older ones mumbling "this can't be happening," but they studied the map as seriously as the younger ones.

They marked the paces as directed, but no luck. Adult pacing is with wider steps than kid pacing. This was figured out and applied. After a few minutes of wild digging, Clunk! It was an old Eaton's cast iron cauldron with Eaton's etched on the lid. Jessica perks up with, "I didn't know they had an Eaton's in 1763." Such a great memory watching them carry the treasure together on the beach to take home and share the jewellery Grandma gathered over the year. It was one of the best days for us on Piers!

I think the best time of any given day is bedtime. We chose to sleep in the 'grand room' on our sofa bed to listen to the waves, fall asleep looking at the moon, and hear the fireplace crackle.

Then, reality. Murray's fish and chips business became so popular we were run off our feet. The constant commute back and forth to the shop, always working and no quality time together was taking its toll. We made the heart-wrenching decision to sell our little piece of Piers paradise and shortly after, our fish and chip shop was also sold. Retirement followed.

We may not have gotten our 70-year retirement on Piers, but we had our seven-year honeymoon there. How many people get to say that?

Jeanette and Murray Elsom

Lot 77 - Frances and Gary Glover

The Joy Of Friendship and The Rewards of Volunteering

In 1999, we decided to have a look at Piers in anticipation of moving onto the island. We had previously experienced the joy of spending time on a very small B.C. Gulf island and realized we wanted to do so full-time. Piers looked like the perfect island.

One sunny afternoon, we docked our boat at the Piers government dock and proceeded to take the path up to McKenzie Crescent to walk the road and get a feel for the island.

Little did we realize we were going to have an encounter that would have a dramatic impact on our lives. There at the roadway was Mary Tucker and her dogs. Her first words were, "Who are you and what are you doing here?" We were a bit startled and tried not to sound defensive when we responded.

As it turns out, Mary became our dear friend. Initially we bonded with her over our dogs and then spent lots of time just hanging out together. Mary and her friend Enid Houghland were a couple of the originals on Piers. Mary, in particular, did much of the work on the cottage and house at Lot 50. She was involved in many aspects of the island's infrastructure, was a volunteer in many positions and had strong opinions about everything. Her friendships were many and varied.

Frances Glover and Mary Tucker

During our time on Piers, Gary and I have been happily involved in volunteering. Gary has been a member of the emergency program and the PIVFD, including time as Deputy Chief and as a first responder. I have been the Emergency Program coordinator for sixteen years. Together we initiated the Canada Day Parade, the yearly wreath-making event for the Christmas party fundraiser and the Red Hat and Black Hat dinners, as described below.

In 1999, Marion Perkins (Lot 97), who was sister to Mary Tucker (Lot 50), owned one functioning gas-powered golf cart. We referred to Marion as Marion Andretti, a salute to Mario Andretti, the famous racing car driver. Marion happily traveled around the ring road at top speed with her dog as passenger. Although we may have looked askance at the dust she stirred up, we saw the value in golf cart ownership, mainly because we had elderly mothers who liked to visit Piers but were unable to walk any distance. We soon purchased an electric golf cart. A few years later we organized a Canada Day golf cart parade that is still going on every July 1st.

Red Hat and Black Hat dinners: In the Spring of 2004, a Piers Island full-time resident, Karen Boyette (Lot 60) and I talked to several other island women about an international organization called the Red Hat Society, and wondered if we should start up our own group on Piers. We did some research and discovered the Red Hat Society was formed primarily to encourage women to celebrate aging in a joyful manner. Even though many groups were made up of women older than 50, we invited all the women from Piers Island to take part, regardless of age.

Our first gathering (see previous photo) was held on a sunny day in June 2004 at Lot 77. Women over 50 wore red hats, and those under 50 wore pink hats. Twenty women attended that inaugural gathering. Dinners carried on monthly, uninterrupted for 16 years, until Covid-19 hit, and we had to cease getting together. Over those years, each dinner was hosted by a volunteer and we had plenty of hosts and many incredible potluck dinners.

Although we initially wore red or pink hats, we soon discovered we were simply interested in an evening of good food and tasty beverages. So, the hats were forgotten, but the camaraderie continued. The name stayed.

It became apparent to the men of the island that the women were having a splendid time getting together for a monthly potluck meal. Therefore, my husband Gary, along with Wayne Morson (Lot 113), decided to create Piers Island's own men's group called the 'Black Hatters.' All island men were invited to attend a men's monthly dinner hosted by a volunteer.

The tradition of monthly women's and men's dinners continued until January of 2020, and will resume when we are given the 'go ahead' after the pandemic. The dinners are a great way to get to know other Piers Islanders and have been particularly helpful to newcomers.

Gary and Frances Glover

Lot 78 - Wendy Eden and Gary Barker and Bob Snelling

A Wonderful Life On Piers

I first heard about Piers Island from my brother Alan Bryce in 1990. His friend Bob Byers and family had a cabin there. Alan knew that my former husband Gary Barker and I were looking for a recreation/retirement property and felt Piers just might be a good fit. Bob generously agreed to take us over to see the island in his tin boat on a wet, cold and blowy November afternoon. That was my first of many such boat trips to Piers.

We looked at a few west-side properties that were not built on and selected some possibilities. Bob provided us with the contact information and I wrote letters to the owners inquiring about a possible sale. As luck would have it, the owner of Lot 78 was ready to sell. We made a deal and were the owners before that coming new year.

Gary and I worked like all Piers islanders did, very hard, to clear years of fallen trees and debris so we could assess more clearly just what we had really bought. It was lots of fun and we very much enjoyed those days. We set up a serious campsite and spent many, many weekends and holidays on our property. Later on I became the sole owner and built a 700 square foot cabin on site. In 1998 I moved there permanently, commuting daily in my 11-foot Avon inflatable. Those were challenging times.

In 2001 Bob Snelling joined me on Piers and in time we added a wonderful addition plus many decks and eventually the dock. We both retired there and were actively involved in volunteering on the island.

Our favourite event on Piers was the Christmas dinner and wreath sale. Being involved in the fire department and the emergency program were also highlights. We left the island in 2015 with mixed emotions but our move to Parksville has met and exceeded our present needs and desires. Our biggest loss is not seeing the very dear friends we made while on Piers. I particularly miss the music group and being closer to my brother and his terrific family. Fortunately good friends aren't lost and Alan can't get rid of me. We still chat regularly with several islanders and visit when we can. I feel I was most fortunate to share island life with the folks there for 25 years and with two great partners. Life has been very good to all of us.

Gary Barker and Wendy Eden

Wendy Eden and Bob Snelling

Lot 79 - Sally and Dick Tuckey

Our Home Away from Home

We purchased our place here on Piers Island in the mid-1990s. We love the island and its bucolic atmosphere that always feels right to us. We have even taken to commenting on that each time we return. We feel so very fortunate to have this 'home away from home,' which provides respite from cares and concerns, as well as a place for our expanding family to join us in fun and relaxation. Those things are so needed in the world at this time. Piers is the perfect antidote to worries and concerns.

Having grown up on Pender Island, Sally had hoped for a similar island lifestyle to the one she had experienced there. When the discussion arose about where we might find a weekend place, she thought that Salt Spring (being closer to Victoria than Pender) might fill the bill. However, Dick had fallen in love with Piers on a previous visit, so we had a look, and ended up buying our Lot 79. The lifestyle was different from that of the larger Gulf Islands - no ferry and no grocery store for two things, but Sally came to love Piers Island for just that. Our arrivals to and departures from the island are not conditional upon a public ferry, but instead our timing is our own in that regard. Thanks to the kindness of nearby resident Bert Johnson we docked at his wharf for several years before starting a dock project of our own. As far as food is concerned, if we have forgotten it, we simply do without. So simple.

A brief humorous story: Shortly after we purchased our lot, Sally overheard Dick telling someone that she had thought of Salt Spring and he had thought of Piers. "So we compromised," he said. Sally immediately asked, "What was the compromise?" His cocky reply? "Piers is halfway to Salt Spring."

We have celebrated various family events here over the 25 years we have owned our property. One that comes to mind was the 40th birthday surprise party for our eldest son Dave. His family and the two of us were on Piers relaxing in the early afternoon when the shuttle appeared on the horizon. Dave had been reading to his daughter and he didn't know that he had been strategically placed so that he would not see the shuttle arriving. It finally dawned on him that this arrival was different - it was full of partygoers. They were very soon identified as family and friends! Great fun ensued, and Dave rose to the surprise occasion manfully.

Piers Island's July 1 golf-cart parade is a wonderful and unique memory. In 2020, when COVID-19 struck throughout the world, many changes had to be made. It was decided that the parade would go on, but without the usual gathering and social time afterward. Our grandchildren have grown up attending the annual event, at first by cheering at the side of the road as horse and rider, carts, and fire truck passed by, and later on by decorating our cart and taking part in the parade itself. In the pandemic years, the wearing of face masks was mandatory but did not deter our crew one bit.

Another annual event looked forward to by all our family is the Piers Island Picnic, with so much fun, arranged by hardworking volunteers. The variety of races is amazing, and reminiscent of old time gatherings. Here I must salute Gerry Kristianson, who for years has officiated the games with great enthusiasm and ability. There is something for everyone from the start-off candy toss, to the age appropriate races, to the hammer/nail contest, and much more. Definitely a Must attend for our family.

We heartily hope to continue enjoying this wonderful island in the years to come. We need it!

Dick and Sally Tuckey

Lot 84 - Gordon and Lynne Neufeld

A Piers Life Too Short

(told by Jackie Charlesworth Lot 135)

Lynne Neufield and I had been friends in Edmonton since childhood. In 1998, Lynne's daughter got married in Edmonton and Lynn and her husband Gordon stayed at our house. They were living in the U.S. at the time. Around the same time there was a family funeral, and Henry and I came to Victoria to be with family (the van der Kamps and the Changs). Lynne was with me. She loved B.C. and made the comment that she would like to buy a house around here. Lydia Chang (Lot 91) jumped in and said, "There's a lovely house for sale on our island." Lynne had no intention of living on an island but when she came to Piers for a visit she fell in love with both the house (Lot 84) and the island. She saw it on Monday and by Thursday there was an accepted offer.

Lynne yearned to return to Canada and so did Gordon. Gordon loved sailing and holidays were either spent sailing the Greek Islands or the east coast of Northern Maine. Coming here to Piers with the open sea all year round was part of the impetus for the move.

Gordon was a physician working with the Navajo Indians in New Mexico and finishing a three-year contract, so it was mostly Lynne and I who came out to Piers together for a couple of years. Lynne and Gordon ultimately moved to Piers full-time, although they still had a home in the US. In the meantime, I was working 14 hours a day full-time so I decided that it was time to retire. I had fallen in love with Piers as well, and since Henry was already retired, we decided to buy a place on Piers too.

Lynne tried to be a gardener, developing the garden on the property to the east on Lot 82, which they bought early on in their stay here. Then sister Penny from Edmonton fell in love with Piers, and bought the vacant lot at Lot 76. Walter van der Kamp designed and built that house. He also built our house at Lot 135 that my husband Henry had designed. He built several other houses on Piers too.

Soon after moving to Piers, Lynne and Gordon got their dog Lucky, who instantly became Lynne's dog. The funniest thing to see was Lynne in the morning doing her exercises lying on her back stretching her legs. Lucky would lie on his back beside her, imitating her every move. Lucky was good with kids. My grandkids would ride on him or lie on him and Lucky just sighed. Some islanders might remember Lynne biking as fast as possible around the island with Lucky alongside her, twice maybe three times, until finally he would stop and howl, almost as if he said, "Enough, enough!"

Lynn tragically died in a car accident in 2006 along with Lucky. Gordon returned to the U.S. and found Piers was not the same without Lynne, so he sold the property a year later. Lynne's sister Penny also sold her place shortly after Lynne died. Gordon commisioned a bronze sculpture with Nathan Scott, a local artist, dedicated to Lynne and Lucky. The beautiful scupture of 'Lucky waiting for Lynne' still stands at Biscoe Beach on Piers today.

'Lucky' sculpture at Biscoe Beach

Lot 95 - Mary and Bill Jordan

Loving Life On Piers Island

In 1998, we decided that we would like to have a cottage on the water. We saw a newspaper ad for a cute one on Piers Island being sold by the McNeelys at Lot 95. Besides the cottage, there was a 600-square-foot workshop and also a large dock shared with a neighbour. It didn't take long for us to make up our minds. We bought it and for several years used it on the weekends.

Over the years, we had the shed made into a 400-square- foot stone cottage with two bedrooms, a three-piece bathroom, kitchenette and living room with a fireplace and a large covered patio at the front. In May 2005, we had the old cottage taken down and began the building of our architecturally designed, full-time stone house and seawall.

We lived in the new cottage during the building of the house and moved into our new house in March 2006. We were novices in operating a boat, but in spite of that, we bought a 22' Lifetimer and called it *Wave Dancer*. Even though we took the Power Squadron course, trying to dock it was not fun in the wind.

We loved life on Piers Island. Everyone was so friendly and eager to help out (as well as recruit us). Bill was chair of the PIID (Piers Island Improvement District) for six years. For years, I was one of the Water Trustees, and also volunteered as a member and then director of the Piers ESS (Emergency Support Services).

The scariest time on Piers was when Bill had a heart attack. The first responders were at the house within minutes. He was taken to the government dock on Barnacle Road by islander Kelly Stevenson's boat, and then to the Royal Jubilee Hospital in Victoria for a pacemaker and stents. All was so well managed by our medical first responders and our fire department. We are both so grateful to all of those amazing volunteers.

The social life was great on Piers - the Canada Day parade, the art walkabout, pancake breakfast, dances (loved it at the old firehall), Christmas dinners, the roadside collections of treasures, the farm, the boat parade for Bill's 80th birthday, the emergency services group, the games and picnic at Biscoe Beach, weekly group exercises, gardening, oil painting with Evey Gabille (Lot 129), showing my art at the PIG (Piers Island Gallery), picking apples and juicing day at Jackie Charlesworth's (Lot 135) garden, Halloween dress up days at Sandy and Bob Brunhams (Lot 64), and the New Year's

Day ocean dip at Garth and Brent's (Lot 20), fun events at Libby and Tony Kahls (Lot 36), beachcombing, and kayak and ferry watching from our dock.

It was so sad that we had to move from Piers to Sidney for medical reasons in October 2020. We loved it all and miss it even more.

Bill and Mary Jordan

Mary Jordan skydiving her 75th birthday

Lot 97 - Marion Perkins

My Mom and Queen Mary

(written by Marion's daughter Lizzie Walton)

The first time I stayed on Piers with my mother, it was very scary at night for me. I kept hearing bumps in the night or the wind whipping by. I wasn't used to this. My mother would always laugh at my fear and say, "Oh, Lizzie, it's a deer." or "It's the wind." Well, one night it wasn't just the wind or some stray deer.

I was sleeping in the downstairs bedroom facing Salt Spring Island. It was a calm night. I was looking out the window over the ramp and the dock. Out of the night came a small boat. It puttered along and then landed on my mother's dock. Two big guys got off the boat, tied up and proceeded up the ramp. They continued right past my mother's house and disappeared into the night. Well, I lay there for I don't know how long, but eventually I fell asleep. The next morning I asked my mother about it and she calmly replied, "Oh, that was just Frank and Guy. I let them use my dock sometimes." That's how I came to know about Frank and Guy.

Going for a walk with my mother through the woods was like a lesson in botany. She knew the English and the Latin name for almost every plant on the island. If you are walking on the road near the old firehall, there is a pathway that leads into the woods. Right near there is a tree that my mother grafted together with something else. I can't remember, but I think it was a tree that is endemic to Piers, a sequoia.

My Auntie Mary (Lot 50) was my mom's sister. She was also known as Queen Mary. I remember one time Amy (my daughter) and I were at her house and she said, "Feel free to go check out the house they are building down the road beside Berneice's." Well, away we went. We just walked right on down through this masterpiece concrete house and onto the beach, where we ran into the owner sunbathing on her own beach. She was not expecting us and wondered what we were doing on her property. I started to explain about Auntie Mary. She immediately understood, even making a reference to the Queen Mary moniker. We were made welcome and allowed to look around, but needless to say, we scrambled our way out of there as soon as we could. So embarrassed.

I wish I had some old-time stories about my aunt. I do know she bought her lot for about $1,000 in the early 1960s, and was one of the first owners on Piers Island. Mary and Enid were friends and went together to buy two lots. They built a tiny cabin that I believe Mary lived in full-time for a while, while teaching in Sidney. She would get up early in the morning and take her little dingy over to the government dock and drive to her teaching job every day. Talk about roughing it.

Marion Perkins and Berneice Archibald

Lot 104 - Gisele Dallaire and Larry Day

Piers is Special!

Larry and I bought our home on Piers in 1999 - the same year we got married. At the time we were travelling to Victoria from the States, every six weeks to help his Dad and we were tired of hotels. On the day we were leaving in September, Larry was surfing real estate on the web and asked if I'd consider living on an island. Of course! He called the realtor to arrange to see the house before our flight back home. Little did we know how hard he had to work to arrange the visit. It was pouring rain. I stepped out of the boat and promptly fell on my butt. I asked if I could wash up. "No, no water." It had to be one of the worst house visits ever. We moved in four weeks later. It was obviously love at first sight!

Larry's father was in the Navy and worked at the dockyards his whole life. We were very fortunate to be able to have him visit us many times on Piers. Every time he set foot on the shuttle, he had an ear-to-ear smile. Piers changed Larry's final memory of his dad from sadness and illness to sitting on the deck watching the world go by, together.

No matter where in the world we were living, we did our best to get time off to spend on Piers. We loved it no matter the season or weather. Part of what made Piers so special were the unique individuals - Frank Williams (Lot 13) selling picnic tickets wearing his umbrella hat and Berneice (Lot 66), who we met the day we moved in. The only woman on earth who could rock a Hermès scarf with full make-up on the shuttle at 9 a.m. She would always offer treats (one for the girls, two for the boys). And, of course, our many dear friends who have become family.

Larry suffered a very severe stroke in 2016. He lost most of his memory (including my name), but always remembers Piers. We celebrated his 75th birthday in 2017 with much help from our island friends. We were able to fly in friends from China, Scotland, England, Alberta, and all over the U.S., thanks to Piersians. Every out-of-town friend had a comfortable bed and made new friends on Piers. I will always be grateful for all of the big hearts on this island. I can't imagine another place where there were more beds offered than there were guests. All our friends were with us to celebrate what I will always think of as Larry's 'celebration of life'. It was soo much better to celebrate it with Larry than without.

Piers is special. It is a rural community of neighbours, nothing like living in the suburbs. It clears the mind, gives you opportunities to truly enjoy solitude in nature, and recharges your batteries. My best memories are all of our friends. And through 'tech talks', where I was able to help with computer issues, we made many friends.

Larry Day and Gisele Dallaire

Lot 123 - Steve Cruise and Pauline Olesen

Fate, Kismet, Zen

We found our Piers Island paradise in the fall of 1989. Steve had been introduced to Piers several years earlier when investigating a claim with an organ being transported by helicopter to Piers. The organ had landed on the beach instead and smashed. That was when he met long-time resident Earla Fitzgerald at Lot 27.

Several years passed and we were looking for an island cottage close to Sidney. We came to Piers in a little zodiac and wandered the beach. 'Zala Zoo' (Lot 99), as it was called, was for sale. We put in an offer, which was rejected. We came back to look at Piers again and wandered the shore. It was a bit of a grey November day and then the sun shone a ray on Lot 123. It was a sweet little Japanese style cottage that captured our hearts. Alas, it was not for sale. After searching and talking, we finally convinced Scott and Penny Denoon, who owned the property, that they would not regret selling to us. On June 30, 1990, it became ours. After selling, the Denoons missed Piers and soon afterwards bought a place a few doors down, with a shared dock, which was what they had been wishing for. We are so thankful that they entrusted us with this beautiful spot and Scott still tells us how much he loves what we've done to the place.

After tiring of "sad Sundays" returning back home, we added to our cabin to make it a full-time home. We added a pod, so we could keep the Japanese flair. Years later we found plans in the rafters from the original owner, for the same style we chose. Fate, kismet, zen, whatever...we love our island home.

Pauline Olesen and Steve Cruise

Lot 139 - Philippa White and Steve Barnes

The ad in the Times Colonist said "2.5 acres, five minutes from Swartz Bay." I'd been looking far and wide for a place to live where I could share land with my two horses. I was working in Sidney, which is five minutes from Swartz Bay, so I called the number. The ad didn't actually say the acreage was on an island.

My realtor was away, so I spoke to the listing agent who told me to go and stand on the dock at Barnacle Road and someone would surely give me a ride. She also asked me to pick up her shoes that she had left leaning against a tree two weeks earlier. That sounded a bit far-fetched.

I arrived at the dock in time to witness the startling departure of a small aluminum skiff that shot vertically into the air before levelling off and rocketing towards the island. Having never been around the ocean or near boats, I thought that's how all boats were supposed to be driven. I later learned it was only 'those Armstrongs' that drove like that.

After awhile, Andy Eastham (Lot 82) came along and gave me a ride over and even offered to give me a lift back after I'd had a look around. Turned out it was his Mom, Carol Popp, who was selling the property at Lot 139. It was July 15, 1993 and a beautiful sunny evening. There were goldfinches flying around the meadow, the sun was setting, and the grass was so tall it was over my head. I found the shoes that were still leaning up against a tree. There was city water to the property, which is a rare thing for rural properties and a big plus for someone with horses. On the property there was flat open space, grass for the horses and my intuition said "yes!" even though I'd never driven a boat before and can't swim. I made an offer the next day and took possession August 1st. I moved over to Piers on August 15th with two horses, a blue heeler dog, and a load of hay. Steve moved in a couple of years later and a couple of years after that we started the market garden.

Gee, I'm supposed to write about highlights of our time on Piers Island. I couldn't even begin to say what they are, other than life is good here, and Steve and I feel very fortunate. We don't all have to be best friends, but we can all be good neighbours and that's what we strive for. Even when we don't get along, it's usually because we all care deeply about the island and are passionate about what happens to it.

We come together during storms, boat sinkings, power outages, snowstorms, heat waves, floods, births, deaths, tsunami warnings, fires, accidents, weddings, dances, and picnics. We share and are generous with our time to keep our community supported and our infrastructure running smoothly. All this just five minutes from Swartz Bay.

Philippa White and Steve Barnes

2000 - 2010
THINGS ARE ABUZZ!

A lot was happening as the population of the island remained constant with around 100 full-time residents. At the turn of the century there was worldwide concern about Y2K (a short term for 'the year 2000') about widespread computer programming problems that would cause much havoc around the world, precisely as the year changed from 1999-2000. On New Years Eve 2000, a lot of islanders came to Piers, because many considered it to be the safest place in the world. One part-time family came all the way from Portugal.

In the early 2000s, people mostly walked and biked around the island, but interest was beginning for golf carts, especially when a local golf course sold many carts to Piers islanders. In 2003, Frances and Gary Glover (Lot 77) organized the island's first Canada Day parade with five decorated carts and a few spectators along the route. Over the years, more golf carts joined in, with Philippa White (Lot 135) and her horse leading the way, followed by kids on bicycles, dogs, wagons, a motorized wheelchair, and the fire truck loaded with firefighters and children. The number of spectators grew and, at the end of each year's parade everyone gathered at the firehall for the singing of O Canada, with a barbecue and a Canada Day strawberry cake.

The yearly art show had turned into a summer 'Walkabout' around the ring road. Many islanders (including creative children) put up tables and displayed and sold their crafts. There was lots of food, including baking and refreshments. Guy Plante (Lot 81) made amazing quiches and sorbets that always sold out. A monthly Red Hat 'meeting' started for all the women on Piers, and the men quickly followed with a monthly 'Black Hat' group.

Canada Day Parade led by Philippa White

The Piers Fire Department (PIVFD) was going strong with a number of islanders taking on the role of fire chief: Steve Barnes (2000-2006), Bob Snelling (2006-2009), and Brian Wheeler (2009-2014). There continued to be an active team of trained first responders for medical emergencies. The two managing groups on Piers, the Piers Island Improvement District and the Piers Island Association continued to be the backbone of Piers with yearly AGMs held during the June/July long weekend. An emergency group (preparing islanders for storms, earthquakes and other disasters) was formed, coordinated for years by Frances Glover (Lot 77).

On a daily basis, the Piers spirit remained high and islanders continued to volunteer on various day-to-day activities to help their fellow neighbours and the community.

Lots 35, 37 - Jim and Debra Hills

Piers Changed Our Lives

When we purchased Mrs. Morrison's cottage (Lot 35), she stipulated she would only sell it to us if all of the funds could be donated to a non-profit orphanage in Haiti and she got the BC Government to allow her to use all the funds from the sale to go towards that cause.

We also made a promise to Mrs. Morrison, that she could return and stay at the cottage at any time. Since we had two other houses on Lot 37, we could easily agree to that. I think that promise helped her in the decision to sell her Piers cottage. The best part of that story is that when we sold Lot 35 to Grant Warrington, he made a similar promise to us that that we could use the cottage any time, and he continues to remind us of that promise.

Mrs. Morrison was a religious woman and Deb and I would visit her in her home in Victoria, often on Sunday afternoons, just down the street from Emily Carr's home. We listened to her stories about Piers and Victoria during the early years, munching on chocolate cookies and sipping tea.

We bought Lot 35, at Schmidt Point, from Mrs. Morrison. It was her opinion that it was the best lot on Piers, which is why she and her husband made the purchase in the 1960s. My wife Debra and I felt the same about Mrs. Morrison's cottage and found selling this property one of the more difficult events in our married life. During 15 years, we owned two properties on Piers (Lots 35 and 37 next to one another), where our four grandchildren and their parents came to visit every summer.

Living on Piers for only a few weeks each summer changed their lives, and ours, and it is still a major topic of conversation when we all get together for the holidays. Each of our grandchildren still have dreams of Piers: the forest trails; the glowing sunsets at dusk; taking their log raft from Mrs. Morrison's beach across to Clive Island; night games in the meadow; Pauline's 'secret garden;' the 'walkabout' and selling crafts; and so much more. They all want a 'Piers experience' for their kids today, and they relive those summer memories each night and at family discussions wherever they may be.

Debra and Jim Hills

Lot 50 - Burke, Kacey and Quinn Stancill

Shipwrecked On Piers Island

We've come to feel that we didn't choose Piers Island, but that Piers Island chose us. We'd like to tell you why.

Our connection to Piers started in 2009 when we met the Thornton family (Steve, Tina, Grace and Billy) at the anchorage in Manzanillo, Mexico after we helped a young man in medical distress in a remote spot a few miles away. We transported him to a hospital for surgery, after which Burke met the Thorntons while looking for a dingy ride back out to the anchorage. That chance encounter led very directly to Piers, where we've been ever since. It all feels a bit like destiny.

The boat we were sailing was *Isis*, a modest but rough little 36-footer, that we sailed along the Pacific coast of Mexico, to Hawaii, to Hot Springs Cove on the B.C. West Coast, then to Piers where we moored her in front of Steve and Tina's place (Lot 32). Perhaps this is obvious, but after two years with the family aboard, with two three-week passages, countless beautiful beaches and sunsets, and the best of memories - not to mention months in Mexican boatyards working on her - *Isis* had become a family member. Our hearts and souls were in that old boat.

About 18 months after we arrived, in March 2012, we took a road trip back to Tofino and Hot Springs Cove to re-visit the place where we first landed in Canada. We saw the spot where, with countless other boaters, we carved our boat's name in the boardwalk. We talked about our plans to sail her up and around Vancouver Island the following summer.

As luck would have it, that trip never came to pass. Instead, we woke up the next morning to classic west coast storm winds - and a series of disturbing phone messages from our Piers neighbours. "You need to call. Something has happened to *Isis*. You need to get home."

By the time we had coffee, we learned that our beautiful boat had broken from her mooring and was sinking - or had sunk - right next to Primrose's dock (Lot 38). The winds in Swartz Bay blew to full gale/near-hurricane force for several hours, causing the mooring lines to fail, and pinning *Isis* by her rigging against the dock pilings, stoving in her tough old hull, and putting her on the bottom. A worst case scenario.

The five-hour drive home was awful. What were we going to do? Could we save her? Half our belongings were still on board, including most of our tools, outdoor gear, the logbook, clothing, bedding and the keepsakes and trinkets one accumulates voyaging.

What we found when we came across Swartz Bay to Piers was stunning. The wreckage was heartbreaking. Our once beautiful boat was crushed under the power of the waves. But there was much more. There was a fire-line of neighbours salvaging our belongings. Steve Thornton had his tug and barge hooked up, and was painstakingly extracting the boat from the side of the Primrose's dock, doing an amazing job salvaging what could be saved. Alan and Uta, the Warriors, Mike Smart, and Lorne and Barbara were all there working hard in rotten conditions for us.

With the help of the village (especially Steve), we were able that night and the next morning to put *Isis* on the beach and patch the massive hole with door skin and roofing tar, eventually floating her off and moving her across to Vancouver Island to be hauled away and scrapped.

We spent the next few weeks drying out what we could, cleaning up the mess, and working through the options. We were pretty devastated.

A few days after the wreck, Miles and Fran Primrose contacted us to say that they didn't want us to pay to repair the substantial damage to their dock. Considering that our insurance company was helpfully denying what we thought was our liability coverage, this is among the most generous things anyone, family or friend, ever did for us. Other neighbours brought us food and helped in so many ways with the aftermath. The silver linings were hard to ignore.

The demise of Isis was one of the worst things that had ever happened to us, but it also reinforced what we had started to realize - that we had found our 'forever home.' As newcomers, as immigrants, this was a big deal. There were people on Piers who cared for us, and would help us and work with us through the worst of times. We will never forget that.

Mary Tucker and Quinn Stancill

Kacey and Burke Stancill

Lot 57 - Brian and Kerry Wheeler

The Event That Changed Our Lives

In 2005, Brian and I were at a transition point in our lives. Our children had left home to travel and attend school. Brian and I were both working full-time and cruising on our powerboat on weekends and holidays. It seemed time to sell the big family home and make a change. We were mulling over lots of possibilities for our next place. Should we live on a boat, buy a townhouse or condo, or rent for awhile? Then we received a call from Gloria Morson (Lot 113) that changed our lives. She told us that two houses were for sale on Piers Island. We contacted realtor Patti L-L, made a quick trip to the island and quickly negotiated a deal.

Our first clue about how life was going to be different was deciding on a moving date. We suggested the beginning of September. Patti whipped out her tide book and pointed out that because of the tide requirements for the barge, we'd be looking at moving in the middle of the night. We decided the following week would be just fine.

Other changes we encountered that first year were boating in the dark, stormy, rainy nights and the pea-soup fog. I also had to learn how to dock a small boat in all kinds of weather. Luckily we have a strong aluminum boat built by Mike Smart (Lot 6), so my clumsy attempts at docking didn't result in any damage.

Other differences between our old city life and life on Piers was how dark at night we found it, at first. Coming home from the government dock or a neighbour's house at night could result in getting lost, as there are no street-lights. Mike Smart helpfully suggested looking up when walking at night. As long as you can see the sky, you likely will avoid wandering into the forest. We also had to get used to no morning paper and being organized with grocery shopping, since running to the store wasn't as easy as in the city.

The benefits of living here soon became obvious. Our neighbours were all friendly and said "Hello" or stopped to chat when we were out. We quickly discovered it could take a long time to walk around the island, since we would stop to chat and catch up on the news. Our commutes to work and seeing the sun rise and set were often spectacular. We took up kayaking, prawning and crabbing. We discovered that it was easy to get involved in island life. We joined the fire department, attended work parties, played music with the 'Scotch-drinking and chocolate-eating ukulele group' and went to the many organized social events throughout the year.

We have a grandson now and are enjoying introducing him to island life. He loves to come here and play on the beach, throw rocks in the water, hike through the woods, look at the horses, eat blackberries by the roadside, jump in puddles and kick a soccer ball down the road.

I am so glad Gloria called us that evening, and caused us to make the life-changing decision to move to Piers.

Karen and Brian Wheeler

Lot 59 - The Freedmans

The Magic Of Piers

(written by Bill Freedman)

In the fall of 2001, the Freedman brothers decided it would be a good idea to find a place where our families could build traditions, memories and experiences. Having grown up in New York and spent many summers along the eastern coast from Maine to North Carolina, a coastal experience seemed like the perfect objective. Bill, Charlie and Jonathan's father, Eugene's best friend Richard Donner of Hollywood fame, had an incredible estate in Maui and also on Orcas Island in Washington State. He often said that between the two, Orcas was his favourite. This was when Bill started his search for a property throughout the Pacific Northwest. After speaking with several real estate professionals who listened to his dreams for their family getaway, one suggested he contact Patti L-L and consider Piers Island.

On a brisk but clear day in November, Bill took a camera and caught the ferry from Anacortes, Washington to Sidney, B.C. This is when the love affair with Piers Island began. He believed he had made a good decision by purchasing Lot 59, but that was cemented on 'move-in day,' the first weekend in February 2002. We showed up with a group of about 10 friends and a moving truck, and began an on and off tradition we call 'PISBAW' or Piers Island Annual Superbowl Weekend. All went smoothly until the last item we had to move, which was a large hot tub. We had assumed 10 guys would be able to figure out how to get it down the slope to the house, around the side, and then elevate it to the deck. This task, however, was too much of a mental and physical challenge for four highly educated lawyers, an actor, an administrator of a large healthcare facility, and four retail entrepreneurs. Enter stage left - Gerry Kristianson, our neighbour at Lot 67. Gerry somehow sensed our struggle from three doors and dense forest away and showed up just at the right time with tools, rope and most of all, the brain of a self-taught mechanical engineer. Within a short time, Gerry had rigged a system of come-a-longs and pulleys that allowed us to lower the tub down the hill. He also came up with the plan to remove the deck rail, which allowed us to hoist the hot tub safely on the deck. When it was time for the Superbowl, Gerry then appeared with a freshly cooked pot of crab that we could hardly believe came from the end of his dock.

Since that time, Piers has continued to reveal her magic. It lies in its raw and bountiful coast, wild interior, and to a group of independent, accomplished humans who know how to persevere and accomplish a task like few groups I have ever known in my life. We have only had the privilege to know a fraction of the island very personally, but those people have become family to us. In particular, they include the Thompsons (Lot 61), Bransons (Lot 63) and Kristiansons (Lot 67), as well as Frank Williams (Lot 13), who only drove the tractor better after a few glasses of his homemade ale. Piers has been an education in appreciation for God's creative genius. While most dream of the experience to taste the ocean at a base level, navigate through fog to find literal clarity on the other side, and bathe in both sharp raindrops and magical sunlight, Piers delivers on that dream and a lot more.

The Freedman family

Lots 63, 81 - Frank Simpson and Guy Plante

We moved to Piers in March 2000 as renters. For the first five years on Piers, we lived at Lot 81. For a long time we were known as "the guys who lived in the Hoytes' house." George and Mrs. Hoyte were the former and original owners of Lot 81.

As with all Piers Islanders, we were finally accepted and became part of the Piers community. We got our dog Cosmo in 2011 and he has also been part of the community too; sadly Cosmo left us just a few months ago.

In 2017, Frank left a pot of fat on the stove, and burned part of the inside of the house at Lot 81. We were especially fortunate to have the backing of Piers islanders, especially Don and Anne Branson (Lot 63), who graciously let us rent their cottage. Five years later, we are still here. We had hoped to buy the house eventually, and our dream to become full-time owners rather than full-time renters finally came true in January 2022, when we bought the house at Lot 63.

We both recently went through some health issues. Islanders were there again for us.

Over the years, Guy catered birthday parties and made quiches and cakes for the community, especially during the Walkabout. He did a lot of baking for birthday parties. A few years ago, Guy taught Argentinian dance classes with Sandy Brunham and a number of other islanders. Guy loves the Ukelele group, where he plays his guitar.

Frank has enjoyed his role of Santa for the past three years. He says his favourite part is making the children happy.

Guy Plante, Cosmo and 'Santa' Frank Simpson

Lot 76 - Brad and Marion Miller

Feeling Blessed On Piers

Our Piers story began in the summer of 2008, when we were trying to find property with a dock on one of the Gulf Islands. We wanted a place where we could tie up our boat and enjoy the beautiful surroundings. We were looking on Salt Spring Island and stumbled across an article about Piers Island. We contacted realtor, Patti L-L, to see if we could look at some places on the island. Since it was Canada Day, she cautioned us that we would have to stop and watch the parade partway through. Sure enough, partway through the day, the traditional Piers Island Canada Day parade rolled through. A couple of horses, some golf carts, kids on bikes and a bunch of other enthusiastic participants. We were hooked before we even put an offer in.

After we bought our place at Lot 76 and hauled our belongings up all 80 steps, we got in a rhythm of regularly visiting our 'island paradise' and getting to know other islanders. As awesome as Piers Island is, we feel the islanders in the community are equally as awesome. The countless hours people spend volunteering as directors, first responders, and helping with endless community projects is truly inspiring. Even more amazing is the fact that if we ever need a hand with something, our Piers neighbours step up without hesitation or any expectation of anything in return.

From the summer picnic, to the Moonlight Madness dance, to the Christmas auction where we bought half a dozen teddy bears lovingly crafted by Mary Jordan (Lot 95), we realized that Piers was a unique place with wonderful, generous residents. We stopped saying "cheers" and started saying "Piers" when we toasted the endless amazing sunsets or watched a ferry ghosting by in the fog. Our three children and their spouses, and now our three grandchildren, all have a strong bond with the island as well.

As all Piersians know, quirky things can happen when living on an island. Some experiences that stand out for us are when our contractor decided it would be 'efficient' to push our old hot tub over the bank, resulting in a Styrofoam explosion and a big mess. Of course, there was the request for a Naloxone kit from the Coast Guard for an overdosed boater drifting by Arbutus Island. Charging out through the kelp bed in *Spirit Bear* after dark with our Piers first responders, is something we will never forget. In 2020, Mother Nature provided a great learning opportunity about dock repair and submersible floatation, after dismantling ours in spectacular fashion.

Despite a few minor challenges, we truly feel grateful and blessed to have Piers as part of our lives.

Brad and Marion Miller

Lot 135 - Jackie and Henry Charlesworth

What Lures Me To Green And Blue Space

I was always a wanderer. While my parents and brothers were sleeping, at the age of four I would get up, dress and go out to the North Saskatchewan River, which had cut a deep valley as it travelled through Edmonton.

Along the valley banks of the river, there were vegetable gardens, mainly tended by Chinese gardeners who lived there. At the time, my home was about two city blocks from the brow of the valley. It was normal for me to wend my way down to the shared paths along the river. I loved the peace and imagined myself as coming from another era, as if I had lived years before, as if I understood the paths and their history. There were little rivulets of water draining out of the banks and I drank that iron-tasting water, while eating stolen peas from the gardens. When you imagine that time, it is surprising that I never met anyone, never felt at risk. I would eventually wander back home about 10 a.m., having left around 6 a.m., rarely having been missed.

Two years later, we moved to a cheaper place. My mother, being a war widow, was eligible for accommodation in abandoned army camps left by the U.S. army. These were essentially out in the country. There was a two-room schoolhouse with three grades to a classroom. There was a swamp-like area, where we would wander on a raft and collect tadpoles and frogs. In the winter, there was a small stable and one of the students rode a farm horse, and if we were lucky enough to meet up with her, we would clamber up on the horse's back. The bushy pathway to the school went through fields. There was a root cellar full of preserves and vegetables, and an old man who protected it from us. Living in the country, although part of the city, was special again, confirming to me my love of quiet and, to a certain extent, isolation.

Many years passed. At age 20, I took a year off university and wandered all over Europe. I married and, with my husband Henry, we travelled and lived in many countries. It was a great life. His parents lived in a country village in Northern Ireland and we summered there often. Being in places where the population was small suited me. Often we would be in cities, but always coming back to a countryside place felt like home.

Years pass and it is the late 1990s. My husband is retired, but I am still working, a big-city girl in a big-city job. Suddenly, our son and his wife who lived in Victoria, had the terrible tragedy of having their first baby die just hours before being born. My oldest friend, Lynne Neufeld, came with me a week later when there was a family gathering of sorrow and consolation. While in Victoria, a Piers Islander, Lydia Chang (Lot 91), who was aunt to my daughter-in-law, said there was a house for sale on Piers. Lynne, who was always interested in real estate, said she would like to see the house.

On Monday, we all gathered at Dolphin Road (Barnacle Road dock) and, having missed the shuttle, someone offered us a lift across. The realtor, Patti L-L, met us and we walked slowly around the island. It was a magical, warm, blue-sky day. We passed a property with a sign posted outside that said, "Cinnamon buns. Put your money in the box." Another sign said "Here is your necklace." Such a feeling of trust and peace permeated the walk and I thought I never wanted to leave. We all looked at several houses for sale and finally we reached the house that was owned by people called 'Thomas.' (Lot 84). We climbed up the steep bank. The house had windows, which from the porch, looked across the living room to more windows and then uninterrupted to the sea. Again, magical…

Lynne bought this house on Thursday. She and her husband, Gordon, could not immediately move in, but eventually, my friend and I would spend many long weekends at the house together. Finally, my husband Henry and I moved into their house for three months during the winter. I loved sitting at the kitchen's open French doors, hearing the lapping waves and seeing the stars at night. It was such a contrast to our Edmonton home where we lived off and on (always renting it out when we lived in other countries) and loved well enough. However, I did not miss the loud hollow sound of the winter protecting doors of our house in Edmonton. I wanted to be able to sit near the fresh air, day or night, to be able to see the stars and hear the wind and the waves, and be at peace with the world.

So, we began to look for a place on Piers. Henry and I both enjoyed gardening. Our lot at 135 was owned by a single woman, Margo, who worked as a nurse and who had lived on the island for nearly 12 years. She had a 'calling' to nurse in Northern Saskatchewan, so she put her house up for sale. The small place where Margot lived was essentially a converted shack, with electricity but no plumbing. It had a lovely little deck with views of the pond and the wetlands, which seemed to make up a lot of the property. We hired a hydrologist to inspect and to advise us if the land could be safely drained and built upon. We had to search for a proper place for a septic field. Then the negotiation of price. Finally, it was agreed.

One day in a bin of old software, I came across an architectural CD. With this in hand, my husband designed the house we had built. The garden plot at the side of the house was built up from the surrounding soil. After moving in, we walked the length and breadth of our land, picking up stones to make the rock walls around the house and along the far side of the land next to the public meadow and orchard.

The raised area for our vegetable garden, measuring about 30 feet by 30 feet with arable sloping sides, was well cultivated and we grew much produce for the first five years. Much of that work was done by my husband, while I developed flower, bush and shrub gardens of annual and perennial varieties.

The land we owned is essentially two acres, part of a six-acre lot, divided roughly into three pie-shaped lots. We fenced a portion of it to protect our gardening efforts from the deer and left a fairly large section of it treed and wild. We cultivated only so much of the area. My husband died five years after arriving on the island. It amused my children and me that people would ask whether or not I would stay on. What a question - leaving was the furthest thing from my mind.

The land came with old apple trees that were planted along a pathway going into the forest. We hired a specialist to prune and bring the trees back into production, and over the years the yield of apples has been so abundant that we are now able to hold a yearly 'apple press day', inviting the entire Piers Island population. With all of their help, the resulting harvest yield is usually up to 1,000 litres of juice.

I feel the apple trees are a trust, and recent tree cutting and clearing on Piers has made me feel that I shall have to do something to protect the trees from wanton destruction if the property moves out of the hands of my family. I also had an area cleared out, revealing quite a large piece of arable land. Suddenly, we were immersed in the COVID pandemic and concerns for fresh vegetable supply caused a group of people to approach me, to ask if the freshly revealed area could be used as a community garden. There are already many people on the island who are skilled gardeners, in particular, Phillipa who is part of the six-acre parcel and who has a small market garden and chickens, horses, and ducks. I decided to employ Philippa as a 'giver of advice' and a supplier of bedding plants. Seventeen families worked very, very hard, hand-digging and cleaning, and riddling the soil. My land, as is much of Piers Island, was the result of glaciers receding and leaving masses of glacial till; hence every fork-load of dirt dug had big rocks and small stones to be cleared away. A rototiller would not have worked. Such a triumph, and the adage, 'Many hands make light work,' was made truth.

At the same time, there were many young children supposedly starting or continuing school, but with COVID restrictions it seemed sensible to start up an island school. One of their extra curricular activities was to learn to garden. So, on my property, three raised beds were started with triangle, square and hexagonal shapes and put together to form a children's garden. They learned how to break down hard, stony ground into productive land. After two years now, their hard work is paying off with peas and potatoes and radishes as the result. The children are eager to water and to support the fledging peas and a sort of 'joie de vivre' in the group happens.

The recent addition to the garden, started by two other islanders, is the arrival of two beehives, which can be seen at the apex of my pie shaped property. The schoolchildren came to learn about them and I loved one child's comment: "Honey is bee vomit."

Recently, in other parts of the province, there have been discoveries of unmarked graves of indigenous children. This makes us so aware that we are recent settlers on the land. I am glad that I can share its bounty with those who live here. It is so good to see the land being used for good purposes.

I have seven granddaughters; eight including the child who did not make it into this world alive. Everyone of them love the island. Many of them spent summers here from the time they were newborns and now in adulthood, they dream of summers on Piers with their own offspring. My adult children will inherit the house and land someday and I know they will honour the land and the joy.

Jackie and friends at the annual apple pressing

Henry Charlesworth

Jackie Charlesworth

2010 - 2020
LOTS OF CHANGES

The biggest change on Piers in this decade has been the wonderful influx of younger families to the island. This has made for a diverse population who are enjoying life together and learning from each other. People saw what they could afford in the big cities versus a more peaceful nature-loving lifestyle on a small island community and chose Piers.

The full-time population of the island has now swelled to more than 125 residents, with over 20 of them children. In fact, between 2014 and 2021, there have been eight babies born to full-time islanders. The advent of more home-based businesses has also made a big difference, with a lot of people being able to earn a living from their island home, although some still commute to work off-island. Many others are retired.

The major event this decade has been the building of the new water tower. The need for its replacement had been discussed for decades, and with monies collected by the Piers Island Improvement District (PIID) from owners' fees over the years, the tower was finally completed in January 2021. There were dozens of volunteers involved in this endeavour especially Maureen and Bob Crooks, Charlie and Nancy Troger, Ander Wynne-Edwards, Steve Thorton, Colin Robertson, Julien Bahain, Monique Joubarne, Brent Irvine, all the water operators and many, many others.

We have always had informal musical get-togethers between talented neighbours. For the past few years, Piers has had a weekly Monday night 'Ukelele playing, Scotch drinking, Chocolate Eating Group.' In addition to the endless artistic talent on Piers, since 2016, we now have a co-op style art gallery called PIG (Piers Island Gallery) featuring the creations of over 20 island artists. Pot-luck dinners thrive for all occasions from neighbours' get-togethers, special birthdays, and Red Hat/Black Hat gatherings.

In 2017, our community was the scene of a film production called 'All-In-Madonna,' which was co-ordinated by Libby and Tony Kahl (Lot 36) with son Octavian in the training roles of filming and editing. There were dozens of Piers volunteers during the crew's days on Piers - loaning their homes as film sets, transporting film crew back and forth to Piers, hosting crew in their cottages, preparing and serving meals, and islanders acting as extras, collecting props, and many other activities. According to Libby, "The crew voiced what a unique place it is and how friendly and kind the residents are. The director Arnold Lim said that Piers Island really MADE this film."

There have been a few events that have come and gone, including the popular Octoberfests and Winefests (held in the old firehall). Jacquie Troger (Lot 78) organized Piers University (PU) featuring our very own island presenters on such subjects as training gorillas by former zoo keeper Garth Irvine (Lot 20); SARS researcher Bob Brunham (Lot 64); Olympic rower Julien Bahain (Lot 83); and beer expert Jake Clark (Lot 97), to name a diverse few. The Piers library sponsored one session of 'Piers Reads' (named after the popular CBC Canada Reads) with books that portray the importance of community, a terrific topic for Piers. Hopefully, some of these wonderful community events will be resurrected again.

Some things have hardly changed. The summer picnic/race and Moonlight Madness dance have both been enthusiastically happening for over 50 years now. Other long-time events are the Pancake Breakfast in September (a fundraiser for the fire department) and the annual community Christmas dinner. This event now includes an amazing fund-raising auction of island-handmade Christmas wreaths and table settings. Each year this auction generates thousands of dollars that islanders donate to the Sidney Food Bank and other local charities. The Walkabout for artists of all ages has, on occasion, included an informal beer garden. The Canada Day festivities continue with the addition of a 10-20 kilometer race, where islanders run, jog or walk several times around the island. Islanders Chris Schran and Mona Rosenberg (Lot 86) took over private ownership of the Piers shuttle.

Volunteering is still a major backbone to our island. The dedicated Piers volunteer firefighters have been fortunate to have Steve Cruise (Lot 123) as their hard-working Fire Chief for eight years now, since 2014. Steve's wife, Pauline Olesen, has coordinated the community's FireSmart program since 2016. There is a valuable team of 12-14 trained medical volunteer first responders thanks to Gerry Kristianson and Sandy Brunham. The PIID (Piers Island Improvement System) the PIA (Piers Island Association) are still going strong with their dedicated volunteer members.

A tireless weekly Monday morning work group deals with general maintenance such as clearing downed trees and dozens of other jobs on Piers common grounds. A group looks after the public orchard and a group of forest caretakers looks after trees in the centre of the island. The emergency group keeps us prepared for emergencies and the trained water committee continues to make sure we have safe drinking water. The Piers library, located in a section of the firehall training room, has a library committee that organizes hundreds of books. In 2019 Biscoe beach had an upgrade of a new shelter and tables, all done by a Piers Island group of volunteers, of course.

New water tower

New Biscoe Beach shelter

Lot 2 - Tracey Landerkin and Ian Moskaluk

Cheers To Piers!

One of the first questions that is asked of new islanders is, "How did you hear about Piers Island?"

Ian and I were looking for a retirement home, preferably on the ocean. Oceanfront properties on the big Island were quite expensive and Piers Island came up in our search, given the Sidney postal code. We found a realtor and arranged a day to explore. As soon as the water taxi pulled up, we were in love! We had a grand tour of the island with Frank Simpson and met lots of friendly people along the way. Needless to say, we bought our retirement home.

Piers Island is made up of many unique individuals. However, together we make a wonderful community. This is a community of volunteers: the fire department, first responders, Monday morning work crew, invasive plant management, and looking after the roadway, to name a few.

As a community, we help each other. This is not always found in today's society. However, Piers Island is quite special. From offering to carry items up the government dock ramp when you have a free hand, or picking up some groceries for a neighbour who can't get out that day. These 'little' gestures happen all the time on Piers Island and this is what brings a smile to our faces. Cheers to Piers!

Tracey Landerkin and Ian Moskaluk

Lot 20 - Garth Irvine and Brent Schorr

West Coast Island Living

We discovered Piers Island through a search on the internet from Calgary in 2013, using 'waterfront' in the search criteria. We looked Piers up on the map and soon learned that we had passed all around this small island several times on BC Ferries, wondering who were the lucky people that lived on that island?

We moved all our belongings to our island in April 2014, on a rainy day. We are two born-and-bred prairie boys who suddenly learned the importance of tide tables in scheduling a barge and moving truck to get all of our possessions across Colburne Passage. We also were indebted to our friends who helped us move everything from McKenzie Crescent, in the rain and the slippery mud, down two hundred meters to our new home, Lot 20. Then, dealing with all the stuff that was left behind by the previous owner, we all moved back up to the moving truck for the return trip to Vancouver Island. Since moving to the island, we have had boatloads of visitors, most wondering if we had lost our minds moving from the prairies to a small island on the west coast.

Especially because we came from Calgary, with its long cold winters, Victoria was the most exotic place for us to move to in Canada. So, we take advantage of the beautiful year-round weather by always wearing shorts. We have shorts for every occasion and have unintentionally earned a reputation for our year-round attire. Islanders recognize us coming from the distance on our ring road walking our dog, Rundle, because of our exposed knees year-round.

Garth almost immediately was recruited to join the Piers Island Volunteer Fire Department and continues to volunteer today. He is also one of the volunteers that issues fire permits. In 2016, I assumed the role of Piers Island Improvement District Financial Administrator and soon became known not only for my wardrobe choice, but also for all island invoices and annual water bills and taxes. Suddenly everyone knew our home because it has one of the only mailboxes on our island that is posted at the entrance to our property; it is used to conduct all island business with our neighbours. This past year, I took over the project management and island interface role in the construction of our new water tower.

I got involved with the Victoria Master Gardeners Association and was recruited by the Piers Island Volunteer Fire Department to volunteer in our Fire Smart program, specifically regarding our wild-land urban interface and yard and landscaping. This included becoming an island zone leader and giving a few presentations and other island activities all aimed at keeping our island safe. Word travelled and I have since participated in Fire Smart presentations on Vancouver Island and the Gulf Islands and worked with the BC Government to produce a provincial Fire Smart guide.

Friends from Vancouver Island, the same ones who helped us move, advised us to change from wine bottles to boxes now that we live on an island, for ease of transportation and recycling on and off the island. We soon found that we were not the only Piers Islanders that poured from the box. We hosted an island wine tasting by the box, Card Bordeaux, paired with food. We had all attendees rate the wines and we sent out our island's first wine ratings and review for our neighbours to consult.

Garth also served four years on the Piers Island Association, including a term as vice-president and president. Among the many things he accomplished were documenting and organizing policies, procedures and work parties regarding our island's constant struggle with invasive species, including broom and gorse. He also organized one of our largest family day picnics, including food and games.

Garth worked at the Calgary Zoo for 25 years and was one of the first people asked to present at the 'Piers University' (PU) held at our firehall. He talked about his fascinating experiences with the great ape, both as a Gorilla keeper at the zoo and his many interactions with them in the wild. We have also led two trips to Africa to see the majestic gorillas since arriving on Piers. On both trips, other islanders joined us.

We hosted the annual Piers Island Polar Bear dip for a few years. The first time attracted more spectators than brave dippers. Nonetheless, we had over 50 people make the plunge on New Year's Day, ranging in age from the eights to eighties.

Rundle, our Bernese Mountain Dog-Lab cross, moved with us from the prairies, but immediately adapted to the west coast which provided two of his favourite things - endless sticks and water to play in and swim. He loves kayaking and boating, and is rarely allowed to be left behind. He helped organize Sunday morning off-leash play sessions for all island dogs, especially all the new puppies that arrived during the pandemic. We invited island experts to share training and obedience tips, and provided a place to share and learn from each other's dogs and experiences.

Until 2020 our island was rat free. Garth worked with Keegan Meyers (Lot 11) over the past year to control our new rat population. This involved education of islanders and daily checking of traps. The battle continues. Garth joined the volunteer water team this year. He is currently being trained on management of our water supply.

Since we retired to the island, Garth has had more time to enjoy two of his favourite hobbies, photography and stained glass. His art has been exhibited in our island gallery, Piers Island Gallery, or PIG, as well as a gallery in Sidney. He has also taught stained glass classes on the island, and last year was the judge for the island wildlife photo contest sponsored by the Piers Island Association.

We look forward to celebrating our 30th anniversary on Piers in 2022.

Brent Schorr and Garth Irvine

Lot 25 - Phil and Ginny Macoun

Finding Piers Island

We didn't find Piers Island. It found us. Ginny and I were living in Vancouver, where we had both worked. I had the opportunity to relocate to the company's Victoria Office, so we started looking for something to buy which meant frequent ferry trips to Vancouver Island to look at properties.

On one such trip, probably on the old Queen of New Westminster ferry, we asked a crew member if they knew the name of the island that we were passing so close to the Swartz Bay terminal. That was our first introduction to Piers - looking at it from the ferry and thinking: There are lots of houses, but there is no one there.

Not long after that trip, on a Friday night, we got an alert from the real estate website that a property meeting our vague criteria had just been listed. We called our agent to see if we could view it that weekend. He called back to say we should get the 7:00 a.m. ferry from Tsawwassen and that we would get picked at the Government Dock at 10:00 a.m. That was our first inkling that this house wasn't in North Saanich, but maybe on an island.

We met the seller's agent, Patti L-L, at 10:00 a.m. the next day and had a brisk trip over to Piers (not a record - Patti can do the crossing in two minutes, we were told). I think we had mentally bought the house before we stepped inside it. It seemed idyllic. Turns out it was and is for us!

After viewing the house, we decided we should walk around the island to get a better idea of what is here. As we walked the road, we just fell more heavily in love with the island. We even were accosted by the island's gatekeeper and long-time resident Mary Tucker, who with a smile, firmly asked us: "Who are you?" and "What are you doing on the island?" She seemed satisfied with our answers and let us continue our walk.

The next question we had to resolve was access to and from the island. We knew nothing about boats. Easily fixed. We rented a boat from Horseshoe Bay for an hour, took it for a run into Howe Sound on a glorious, sunny, windless day and thought, "How hard can it be? Let's do it."

We had a contract on the house by Monday night, 72 hours after the house hit the market. We haven't regretted it for a minute. We have had sojourns away for work, but have loved coming back to Piers, loved getting to know the people who live here, made firm friends, and shared our house with friends and family from all over the world.

Piers Island has become a sanctuary and a base for our daughter and her family, who have alternated between Switzerland and Canada. They lived in our house for seven months while we were away, using the shuttle as necessary to get on and off the island. Our granddaughter shared her birthday cake and many cuddles with neighbours on the shuttle on her first birthday. Five years later, with COVID spreading rapidly in Europe, Piers provided a sanctuary to their family. They came for a month and stayed for nine. Piers coped.

Two families on the island had already made plans to home school during the pandemic. With two more arrivals from Switzerland, and with another very bright four-and-a-half year old, they had eight kids ready to learn and play together. Gerry and Diana Kristianson (Lot 67) offered 'Kate's Cottage' as a classroom, and hey presto, Piers School was up and running. Over the course of the year, the Piers School has entertained islanders with Christmas carols, Chinese New Year Dragon dances, and an end-of-the-year concert. Morning breaks were spent exploring the beach and the water's edge (and sometimes getting a bit more involved with the water than was planned). With the extraordinary teaching skills of Christina Van der Kamp, and the contributions of mothers and other islanders, the kids had lessons in science, art, library, social studies and French, as well as their regular classroom lessons. The children weren't dis-advantaged by COVID. In fact, they have thrived in the truly unique Piers community.

Phil and Ginny Macoun

We have always been glad that we asked about this island, and that it reached out to us to come and live here. It has provided a home and a sanctuary for us, our children, and now our grandchildren.

Macoun and Ungstad family

Lot 35 - Grant Warrington

Dear Piers,

I've been coming to see you for two decades now, and for the past eight years I have been blessed to be part owner of a stunning property and little cabin that looks east, to the rising of sun and moon.

Every time I set foot on your shores I feel like I've died and gone to heaven ... you are such an incredibly beautiful and convenient escape from the pressures and ever quickening pace of life on Vancouver Island, the mainland and the rest of the world.

You represent to me a community of people who say hello or wave to one another when they pass each other on foot, bicycles, and tricycles, in golf carts or watercraft.

People who, for the most part, respect each other's differences and who encourage creative responses to challenges the community faces. People who support the arts, music and local food production. People who respect and care for the land, and who volunteer for the common good.

There are times when the calm waters that surround you shimmer bright light into the soul. That light is visible in our smiles. When winter storms or hot dry conditions threaten, there is always a sense we will endure.

Grant Warrington

That even COVID could not really divide us. That neighbours care and do their best for each other. If we ever quarrel it can soon end, like turning a page without damaging the book. These things matter, now more than ever.

Thank you, Piers.

Lot 45 - Valerie Rolfe and Peter Lupini

Our Piers Experience

Popping juicy blackberries into our mouths with maroon fingers, we paid little attention to our realtor pacing the dusty road. "C'mon! We're late!" It was our first time on Piers Island, and we were already sold on the free fruit.

We'd hoped for a mouse-and-outhouse cottage like the one where I grew up on Gambier Island, but we ended up with a proper house, insulated, well-loved, and alpine-like. There was already a fenced area for our three dogs and a doghouse for Pete. The typical west coast cast of characters - mosses, lichen, salal, ferns, and firs - blanketed our property and settled our systems. One thing was clear: this place was restorative.

We bought a boat and named her *Mariah* after our indomitable Lab. Our neighbours settled in for 'The new people learning-how-to-dock show' as our cries filled the sea air with, "REVERSE!" and "ROCKS!" and that old family favourite, "STOP YELLING AT ME!" followed by, "I'M NOT YELLING!"

Once we'd lightly furnished the place with friends' cast-offs and the requisite nautical charts and laminated bird ID posters, we focused on figuring out the physical and cultural terrain, expecting it to resemble the years we lived on Bowen Island when the kids were small. Certainly, we lucked out with neighbours and the wider welcoming community, jumping into the pancake breakfasts, dances, and bonfires. What a delight to walk along the road to North Meadow Farm (Lot 139), finding friends along the way or making new ones, returning home with armfuls of greens and eggs from the Saturday market, the dogs ambling along in the dappled light.

The beauty of Piers for us is that, despite it effectively being a suburb of Sidney, the brief boat ride across the channel feels like we're miles from civilization. We vow to read on the porch but never do, happily distracted by the heron, hummingbird, raven, eagle, otter, or that scoundrel mink who cheekily preps meals in our pond. Reading happens inside with our backs to the windows.

What we love about Piers is the sanctuary of the forest, the shelly beach, PIG (Piers Island Gallery), the farm, the orchard, and the restful road, safe to travel by day or moonlight, bats feasting on bugs at dusk, deer browsing at its margins. We love sliding through the water in our kayaks, curious seals like periscopes, belted kingfishers winging from crag to pile, and friendly waves from people on porches and docks, chairs angling like sunflowers catching the day's last rays.

There's much kindness and volunteering on Piers - work parties and lending a hand, scrap plywood, transportation, local knowledge. We depend on one another for safety and services, but I also think that islanders are conspiratorially aware of the magic that is ours, and that requires nurturing and cherishing. I feel there's a collective amazement at our great good fortune, for even having found Piers Island at all. Whatever differences arise, I think we have that one thing that unites us. That, and an abundance of blackberries.

Peter Lupini, Val Rolfe and Jack

Lot 46 – Sharon Stewart

Thank You Piers!

When I found Piers in 2014, I found a little miracle. I had been living in Alberta but I grew up on Salt Spring Island, so when the opportunity arose to come back to the Coast, I jumped at the opportunity. Patti L-L introduced me to Piers. Lot 46 "spoke to me". I could see that the original owner, Bill Oldfield, had once had lovely gardens, although they were at that time totally overgrown and neglected. I looked forward to developing my own little garden oasis.

The island has a charm with its lack of streetlights, using a golf cart instead of a car, and always having a wheelbarrow handy for all the packing to and from the dock. Who needs a gym when you live on an island? Enjoying the fresh ocean air was a delight. On a hot day, you just dip your feet in the ocean with its crystal-clear water. The water was so clear near my neighbour's dock that I was able to retrieve a couple bottles of wine (months later) that had inadvertently fallen in when I was trying to get them onto the dock. Oh yes, there are those "not so lovely" waves that catch you by surprise… especially when you're a novice boater! Don't get me started about boating! But the chilled wine was a nice treat.

Happy memories also include my 'special' friends… the island critters. I feel blessed that a couple seagulls adopted me and came to visit regularly. They truly are the acrobats of the sky. One in particular would always seek my attention and would come to sit with me. That gorgeous bird became my "Buddy". When my Edmonton friends came to visit, they were in awe of my intriguing lifestyle and magnificent views.

Patti, Vicki and Sharon Stewart

Thank you Piers for happy memories.

Lot 56- Greg Miller and Abby Brooks

Piers Is Our Home

When we moved to Piers in 2013, we moved into our first purchased home. We moved, not only into a wonderful first home, but we moved into so much more.

We moved into a way of life. A lifestyle of wandering to neighbours for a quick hello and staying for a long dinner… You never know how a day will end. A lifestyle of starting out for a midday 3.14 km run and finding yourself home after three hours because of many chats and visits… Anyone from Piers knows how that is. A lifestyle where children embrace nature by feeling sand and rocks beneath their bare feet and scamper up mossy bluffs wondering where their forest adventure will lead them. A lifestyle that includes finding your hobbies right out your front door. Fishing, biking, walking, soccer, ukelele, gardening and so much more, just outside our backyard. Those are the things about Piers Island - which are absolutely amazing. But the people, the people are so much more.

Even before moving our endless boatloads of furniture and items into our new home, we were welcomed by Piers Islanders. Our family has grown over the last eight years and our Piers community is giving our children, Cade and Veda, a childhood that will carry them through life with pride and confidence. Islanders host surprise baby showers, celebrate the arrival of a second child with a brand new ukulele, drop off second-hand clothes, invite us for outdoor movies, join us on the beach for happy-hour swims, pass out high-fives, cheer the kids on when they learn to ride bikes and, of course, yes of course, accept delicious food made of leaves and sticks by our three-year-old at her roadside burger stand.

I once heard a quote about how people do not remember what others do or say; they remember how others make them feel. Our Piers Island friends make our children feel welcomed, valued, trusted and appreciated everyday and this is what will help carry them though life.

"Number 56 is our house; Piers is our home. Thanks to our wonderful friends and neighbours, Piers is our home."

Abby Brooks, Greg Miller, Veda and Cade

Lot 60 - Steve and Michelin Tait

The Simplicity Of Life On Piers

Piers Island entered our lives in the year 2013 by way of a chance elevator meeting with Howie and Barbara Eckman in our Vancouver condominium building. Michelin and I had seen this lovely couple, who at the time were in their early 80s, on previous occasions after they'd returned from their cottage (Lots 31 and 33) on Piers looking refreshed and very, well, youthful. When they told us where they'd been, we both exclaimed, "We must learn more about this hidden gem of an island." What followed next was an internet search to find out more about Piers, followed by a couple of quick visits and a rather swift purchase of our home-away-from-home. Every once in a while life deals you an 'ace' and this was clearly one of those opportunities for us.

The interior of the home we purchased had been totally redone by the previous owners, Karen and Jim Boyette, who we have never had the pleasure to meet. Their tastes aligned well with ours and the home inside was immaculately revised to an exceptionally high standard. As a result, we were able to focus our energies on the areas we loved the most, namely the garden and the yard. Along the way we've completed a number of our own improvements, including a workshop which one longtime island resident referred to as "the Pavilion", and our bunkhouse, which we call "the Spa."

But while we thought we were merely purchasing a vacation property, what we soon learned was that we'd really acquired was a whole new and welcoming community. We've become involved at various times with the Monday morning work crew, the Ukulele Group, the Victory Garden team, the rat patrol, and volunteer caretaking stewards of the hillside and giant rhododendron at the new firehall.

The friendships we've developed on Piers have been numerous, deep and genuine. Immediately prior to returning to Vancouver (our birth home) and coming to Piers, we had been expatriates for over 16 years, both in the UK (London) and Asia (Hong Kong). We'd grown used to the ex-pat life, where every two to three years people would arrive, live and contribute, and then move on to their next corporate assignment elsewhere in the world. Being an ex-pat can be a transient lifestyle and, exciting as it was, the joy that comes with stability and with friends being more than brief acquaintances, now has great appeal and personal value.

Our kids and grandkids love Piers and cherish the opportunities they have to spend summers here. Given our eldest, Ashleigh, and her family live in Calgary, and Stephanie, our youngest, and her family live in Toronto, it's no small event for them to get to Piers but they all prioritize it and to a person call our home on Piers, "Ours." It is for this reason we feel Lot 60 will remain in our family long after Michelin and I have left this natural earth.

When preparing this piece, I asked one of grandsons what he most enjoyed about Piers. His answer was simple, as he commented on the bike rides, the Uke group, the friendly people, the Saturday morning farm market line-up gathering, the chance to spend time with his grandparents and family. But, mostly he loved the simplicity of life here. On that count, we can all agree.

Steve and Michelin Tait and family

Lot 61 - Chad and Lisa Rintoul

Life Lessons And New Chapters

We moved to Piers Island in December of 2017, from Deep Cove, in North Saanich, where we had lived since we returned to Canada in 2003 following a decade working overseas (Vladivostok, Almaty, London). Having recently sold our interest in a cottage on Lake Cowichan, we wanted to be 'on the water,' and loved the tranquility and adventure that Piers offered.

Living on Piers has been a challenge for our teenage children. Nolan found out quickly that the centre of the island isn't the "mountain bike terrain park" that he had hoped. Clara decided that the "pre-historic internet service" would be inadequate. They have coped and managed to keep busy. We decided when we moved here, that living on Piers would not be an excuse to miss out on the activities that they'd always enjoyed. So, we have been regular commuters, ensuring they made every early-morning band practice, soccer or hockey practice or game, and that they never missed a shift at their part-time jobs. Learning to boat, and the responsibilities that come with living on a small island have been good life lessons for both of them, and one day they will realize how fortunate they were to live here.

For now, I continue to travel provincially with my work and remain very much connected to Sidney, through my involvement with the municipality. Lisa is a Registered Nurse who works full-time and has been exceptionally busy throughout the pandemic. Piers is a great place to connect as a family when we are all here. There are fewer distractions, and time slows. That time together has been important. With Nolan off to university now and Clara graduating from high school soon, our family will soon begin new chapters, and we look forward to spending more of our time on Piers and less in the boat!

Clara Rintoul

Nolan Rintoul

Lot 73 - Michal Pawlik and Ming Huey Chang

(written by Ming)

When I first came to Piers Island, I was what's called a "thousand gold lady" (千金小姐) in Chinese. The term describes a delicate lady living a sheltered life. I don't know if and how fast other people are changed by life on Piers. For me, it is a humbling process, and I have gone through leaps of changes and am still learning a lot.

Being someone who had only lived in big cities before, I was very apprehensive about this 'boat access only' island. I could not imagine how I would do grocery shopping or any of the fun things that I used to enjoy in the city. I also had a fear about boating, about the waves and the wind, and about being trapped on an island. It seemed ludicrous having to use a wheelbarrow to bring in groceries, never mind that everything had to be hauled in on a boat. Not knowing anyone on the island, I had all sorts of assumptions and prejudices about people choosing this lifestyle, which only reflected my own bias.

Nevertheless, I resisted hard in the beginning. I was scared and delayed my actual move as long as I could. I compared and complained based on the conveniences I had in the city, but refused to take in what I could do here. Then, like the new veggies growing in my garden, I grew new abilities. I don't know where I dropped my pride and resistance, but I remember the day I was astonished by Mary Jordan. This tiny lady of my mother's age had the most regal house on Piers. I have always said, "If the Queen ever visits Piers Island, she would stay in Mary's house."

However, Mary was no 'thousand gold lady.' She picked every stone and planted every plant on her property. I remember one day she was going through the debris of the stone chimney taken out of her guest cottage. She was breaking up big, heavy chunks of stones and cement and salvaging the stones for her garden. Mary never had a golf cart, so she had to wheelbarrow the debris out to hide. I was there to pick up some of her plant cuttings and volunteered to help. Enthusiastically, I loaded up her wheelbarrow and started to push. Strangely, I could not walk a straight line and kept leaning over to my left side. It was very heavy, indeed, but I did not think it was my problem. I said to Mary, "I think there's something wrong with your wheelbarrow. Maybe the tire needs more air." She said, "Really? But it was fine when I was using it." I tried again and still couldn't walk straight or far. So Mary picked it up and charged ahead. I could not believe it. This 80-year-old tiny woman was able to push a full load of cement and rocks easy-peasy.

One cold winter our heat pump quit. Mary gave me some firewood and told me that she used to chop her own firewood. Again, picking up an axe and splitting wood was something I had only watched on TV, or in the Grouse Mountain lumberjack show. Inspired, I picked up the axe and chopped all the logs I got from Mary. I think I made my husband proud that day. Perhaps my parents would cry if they saw their pampered daughter doing such heavy work, but maybe not. Maybe they are happy to see their daughter finally learning the value of hard work and not always choosing the easiest way from living on Piers.

Ming Huey Chang and Michal Pawlik

Lot 83 - Julien Bahain and Katie Steenman

A Special Community Like A Small Village In Europe

We came here to the West Coast of Canada (Julien from France and Katie from the Netherlands) to raise a family. We wanted something special, not just a condo in town. We wanted a house in the middle of nowhere and on the oceanfront because both of us are rowers. The challenge was that we only had so much money. We looked for a long time and we were close to going back to Europe since we could not find our diamond in the rough.

Then Katie found the house on the map on realtor.ca, and it looked like it was on the Saanich Peninsula. The price was too good to be true and we wondered what was wrong with the house. Katie enquired more and then told me it sounded great, but one hitch was that we had to row to go to work. Perfect! Jade was six months old at the time and somehow we just got enough money to afford the mortgage. We didn't know anyone on Piers. We would give it a year, and then decide if we would stay. We have been here now for five years and intend to stay forever.

What is important to us is creating our roots here on Piers and connecting with the great people, especially because we don't have family in Canada. We find raising a family here is so special, with us all living life to the fullest. For our children, being safe to bike around the island and talk with adults, it's all great. We got involved in volunteering on Piers (the PIID and PIA) to keep it a wonderful place. The volunteering aspects of the island are so special. Yes, it is taxing and a lot of work, but so rewarding. We hope Piers will always have volunteers with their own knowledge and experience, rather than tendering jobs out. Katie has learnt very important skills as a water volunteer, and we both have learnt lots with our committee work.

Everyday living on Piers is the highlight. We are both working full-time, and have young kids, and volunteer a lot, so we are extremely busy. Things like the storm in the middle of February, brings a level of excitement and uncertainly, which we both embrace. Even sitting in our garden is special.

People are what makes the island what it is. Neighbours helping us when our motor was down, getting together with friends - it's all a highlight. It reminds me of a village in France: A small community, a small market, everyone knows everyone, people get together all the time. We don't all agree with everyone all the time, but you have to get along. If there are problems, it's important to learn to work together despite our differences. Everyone has a place (and has an opportunity to be themselves), whether an artist, a welder or whatever. Piers creates the type of atmosphere where everyone has a sense of belonging. We'd been craving for this type of environment. The very first time we visited Piers and started chatting with islanders, we felt we could belong here.

Piers School is the perfect idea of how Piers found solutions to problems. We could have all suffered terribly on Piers during Covid, especially those of us with young children. It was not safe to commute or have kids in school. The opportunity with Christina (Lot 101) as the teacher at the school was wonderful, and Gerry and Diana (Lot 67) donating their cottage for the school house was amazing to make everything work. Jade probably won't remember Covid, but she'll remember the great time she had at school on Piers.

We are looking forward to the next 15 years, and can't wait to see what Piers will bring to our family. Piers makes the kids really resilient. They ride on the challenges of living on a small island - they need to wait out the fog or a storm and they learn that things don't happen perfectly. Both Jade and Luka are hard workers already. They help move groceries, do whatever they can to help. They just ride the wave the whole time…

Julien Bahain, Luka, Katie Steenman and Jade

2020-2022 COVID

During the Covid pandemic (2020-2022) most of the island's social events were temporarily suspended. The PIID and PIA meetings moved to Zoom (internet meeting platform) and the Christmas party had to be cancelled. The Christmas auction was still held via Zoom to donate monies to local charities. The Monday morning group and orchard group were still able to continue their outdoor activities, keeping spaced safely apart. Jackie Charlesworth (Lot 135) opened up a section of her property for a community 'Victory Garden' as a tribute to islanders over Covid. Many part-timers spent more time on Piers during those years, because they felt more protected than in the city. A special Covid event happened with the opening of a small Piers School during the 2020- 2021 school year. (See teacher Christina van der Kamp's story below)

In 2021, some safer outdoor events were held again, without the picnic/barbeque components, including the Piers Picnic (races only), the art Walkabout, Canada Day golf cart parade, the kayak 'Poker Paddle,' and the Apple Fest. Of course, islanders were always happy to meet each other 'six feet apart' on their daily walks.

Slowly most activities are starting to resume on Piers in 2022. Island meetings are being held as a combination of in-person and Zoom. Despite the challenges of the last few years, Piers Island has remained strong - a wonderful community committed to its people and its 'joie de vie'!

Piers Schoolhouse

(Written by teacher, Christina van der Kamp)

Near the end of summer 2020, we were settling into a prolonged COVID pandemic. I wondered what the upcoming school year would look like for our two kids, Maggie and William. Then, I was approached by Amy Warren (Lot 28) regarding the possibility of me tutoring her three boys. Their family was considering staying on Piers through the school year, rather than returning to Calgary. I also had some conversations with Katie Steenman and Julian Bahain (Lot 83) about schooling options for their daughter, Jade.

Over the next weeks, the idea of island schooling for our three families grew out of these conversations. But where? Our first thought was the firehall, but its draughtiness was not ideal. Luckily, our resourceful Fire Chief Steve Cruise put me in contact with Gerry and Diana Kristianson. They had an empty cabin on their adjacent property at Lot 69 and were happy to have us take a look.

Perfect! Small, easy to heat, with an open living space, cozy little bedrooms, and a big porch with a picnic table. Even the furniture was already painted bright yellow and blue. Isabel (Lot 10) and Manon (Lot 37) came to help dust, scrub, and vacuum. I took some of my classroom supplies out of storage, hung up some coat hooks, and we were up and running.

In November, we were joined by another 'pandemic refugee' family, the Ungstad-Macouns from Switzerland. Carly and Adam, and their two children, had been visiting family on Piers (Lot 27) and decided to stay put because the virus was putting the whole world on lockdown. One play date and we knew that they were meant to join our little group.

Despite our unique location, our school days were not that different from a regular school. In the mornings, we met at our schoolhouse for math and language arts. Conveniently, we really just had two grade levels, Grades 1 and 3, and most of the curriculum came from an online school in Alberta. We had breaks for snack and recess, including beach exploring and forest games behind the cabin. We always ended the morning with sharing books and singing. Then the kids took over the road with laughter and shouts for the bike ride home.

Lunch was at home and then we met up again in the afternoon. The families involved each took a different day for science, social studies, art, library, and gardening. There were many other highlights throughout our year, including caroling for the holidays; an 'open mic' for Writing Day; trips to our 'private' pool; a beach clean-up session for Earth Day; pajama days; and a spring concert and 'graduation.' Along the way we amassed impressive collections of shells, rocks, and bones and every imaginable classroom pet (alive and dead), such as beetles, banana slugs, a mouse, guppies, octopus, lizard, junco, snake, and a mink trapped by Gerry. The circle of life lived every day.

Most importantly, we were fortunate to have so many islanders support our endeavours. Carly and Katie (and Luka) came nearly every day to help with the teaching. Philippa (Lot 139) guided us in building a year-round children's garden on Jackie Charlesworth's property (Lot 135). We even helped to hatch her farm's next generation of laying hens right from an incubator. Lynn Pritchett (Lot 23) took us out to learn about native plant species; Linda Vanden Berg (Lot 43) came to share her knowledge of Indigenous uses of cedar; and Ming (Lot 73) taught us the legend of Chinese New Year and helped us create our own dragon. Pauline Olesen (Lot 123) hosted us for not only a FireSmart training camp, but also shared her studio with us to make fused glass creations. Ann Cooney (Lot 68E) gifted us custom t-shirts, stuffed animals, and other treasures. Sandy Brunham (Lot 64) offered fun contests to challenge us and, along with Frances Glover (Lot 77), made sure we were up-to-date in our emergency preparedness training. We celebrated many birthdays at the schoolhouse with the help of Gloria Morson (Lot 113) and her singing birthday card.

Teaching in a one-room schoolhouse has always been a dream of mine, and the experience included all the hustle and bustle and idyllic moments I had hoped for. On our last day of school, Gerry and Diana gave us permission to sleepover at the schoolhouse. They even provided ice cream (cranked by hand) for our bedtime snack. A huge 'strawberry' moon came up that evening and I had a moment to reflect on our year together.

I thought about how the end of our school year had coincided with the distressing news from the sites of former residential schools in the province. News of unmarked graves signaling the abuse of children, who had deserved the same care and respect that our children had experienced this year. I hoped that my students would remember our learning and experiences together. But mostly, I hoped that they would come to understand just how privileged they are and just how well Piers Island, as a place and community, cared for them this year.

Piers school in session

Piers School 2020 - 2021

EPILOGUE
THE DOUKHOBOR YEARS

The Doukhobor penintenary was located on Piers Island from 1932 to 1935. Harold Skolrood (Lot 92) has written an excellent research documentary of the Doukhobors on Piers in his book 1993 book *Piers Island: A brief history of the island and its people, 1886-1993*. The website at www.doukhobor.com is also an excellent resource for information on Doukhobor history in Canada and on Piers Island.

In 2007, Islander Tony Booker invited members of the Victoria Doukhobor Choir to sing at the Piers Island firehall. The choir of around 30 members sang many traditional heart-felt songs from their heritage. A number of islanders attended this significant event. The choir said the songs they sang were likely the same ones their incarcerated ancestors sang during their imprisonment on Piers. Singing has always been an important part of the Doukhobor heritage and prisoners were known to sing as they worked in the fields and orchards during their captivity. It was also a way for men and women to communicate with each other when they were separated.

After the concert, Matthews (Lot 119) long-time owners on Piers, invited choir members to their property that was the previous location of the men's penitentiary. Remnants of pilings from the former penitentiary dock still remain at that site, just a few minutes walk from the firehall. It was a difficult visit, because the choir members trudged slowly down the graveled pathways, where memories of their grandparents' footsteps during their incarceration 80 years earlier were on their minds. Many choir members and islanders felt the concert and the tour were a healing reconciliation experience. One choir member said, "I always felt sorry for my Grandpa that he was in this terrible place, but now that I see it, I don't feel so badly for him because at least it was a beautiful location on the sea." (Unfortunately, the woman's prison was located on the inside of the island, not on the seashore). She added, "I still feel sad about the tragedy of husbands and wives and children being separated from each other."

In collecting the stories from Piers Islanders, there have been a number of islanders who found out after they had moved here that their family members had a history in the Doukhobor experience on Piers. Vicki Morrison (Lot 7) had a great-uncle who was incarcerated, and Bob Crook's

(Lot 100) grandfather worked as a warder at the Piers prison.

A number of islanders including Primroses (Lot 38) and Benders (Lot 121) gave a tour to Doukhobors, whose ancestors were imprisoned on Piers. A film was made of one visit by the National Film Board of Canada. Our matriarch Mary Tucker years ago gave an impromptu tour when she met a couple of Doukhobor family members, who were moored at the Piers public dock.

The tragic years of the Doukhobors being incarcerated will never be erased from their families' memories or the island's history. Hopefully, over time, with sharing of compassionate experiences on both sides of the story, there will be more of an understanding and forgiveness.

I have been fortunate to be introduced to Vera Maloff, whose mother and paternal grandparents were all interned on Piers Island. In 2021, Vera published a book called *Our Backs Warmed by the Sun: Memories of a Doukhobor Life.* Vera's mother is still alive at the age of 102. Although she tried to forget this terrible time in her life, she told many stories over the years to Vera and other family members.

Vera has written the following submission, based on her mother's stories. Although this is not a positive passion, it is history that needs to be told. Years ago, I heard the expression "It is important to remember the past, so history does not repeat itself." I believe this certainly applies here.

I am indebted to Vera for sharing this painful, yet important part of her family's history.

Image G-606 courtesy of the Royal BC Museum and Archives

The Shadow of Piers Island

by Vera Maloff

Piers Island entices me - tall maple and oak trees shade hiking trails, pebble beaches line its shores and sailboats anchor in a sheltered harbour. A short boat ride from the Saanich Peninsula, close to Sidney and Victoria. I am told that people on this small island work together as a community; they have established a public library and reading room, a school and activities for the residents during the recent pandemic. It seems that this is a place I would enjoy visiting or living.

But for me there is a shadow on the island. A visit there would be to put to rest old ghosts that my family has spoken little of for over ninety years.

In June of 1932, the island was expropriated by the federal penal system. It was considered to be an ideal place to retain a group of non-violent men and women who went askance of the law. My ancestors were three of the 546 prisoners incarcerated there when it was a penal colony for a pacifist sect of Christians, the Doukhobors. Grandmother Lusha Maloff and my Great-grandparents Nikolai and Elizaveta Maloff arrived in the fall of 1932 on the newly constructed pier and walked through the gates of the prison escorted by guards and inspected by the newly hired staff. They spent two years of their lives on this island, but there is little left to mark their existence. They left only their tears and DNA in the soil of the island.

Lusha Maloff, nee Hoodicoff, was twenty-nine years old when she had her children taken under "government care" while she was incarcerated on the island. Nadya, at six months old was placed in foster care in Vancouver; Petya, nine, and twins, Johnnik and Luba, four years old were held at the Alexandra Orphanage; Elizabeth, eleven, was sent to the BC Girls Industrial School, a reform school.

Grandmother Lusha and children

I knew my Grandmother Lusha well. My mother, Elizabeth was her eldest and our family lived next door to our grandparents' market garden farm in Thrums, a community in the West Kootenays. Grandmother Lusha was a slim, lithe woman, her features classic and her long hair silver when I knew her, braided and arranged in a bun at the back of her head.

Lusha was born in Saskatchewan in 1902 to a Doukhobor pioneering family who three years earlier had immigrated from Russia. In 1908 the family moved to British Columbia where they established a farm on the Kootenay River close to Castlegar. Her parents helped build the schoolhouse in Thrums and she enjoyed attending the one-room school, learning arithmetic, that she was good at, and English reading and writing. She remembered the school plays and songs, and even in her nineties, when she suffered from dementia, she could sing many of the songs. Even though she had many admirers, at the age of 18, she married Pete Maloff, a handsome young man who had just arrived from California. In her later years she said, "When I saw your Grandfather Pete, I knew I would marry only him." They were together for 53 years until grandfather died at 71. She mourned, "I never wanted to be a widow," but lived 25 years longer, missing their close relationship and the adventurous life they had together.

As a child, I visited grandmother daily in her welcoming home where everything had its place, organized and clean. She gardened in such a manner, too - bedding plants labeled in orderly rows in the greenhouse. She knew all the good varieties and her customers depended on her expert selection. I loved transplanting flowers, tomato, cucumber and pepper seedlings into larger pots in the early spring while the sun shone in through the greenhouse glass and warmed our backs. In the garden, too, there were long straight rows of cabbages, potatoes, beans and corn that towered over her head, a testament to her gardening skill.

Grandmother Lusha often had company at her house - visitors from far and near that she fed generously with borshch, vegan in the early days as my grandparents did not eat animal products. Even the police who came to arrest grandfather for refusing to register for the national mobilization in the 1940s were fed. It was her nature to be hospitable. She was the beekeeper in the family and, because of her calm manner the bees never stung her.

And I knew Lusha as a great-grandmother. On her first visit to see my baby, she bent over my newborn and, looking into her eyes, said a prayer and gently pulled her ear lobes so that she would grow big, strong and wise. It became a tradition - all the babies in the family had to have a blessing from their great-grandmother.

After she passed away, my mother and I sorted boxes of Lusha's fabric in earthy tones of brown, green, yellow, and orange - the hues of the clothes she sewed. She left flowers too, hydrangeas and clematis that climb the walls of her old home, and grapes that provide us with juice in the fall.

Nikolai Maloff, my grandmother's stareechok, (father-in-law), was 61 when he entered Piers Island prison, though the registry of prisoners on the island states he was 52. Doukhobors did not believe the government had any business keeping records on them, so his age was most likely a guess by the warden - ten years younger than he was.

I know my Great-grandfather Nikolai through family stories, photos and his wooden spoon carvings I have in my cupboard drawer. He was born in the Russian Caucasus mountains to a family who kept a road inn, and he looked after the horses stabled there. When he came of age to serve in the czar's army, he refused and, like many young Doukhobors, was indentured to work for a neighbouring Tatar tribe. He toiled morning till evening building rock walls, a skill he was to use later when he built the foundation and basement for his son's house. It stands strong supporting the Thrums farmhouse a hundred years later. When Doukhobors were released and allowed to come to Canada in 1898, he came with his wife, son and his mother who had remarried and had two young children.

In Saskatchewan he settled with the Doukhobor colonists but when his sons were of school age, he insisted they attend English school. At the time government schools were not accepted by the community, so he left the Christian Community of Universal Brotherhood and took a homestead. He was to regret this act for many years because it meant he had to swear an oath of allegiance to the Crown when he believed his first allegiance was to God.

A restless soul, he could not find a corner of Canada to call his own and joined Doukhobor cooperatives in Oregon, California, in the Kootenays, and, upon the economic dissolution of those, a community in Hilliers on Vancouver Island.

Nikolai loved to be outside and from early morning to evening, my mother said you could hear him singing as he worked in the gardens or woodshed. In summer, he slept outside in a treehouse he built in a tall poplar. On Sunday mornings, he walked his grandchildren to prayer meetings, telling them, "When you pray in the morning, the whole day will be better."

My Great-grandmother Elizaveta Maloff, nee Barisoff, was 63 years old when she arrived on Piers Island, although the prison registry states 57. From a family photograph I see she was beautiful with, as my mother tells me, a heart as big as her bosom. My hazy memory of her, or perhaps it is a story I have been told, was when everyone in the family went huckleberry picking, she looked after me. As the day grew late, my great-grandmother worried, "They won't come back, they are lost," but I confidently replied, "Oh yes they will, and they'll bring huge buckets of huckleberries with them." (Photo below is of Great-Grandparents Nikolai and Elizaveta).

Elizaveta was the midwife who delivered my mother and as Elizabeth grew older, she worked beside her grandmother and learned to bake bread, make fruit leather and weave rag rugs. A treasured memory of my mother's was sinking her teeth into a slice of her grandmother's warm freshly baked bread, and her grandmother's hands lovingly rubbing her shoulders as she told stories of her life.

As a young girl in Georgian Russia, she was the shepherd of the family. According to the custom then, she had an arranged marriage to Nikolai who was younger than her by several years. Perhaps she was aware of life as a prisoner for when Nikolai was indentured in a Tatar village in Georgia, she and her son Nick joined him. She learned some of the Tatar language and songs, but she was always afraid that the village elders would steal their blond, blue-eyed son who at three years old ran about the village. When the family was leaving for Canada, they told her, "Leave your son with us. He'll become a hlawniy, an important man, in our village." Elizaveta hung on to her son even in his sleep and safely brought him to Canada. In Saskatchewan, shortly after their arrival, she birthed my grandfather Pete and his sister Tanya.

She followed the lead of her husband as he moved from community to community and when he died, Elizaveta returned to live with her children and grandchildren, helping where she could.

So why were these gentle people held on an island far away from their home in the Kootenay valleys? This is complex. My grandmother Lusha never talked about the imprisonment and separation from her children and husband. It was through newspaper articles and discussions with my mother years later that I learned about their Piers Island incarceration.

In 1932, my Grandfather Pete Maloff, together with other Doukhobors, was petitioning the government to redirect his tax dollars away from military spending. They refused to pay their land taxes and staged a march on Baker Street in Nelson. They were arrested and sentenced to three years in the B.C. penitentiary on charges of disturbing the peace, and their land was confiscated. The Maloff farm was sold for back taxes of $100. At the time, the Doukhobor spiritual leader, Peter P. Verigin, was also detained for what many Doukhobors believed were trumped-up charges.

A group of Independent and Sons of Freedom Doukhobors gathered in a meeting in Thrums at the home of Ivan Perepolkin looking for a peaceful way of demonstrating against what they saw as social injustice.

When I ask my mother, now a centenarian imbued with a calm wisdom of her years, what her mother and grandparents did to get arrested, she takes a deep breath and, as if she is reviewing a movie in her mind, she starts to tell me of those days, over ninety years ago. "It was a difficult time. There were so many protests and arrests. People were all riled up. Grandfather Nikolai told us he was going to the meeting just to see what the group was proposing to do. Grandmother Elizaveta begged him not to go. With father in jail, he was needed. Grandmother knew that with his passionate character, he would get caught up in the protest."

Ivan Perepolkin was a friend of the family, although my grandfather did not always agree with his lifestyle and tactics. Grandfather Pete called him a Christian anarchist who had used nudity as a peaceful way of protesting. The consensus of the Thrums meeting was, 'If they rob us like that, we may as well show that they have left us naked.'

The Grand Forks Gazette of May 1932 gave detailed reports about the demonstrations and arrests. The provincial police had been patrolling the Perepolkin property along the road allowance in expectation of a nude demonstration. When the police noticed that some at the meeting began undressing, they requested backup from "special constables" who arrived shortly after to arrest and escort the compliant Doukhobors to the provincial jail cells in Nelson. The newspaper report stated, "While the majority of those were in the nude, there were many who were partially clad .... Many who did not disrobe, expressed themselves as sympathetic and declared they would disrobe."

The nudists and those who supported them were all arrested, including the old or infirm. They were charged: "At or near Thrums and without lawful excuse, [the prisoners] did appear in a nude condition on private property not their own, the said property being adjacent to the public highway."

They were sentenced by the judge, within the jurisdiction of a newly created law, to a mandatory three years imprisonment in a federal institution. There was no leniency. Ironically, Ivan Perepolkin, who was instrumental in organizing the protest, was not charged - he was on his own land.

Upon hearing the verdict, Great-grandmother Elizaveta and Grandmother Lusha, without a breadwinner to support the family, decided "We may as well join them." The protests continued and grandmother and great-grandmother, gathering the children, joined the next demonstration and were promptly arrested. From the May 20, 1932 Gazette, "It was about the noon hour that provincial officers patrolling the vicinity of Thrums telephoned to Nelson that Sons of Freedom were breaking the law. Trucks were sent out immediately and without fuss the naked fanatics piled aboard and were brought to join their 'brethren' in jail."

There was dissent from some in the general public at the excessively harsh treatment and wasteful use of government money. The editor of the Daily Province in May 1932 expressed this sentiment,

"It is foolish to suggest that the Doukhobors are dangerous. They are a nuisance; they deliberately outrage the feelings of their neighbors. But they are not violent, and it is idle to hope that a prison term will reform them. The people sentenced at Nelson are religious fanatics, and persecution has no effect on fanaticism except to increase it. Nor can there be much expectation that severe sentences will prevent others from following the course which brought these sentences."

The federal government was responsible for finding a location to intern the prisoners. Harold Skolrood has written about the Piers Island Doukhobor internment in his book, Piers Island: A Brief History of the Island and its People. Reading excerpts of his book in the Doukhobor Genealogy website, I learned that Piers Island was selected and expropriated from the Harvey family under the Penitentiary Act. A prison encompassing 10 acres of the northwest corner of the island was built with "no extravagance whatsoever." Skolrood explained the daily routines and activities of the men and women in the jail: the men worked in the vegetable gardens, cut and brought in firewood, moved stores to the kitchen, did some blacksmithing, shoemaking, woodcarving; the women cooked, washed and in their spare time sewed and made baskets that were sold.

Separate women's and men's penitentiaries on Piers Island

The spartan buildings were most likely not unusual for the Doukhobors, having lived in simple homes. The harshest punishment to the parents, to my grandparents, was that their children were taken away. During the depression year of 1932 the federal and provincial Conservative governments in power seized 361 Doukhobor children between the ages of seven and eighteen and without any formal court intervention placed 75 girls in the BC Girls Industrial School, 92 boys in the BC Boys Industrial School, 75 children in orphanages, and 119 in foster homes in the lower mainland of B.C.

Doukhobors convey their faith through singing their psalms and hymns. As I read Skolrood's book, I find it especially poignant that the mournful singing of their "rich voices in perfect harmony" was heard as far away as Sidney. And then my heart grieves for my grandmother and from that long ago time, a grief-stricken keening resounds in my ears when I read how the "mothers expressed a longing for their children through songs" that were heard throughout the islands close by. My mother told me about the Russian songs they sang at the Industrial School, songs about birds; one who laments that birds of prey harass her, give her no rest or peace to build her nest and another who says she will die in captivity, even if she lives in a golden cage and is fed tea and crunchies.

Grandmother Lusha was doubly sad on Sunday afternoons, when the men and women were allowed to have half-hour conversations behind fences, 300 feet apart that separated the men's and women's compounds, while a guard strolled in between. Lusha's husband was in the New Westminster penitentiary and she feared for his life because she heard he was being harshly treated in solitary confinement.

The Doukhobor community agitated to have the children released to the homes of relatives and after a year my mother Elizabeth, her siblings Peter, Johnnik, Luba and Nayda were taken in by their Hoodicoff grandmother. Lusha, Nikolai, Elizaveta, and Pete Maloff were released after two years for "good behavior," as were many of the Doukhobor prisoners. Skolrood wrote: the ex-prisoners were given a railway ticket home and $10 in their pockets but were otherwise left destitute, many with no property to return to. Due to their diligence and hard work ethic, my grandparents survived, living from the food of their gardens and with extended family support. The emotional scars lasted longer, perhaps for generations.

Vera Maloff and mother Elizabeth (now age 102)

CLOSING THOUGHTS

A Passion For Piers has been a labour of love for me. For two years it has also been my 'Covid project,' which has helped to keep my mind focused on the positive side of life.

So many families have expressed to me how they enjoyed gathering together over the past two years to collect photos and tell stories about their memories of their time on Piers. Comments such as: "It has been a journey of remembering, of love and laughter, and sorrow and grief of those who have passed on." "We were fortunate to have been part of such a wonderful giving community." "We were so lucky to have been able to freely roam and enjoy the island as children, and to have the memories of the island to share in our family." These sentiments express exactly what I wanted this book to represent - "*A Passion For Piers*".

My humble thanks to all those who took time out of their busy lives to share their Piers memories. You each made this book the wonderful creation it has become.

** All profits from this book will be donated back to Piers Community projects.

ABOUT THE AUTHOR

Patti Locke-Lewkowich (Patti L-L to friends and collegues) has lived full-time on Piers Island with her husband Barry Tate since 1996. Being a former Winnipeger, Patti feels she is living in heaven.

In the mid-1990s, she self-published a book called *My Life Story*, a workbook full of thought-provoking questions to encourage others to document their life as a legacy for family and/or as a tool for planning the rest of one's life. Patti gave *My Life Story* workshops and sold the books to accompany the workshops. She also assisted dozens of people to write their own life stories, starting with her father-in-law, who gave copies of his book to family members on his 90th birthday. Patti has been interested in storytelling since childhood. *A Passion For Piers* gives Patti the opportunity to carry on this love of storytelling with her community.

Patti was a counsellor for 20 years, including three years in the early 1990s, on the BC Southern Gulf Islands, serving Salt Spring, Pender, Galiano, Mayne and Saturna. In her second career Patti was a realtor (in Winnipeg and in Greater Victoria), including 1997-2015 when she was the resident realtor on Piers Island. The latter was the favourite part of her real estate career, when she introduced people to become islanders and share the joys of her community. In *A Passion For Piers*, Patti uses her diverse skills to interview and co-ordinate hundreds of people to gather their stories.

Patti sees community as an important part of her lifestyle, and values the spirit of belonging that she and Barry have on their utopic island. She believes that a community like Piers where people know, help and trust each other is so important in today's world.

Made in the USA
Middletown, DE
19 July 2022

69708277R00176